THE
GENERAL THEORY
OF EMPLOYMENT INTEREST
AND CHEATING

THE
GENERAL THEORY
OF EMPLOYMENT INTEREST
AND CHEATING

by Yves Laulan

Originally published in France as *La Triche* by J.C. Lattes.

Translated from the French for Richardson and Snyder, Ltd.
by JAMES WEEKS

Richardson and Snyder, Ltd.
New York

TABLE OF CONTENTS

INTRODUCTION

Yves Laulan has drawn on five years of painstaking research, and a lifetime of economic experience, to pull aside the veil of hypocrisy which normally cloaks diplomatic relations. What he reveals may surprise and shock you. Yet you will find his reasoning difficult to argue with.

The questions Mr. Laulan raises are timely and important:

How did Europe cheat the United States out of hundreds of billions of dollars in precious economic resources?

How did the U.S. retaliate against Europe?

What has OPEC really been up to all these years?

How did the Russians manage to dupe Henry Kissinger?

The answers are all here, neatly and provocatively packaged.

In Laulan's pragmatic interpretation, the world is governed by power relationships among nations. All the rest is rhetoric. Friend or foe, the strong dominate the weak and do not hesitate to use their power.

While peace seems to prevail, the nations of the world are really engaged in a bitter behind-the-scenes battle for economic growth and the power which it brings. The weapons used for the past three decades, Laulan argues, have been those of subterfuge and cheating.

Unless the world stops its cynical cheat-thy-neighbor approach, Laulan believes, disaster is inevitable.

Mr. Laulan is not a pessimist; he is a determined realist. He believes that in the 1980's the major industrialized nations may ultimately be forced by the energy crisis into dealing more fairly with each other.

In the meantime, the cheating game continues. The U.S., says Laulan, has found a new way to cheat the Europeans: high interest rates. Interest is tax deductible in this country, but not in much of Europe. Thus, the U.S. is in a position to grind down Western European economies with high interest rates and a strong dollar at relatively little cost to itself.

Laulan now anticipates what he calls a "greening of the U.S. economy" in the 1980's. He believes the U.S. is in a good position to move out in front of European countries in what he terms the great "Race for growth." He also believes a more balanced East-West relationship is possible in the 1980's as President Reagan rebuilds American defenses. But there's a caveat: if the U.S. moves enormous resources into the economically sterile defense budget, the Europeans may skimp on their own defense spending and again try to overtake the U.S.

Finally, Laulan sees little respite from rising OPEC oil prices. He believes that the current "glut" will end soon after the world economy emerges from recession.

The bulk of this book was written in 1980, though this translation incorporates some updating and a new postscript, "Lafferism, Reaganomics and the No Work Society." Already, some of Mr. Laulan's major predictions have come true. He anticipated the recent exacerbation of tension within the Atlantic Alliance. He foresaw co-financing arrangements now being developed between the World Bank and commercial banks as a solution to petrodollar recycling. He also predicted that persistent high inflation and rising unemployment would lead to an end to the policies of President Giscard d'Estaing, and the coming to power of a socialist government in France.

This is not a book of gloom and doom. Mr. Laulan bubbles over with ideas on a better future for the world. For now, however, the most important thing about this book is the careful explanation it gives of *how we got where we now are*. It is an iconoclastic story that could only have been written by a brilliant economist observing the American scene from a European vantage point.

I have never read anything like it before.

Julian M. Snyder
New York City
July 1, 1981

PROLOGUE:
The Cheating Game

For more than seven years now, since the end of 1973 to be exact, the world has been reeling from a series of shocks stronger than anything suffered since World War II. The impact has been felt not only in the fields of economics, politics and military strategy, but also in our minds. We have lost our bearings. Our carefully constructed system of references, values and deeply-held beliefs is on the brink of collapse.

The years 1973-1975 marked the end of a period of strong economic growth, expanding international trade, and relative monetary stability, all wrapped in a blanket of military and political security which we could feel around us. It was a world in which we no longer felt threatened or oppressed by anything, except possibly by boredom. It was this feeling of security which was responsible for the unusual character of the late 1960's and early 1970's, when a widespread tendency towards introversion and reflection on social change led to such things as the events of May 1968, American campus revolts and the birth of the ecology movement. Meditation of that kind occurs throughout history only at times of great security, when man is free to contemplate his soul.

It took time for the intellectual landscape to change. Fashions die hard. The same political and intellectual arguments continued for several years, stuck in the groove of habit. Then came the first oil crisis, and more recently the second oil crisis and the crises over Iran and Afghanistan. Finally, the whole structure of ideas began to fall apart. The sordid and bloody conspiracy of Marxism was finally exposed for all to see. In France, a new wave of young philosophers, cleverly exploiting the media, achieved fame and glory by "discovering" what we had already known for many years, in fact ever since Soviet defector Victor Kravchenko announced "I chose freedom" in 1946. Now we have the "new" economists, who have in fact invented nothing new at all, but are simply unearthing basic truths from classical economics.

In the 1980's, we shall finally have to adjust to the post-oil crisis realities. Since 1973, little or nothing has been done to prepare for the challenge, so we are way behind schedule. In the U.S. and other industrialized countries, private consumption has continued to be the main engine of economic growth, which is precisely the opposite of what should have happened. The main aim should have been the financing of new energy sources together with a policy of enforced conservation. Instead, from as early as 1975, Detroit abandoned its small car assembly lines and went back to making gas guzzlers as though the oil crisis had never occurred. Despite all the long speeches about the need for industrial restructuring and diversification of energy sources, no fundamental changes have been made. Almost everything remains to be done. It is now obvious that the necessary adjustments *will* be made, either voluntarily or by means of force, under the pressure of harsh new political and economic constraints. More than half a decade late, the industrialized world is going to have to face the music.

The 1980's will be dominated by two issues—energy and defense. You only had to listen to the preliminary themes of election campaigns fought in 1980 on both sides of the Atlantic. It was no longer a question of change or reform or even continuity. Now we were hearing the words of *command* which could have been so useful in the early 1970's. In politics the man of the hour is the one who can articulate most clearly yesterday's problems. Governing consists largely in anticipating the outcome of the next opinion poll. Or to be more precise, it consists in being first to understand what should have been done to keep us from being where we are.

Right now, the key question is no longer whether our living standards are going to rise. It is whether we are going to have enough oil, and whether war is going to break out in the years ahead. Reduced to these elementary terms, our problems become clear. We need to put our intellectual house in order again. In the first place, we must recognize that in economics there are no unalterable rules, theories or laws.

Some years ago, I was asked by the then Secretary General of NATO (North Atlantic Treaty Organization), Manlio Brosio, to explain the mystery of the U.S. balance of payments deficit. I did my best, but obviously without too much success, because at the end of my explanation he exclaimed: "But that means there are no economic laws!" To which I could only reply: "Alas, no, there are only people." In reality, everything comes down to people and their individual and group behavior patterns, which change and adapt themselves to circumstances. This is what makes analysis of the past so difficult. How do we account for the extraordinary adaptability of banks in the aftermath of the first oil crisis? Thirty years ago, the oil shock would have triggered a horrendous world crisis. Today, experts are still amazed at how easily our banking mechanisms and institutions managed to absorb the impact without too much pain. This surprising flexibility is also of course what makes it so hard to predict the future. In making predictions, the only thing we can be just about sure of is that we shall make mistakes. Who can honestly re-read without blushing what he wrote five years ago? Nevertheless, there are certain guidelines we can use to help find our way through the maze.

The first guideline is that in economics everything is dominated by power relationships. A friend of mine, a senior official in the French Ministry of Finance, likes to say: "Money is power." He is absolutely right. Pure economics does not exist. Economics is people—their appetites, their fears and their ambitions. This is why I have always deeply mistrusted plans for international monetary reform. The most ingenious plans serve only to cover up the underlying reality, which is the reality of power relationships. *Either* a solution has already been found, a new balance of power among nations has been established, and reform plans will serve merely to formalize an already existing situation. *Or* a new balance of power has not been established, in which case the plans, however ingenious, will prove meaningless and will inevitably fail.

Political and military power relationships among nations are obviously one of the keys to understanding contemporary history. Problems of national security have always been in the background of the political scene, even if they were largely hidden from view during the 1960's, which may fairly be described as a decade of madness. A whole part of humanity believed it could live, as it were, in a state of weightlessness, in a world blissfully free from external threat. Now, things have changed.

At the beginning of the 1970's, Nixon and Kissinger allowed U.S. defense capabilities to weaken in the name of detente. Now, just a few years later, they have published moralizing books waking the Western world up to the dangers of the situation which they themselves created. It's a surefire recipe for success in politics: always predict things which are actually happening, or better still, things which have already happened—things which will be of concern to everyone in the future, usually when it is too late. This observation is particularly relevant to the present situation. It takes five years to build a weapons system and rebuild a defense system. Whatever grandiose defense programs may be announced today, there is nothing at all that can be accomplished within five years. From now through 1985, we shall have to live with the consequences of defense decisions taken—or rather not taken—five years ago. That means either submitting to foreign domination, or living dangerously on the edge of the precipice. Some choice.

A second guideline, a corollary of the first, is the close links between defense policies and economic policies. Until recently, these links were blithely ignored both by the military and by economists. But now, shrewd economists are beginning to pay more attention to the role of defense issues. This is highly significant. Some economists are a bit like sparrows: when you see them converging on the same spot, you know there is something there to keep them fed and nourished. The fact is that a long-ignored truth is now being rediscovered: that defense and economic issues influence each other in the most intimate way.

In the first place, national security determines economic developments. Conversely, the state of the economy influences the defense posture. For example, France has solved its balance of payments problems largely through arms exports.

Another example is the Iran-Iraq war. In order to boost export earnings, the industrialized West armed both countries. The U.S. armed Iran under the Shah, while Europe armed Iraq. Today, these two countries are tearing each other apart, threatening to send the whole Middle East up in flames and cut off the flow of oil without which our economies will collapse.

Then there is the example of Saudi Arabia, the world's largest oil exporter. Which country benefits the most from the oil which the Saudis sell voluntarily for less than the market will bear—and in amounts which they have no need to sell at all? The U.S. does. Why? Because the U.S. remains the only country capable of guaranteeing protection against the ambitions of the Soviet Union and its satellites.

It is absurd to deny that economic and defense policies have an almost incestuous relationship with each other. Or to pretend that the only thing that matters in economics is the growth rate of the money supply.

The world has been shaken to its foundations by three inter-related crises. The *oil* crisis is there for all to see. So is the *economic* crisis, which is a crisis of growth. Then there is the *defense* crisis, which we are becoming more and more aware of. But it is not enough to identify these crises. We have to analyze them and unravel the ties that bind them together. The fundamental tie is the lust for power, which pits nations against each other in never-ending confrontations. The first confrontation is the one between the East and the West—the Soviet Union and the United States—which has continued since World War II. This is not only a military confrontation, involving attempts by both sides to achieve military supremacy, but also an economic one. Remember how Khrushchev proclaimed the Soviet Union would overtake the U.S. in steel production, and then in grain production?

The second confrontation is within the West, pitting Europe against the U.S., or more precisely, Europe and Japan together against the great American protector, a rival both hated and loved at the same time. This rivalry has frequently taken economic forms. But also, and above all, it is a political-military revolt against the U.S., which was clearly illustrated by de Gaulle's withdrawal of France from NATO and the development of an independent French military strike force.

A third confrontation, dating from December 1973, is that between OPEC (Organization of Petroleum Exporting Countries) and the rest of the world. This confrontation now dominates the rhythm of world events, but it has by no means eclipsed the other two, nor has it diminished the importance of the ever-present North-South conflict, the agonizing conflict between the Haves and the Have-Nots—the industrialized nations and the countries of the Third World.

After World War II, a frenzied race for economic growth began between the U.S., the dominating power, and Europe and Japan, the dominated powers. Until 1973, the race was won by Europe and Japan, because they cheated on defense. They got the U.S. to guarantee their security, and so saved hundreds of billions of dollars of resources, which enabled them to catch up with their American rival and protector. This led to a crisis within the NATO alliance. Then, like a bolt from the blue, came the first oil crisis, which had been anticipated by *no one.*

This marked the beginning of the second stage of postwar world history. Before, we worried about problems such as U.S. frozen chicken exports to Europe. Now we had to worry about whether we would have enough fuel to keep warm in winter, and enough gasoline to drive our cars. In this second stage, it was the United States' turn to cheat—on energy. While Europe and Japan slowed down because of the burden of the oil payments they were forced to make, the U.S. thrived, thanks to its international currency printing privilege. With energy still cheap, the U.S. was able to finance one of the longest and strongest economic expansions in its history, causing a spectacular reversal of positions: after 1973, the U.S. took the lead in the race for growth, leaving Europe and Japan behind.

The history of postwar international relations is thus the history of a game in which everyone cheats. He who cheats the best or the longest is the winner. The Europeans cheated on defense. The Americans cheated through their use of the Dollar Exchange Standard. The Soviet Union, for its part, cheated on detente. And the OPEC countries, after 1973, cheated by selling their resources at prices quite unrelated to cost, and squandering the proceeds. Striving to gain increased power, countries play with their resources as gamblers play with their stakes.

The third stage of postwar history is now beginning. In the 1980's, whether they like it or not, the U.S. will have to pay the real price for energy, and Europe and Japan will be forced to pay the real price for their external security. Who will come out on top? Who will be in the strongest position as we head into the 21st century?

PART ONE:
Three Crises Which Shook The World

The current world economic crisis must be considered in the context of the post-war battle for economic growth between the United States on the one hand and Europe and Japan on the other. From 1945 to 1973, Europe and Japan, acting both as allies and as rivals of the U.S., succeeded in nibbling away at the dominant position of the U.S. by growing at a faster pace: the average annual growth rate of the U.S. economy was only two to three percent, compared with five to six percent for Europe and eight to 12 percent for Japan. Despite all the talk in the early 1970's about the supposed virtues of *zero growth*, economic policies of all nations are still based on pursuit of the fastest possible expansion. The reason is obvious: economic growth is the precondition for power, whether it be economic, political or military power. No country can escape this reality. It is in this light that we must look at the postwar conflicts among the U.S., Europe and Japan, which have often been described, but rarely convincingly explained. Classical analyses of these conflicts are inadequate because they are made in purely economic terms. Economic theory can explain policy means, but not the ends which they are designed to achieve. We cannot afford to limit examination of international economic relations only to the monetary and commercial aspects. To grasp the whole picture, we must take the key policies of a nation—including monetary policy, foreign trade policy, overseas investment policy and defense policy—and study them not individually, but together, as interrelated parts of an overall strategy.

The relationships among the major industrialized nations can be analyzed in terms of rivalry between a dominant power, the U.S., and secondary powers, Europe and Japan, which are trying to escape from U.S. influence. Monetary crises and trade wars are merely the visible signs of an underlying struggle for long-term growth between the U.S. and the rest of the industrialized world. For a quarter of a century, the U.S. has dominated the world scene, through careful exploitation of the international monetary system, through the Dollar Exchange Standard and through its defense capability. But the burdens of being a superpower have taken a heavy toll on available U.S. resources; this in turn has allowed European and Japanese rivals to grow more rapidly, and thus whittle away the U.S. economic lead.

8

The U.S. economy emerged from World War II practically without a rival in the world. The war-ravaged economies of Europe in 1950 still represented only about half the productive power of the U.S. The Japanese economy equalled only five percent of U.S. Gross National Product. This position of dominance was the basis for the whole structure of postwar U.S. foreign policy, which was a unique combination of generosity and lust for power, involving the Marshall Plan, the setting up of an international economic system based on the dollar, and the building of a defense system based on the superiority of U.S. nuclear weapons. The simultaneous pursuit of economic, political and military goals, involving huge currency outflows and intensive use of domestic resources for non-productive (defense) purposes, was made possible by the crushing superiority of the U.S., with its seemingly unlimited resources. But within 20 years, the balance of power had changed radically. Europe had expanded to represent 80 percent of U.S. Gross National Product, up from 55 percent, and Japan 20 percent, up from five percent.[1] All indicators showed how Europe and Japan were catching up.

Between 1959 and 1970, the annual average growth rate in the U.S. hovered around 3.5 percent, compared to rates of almost five percent in Europe and 10 percent in Japan. Productivity per capita surged 150 percent in Japan and 65 percent in Europe, but rose only 32 percent in the U.S. Japan's share of world trade almost doubled to 6.2 percent from 3.2 percent, and the European share rose to 44 percent from 40 percent, while the U.S. share dropped to 13.7 percent from 16 percent.

Between 1960 and 1970, Japanese reserves increased to $5 billion from $1.9 billion, and those of Europe rose to $31 billion from $24 billion, while U.S. reserves fell to $14.3 billion from $19.3 billion (with gold valued at 35 dollars an ounce).

The main reason for the American handicap during this period was the military protection which the U.S. was providing for Europe and Japan. This allowed them to cheat by plowing into growth-generating investments resources which they would otherwise have been forced to use for their own defense. Europe and Japan benefitted from a quarter century of cheap defense costs. Japan was spending only one percent of its GNP (Gross National Product) on defense, and European countries only between two and five percent, while the U.S. was spending between eight and nine percent up to 1960, and six to seven percent up to 1970. According to a recent State Department publication, the U.S. between 1950 and 1970 spent around $1.3 trillion on defense and the Soviet Union about $1 trillion.[2] By comparison European defense outlays in the same period amounted to no more than $300 to $350 billion. These figures give some idea of the resources which Europe and Japan were able to save on defense, and thus devote to economic growth. When the U.S. woke up to the handicap it was suffering from, the Atlantic Alliance was plunged into crisis at the start of the 1970's.

Then came the oil crisis, in December 1973.

---

[1] Movements of floating currencies make international comparisons much less meaningful from 1970 onwards.

[2] Calculated in 1970 dollars.

9

CHAPTER 1
The First Oil Crisis

The crisis initially took the form of an embargo on oil supplies at the time of the Yom Kippur war in early October 1973 between Israel and its Arab neighbors. This was followed within a few months by a fourfold rise in the oil price—or a sixfold rise, depending on which reference points you choose. A few figures suffice to illustrate the effects of what came to be known as the *oil shock*. In 1974, OPEC revenues rose about $70 billion. As a result, the net oil bills of the major importing countries, expressed as percentages of their Gross National Products, jumped to between 3.5 percent (France and West Germany) and four percent (Japan and Britain). Oil purchases suddenly accounted for 17 percent of total imports in France, 18 percent in Germany and a whopping 36 percent in Japan. At the time, despite the embargo and the worries about whether regular supplies would again be available, it was already clear that the biggest problem was going to be prices rather than supplies.[1] The first oil crisis was without doubt one of the most significant events since World War II. To understand its importance in economic terms, we must first understand the true nature of the *coup* of December 1973.

The Coup of December 1973

The word *coup* is perfectly justified, because what we witnessed in December 1973 was an application of force. In the aftermath, analysts debated at length whether the reasons for the crisis were political or economic. In reality, they were both, although it is clear by now that the political causes were secondary to the economic ones. Israel is still intact but, despite that, the flow of oil has not been interrupted again. On the other hand, the price of oil has never fallen back to its earlier levels.

Does the oil price make sense?

It is worth asking ourselves if the price of oil makes any sense in economic terms.

---

[1]Today, the opposite appears true. It can be argued that the most important issue now is the quantity of supplies available, and that price increases are of (relatively) secondary importance.

Many analysts, notably in industrialized nations, have tried to demonstrate that the quadrupling of the price was economically logical. In reality, however, it is safe to say that the price has no economic basis; it is purely arbitrary and political. In the first place, it is impossible to justify the 1973 price increase on the basis of production costs. As we all know, a barrel of pre-crisis oil sold in 1973 for about two dollars; the cost price, which varies greatly from country to country and oilfield to oilfield, ranged at that time in the Middle Eastern area from 10 to 20 cents a barrel. Thus, the margin between cost price and selling price was already huge. Raising the selling price to eight dollars a barrel made that margin still more exorbitant and arbitrary. Some analysts sought economic justification for the price hike elsewhere. They argued that the increased price would encourage the world to cut back its use of a rare and non-renewable commodity, and to manage available supplies better in the long term, by developing alternative energy sources. In other words, these analysts were saying the oil price should be set at a level equal to the marginal cost of alternative energy supplies. Once again, the proposed justification does not stand up to analysis.

During the past six years, no one has been able to demonstrate in economic terms what the marginal cost of new energy sources might be. So far, it seems this marginal cost is always the market price of oil plus 10 percent! Furthermore, to judge from the use which has been made of a significant portion of oil revenues—gambling in Monte Carlo, buying arms—it seems clear that concern over the prudent use of available oil resources is a relatively secondary and peripheral issue.

There is another curious argument which often crops up in analyses trying to justify the quadrupling of the oil price. This argument says in effect that the price hike was justified by the fact that the price of a thermal unit had dropped more than 50 percent between 1962 and 1972. Thus, the argument runs, to multiply the price of energy by four was simply to allow the price to catch up with the prices of other products. Strange logic indeed. What needs to be explained is why the price of a thermal unit should have stayed the same throughout the 10 years in question, and why it should have faithfully kept pace with prices of other products. It's like arguing that in 1973 the relationship between payment for an hour of work and the price of wheat should have been the same as it was in the 19th century.

In truth, the only plausible justification for the price rise was *fiscal:* the oil price now has all the characteristics of a tax. OPEC strategy consisted simply in raising the price as far as possible to a level which the industrialized nations could still pay without major risk of world economic catastrophe. Economic logic was not involved. It was rather a question of fiscal logic. The OPEC aim was to maximize income from oil by judging the ability of taxpayers to make their contributions. That was the heart of the matter. The oil producers are aiming to increase their assets as fast as possible. Thus, the only limit to the oil price lies, on the one hand, in the producers' fear of triggering political and economic catastrophe, and on the other, in the ability of consumer countries to pay their oil taxes. These considerations account for the constant confusion of OPEC's price-setting deliberations. The OPEC countries are a very heterogeneous group, varying greatly in their oil output and the size of their populations. It is obvious that the needs of all of them are not the same. It is the marginal or secondary OPEC producers who are willing to push prices up at the risk of provoking imbalances not only in the oil market but also throughout the world. An oil pricing system which consists in periodically seizing increasingly large amounts of the wealth of consumer nations is by its very nature unstable; one day it may prove untenable.

A Durable Cartel

The short- and medium-term consequences of high oil prices are unpredictable and incalculable. History offers no useful guidance in our present situation, and neither does economic theory. In fact, some of the most basic assumptions of economics have to be re-examined. Take for example the theory of economic rent, invented by the English economist David Ricardo at the beginning of the 19th century. The theory holds that ownership of land justifies receipt of unearned income, the ground rent; for many decades, it has proved to be a more or less satisfactory guide to economic behavior. But now, OPEC nations have changed the name of the game by applying the theory on a gigantic scale, involving hundreds of billions of dollars, and in unprecedented socio-economic conditions. The fact is that OPEC governments took no part in developing the fantastic oil wealth which they are now in a position to appropriate; they made not the slightest financial or technological contribution to lifting the oil or to making use of it once it was above the ground. Their only justification for seizing a substantial portion of the total resources of the world was that they live where they do.

The situation was complicated by the precariousness of certain governments in the Persian Gulf area. It was further complicated by the fact that some of the biggest oil producing countries are very thinly populated, and had only archaic methods for distributing their new-found wealth among their citizens. And yet, despite many 1973 predictions to the contrary, the OPEC cartel has stood the test of time. It has acquired a new member, Nigeria, and, more importantly, it has acquired a number of *implicit* members, in the sense that every oil producing country which approaches self-sufficiency in oil becomes an implicit OPEC member. This was true of Mexico, and it may soon be true of the Ivory Coast and Argentina. You could even say it is true of Britain and Norway; the British and the Norwegians are already called blue-eyed Arabs in some quarters. The point is that all oil exporting countries adopt pricing and production policies identical to those of OPEC; the Soviet Union, which exports oil to its client states and allies in the Eastern bloc, is no exception.

The logic of the oil market dictates there can be only one price. OPEC countries have repeatedly promoted the concept of a two-tier market in order to force through new price increases. But the concept is merely an illusion. When the price is split, the lower price always rises to catch up with the higher one.

It is worth noting that some important structural changes have taken place in the oil market since December 1973. For one thing, Saudi Arabia, although it remains the biggest producer, seems to have lost the almost total control over prices which it appeared to enjoy before. For another, the major oil companies have lost control over production, and even distribution.

The question that remains to be asked is why the coup of December 1973 proved successful. The answers are very simple, even elementary. Oil is an indispensable product, which no nation, rich or poor, can do without. To stockpile it takes an enormous amount of space, and is very costly. And stocks are vulnerable to attack. Finally, the price of oil is very inelastic (even if the price rises sharply, consumption continues); it has become clear from experience that consumers are willing to pay much higher prices for oil than they had expected, rather than significantly reduce their consumption and their living standards. For the time being, oil can hardly be replaced by alternative energy sources.

This combination of circumstances explains why the cartel has endured. But it is obvious that the industrialized world does not work like some perfectly-functioning machine. Repeated crises will inevitably create dangerous instability, not only in the economic system, but also in the political balance of the world. The price of oil is less an economic problem than a geopolitical one.

The Response from the West

The quadrupling of oil prices in December 1973 had the following effects:

• Inflationary effects, which raised world prices to unheard-of heights. Only after two to four years, depending on the country, were governments able to slow the inflation rate; in many cases, the price of their success was a politically unpopular slowdown in the rate of economic growth.

• Deflationary effects, resulting from the fact that the oil tax cut into the real income of nations, leading to production slowdowns and unprecedentedly high levels of unemployment.

• To continue their development, Third World nations were forced rapidly to increase their external indebtedness; some of them are now living with the constant threat of debt payment crises.

• Nonetheless, international trade was maintained, thanks to the dramatic growth of the Eurodollar market. The Eurodollar market served a dual purpose, in recycling petrodollars and in financing the world economy to the benefit of both developing and developed countries.

• The price to pay for all this was chronic world instability, involving increasingly frequent and increasingly serious monetary crises.

• Only the United States was spared the consequences, and enjoyed a burst of prosperity; the price it paid for this was steadily worsening inflation and a large trade deficit.

The Western world did nothing or little to adapt to its changed circumstances. Everywhere, public opinion refused to face the facts. The proof of this is that economic activity was fueled by continued household consumption and not by investment. Industrial activity was based partly on record growth of the automobile industry, which in turn was based largely on production of gas-guzzling cars. The ecological movement was left free to spout its fantasies about the evils of nuclear energy as a replacement for oil. As a result, the growth of the nuclear industry slowed down, or was stopped altogether, as in West Germany and the U.S. Rarely has public opinion been so directly opposed to the necessities of the moment. The bottom line is that standards of living continued to improve. Within four years, using monetary, financial, trade and foreign exchange mechanisms, the industrialized world had succeeded in partially "digesting" the oil shock.

Petrodollar Recycling

The most spectacular response of the West to the oil crisis was the recycling of petrodollars by Western banks. In effect, the commercial banking system came to the relief of official international institutions, which played a relatively modest role in the aftermath of the crisis. Petrodollar 'recycling' is one of those buzz words which enter the language in response to an overwhelming need. What it describes is the process by which the major international banks, since 1974, have succeeded in recycling, i.e. re-injecting, into the world economic system the buying power removed from the system by the accumulation of petrodollar surpluses. These surpluses represent the difference between the export income of the oil producers and their payments for imports of goods and services; between 1974 and 1978, the surpluses totalled $151 billion (See Table 1). The recycling process fulfilled two distinct functions. In the first place, it allowed oil producing countries to find lucrative,

SOURCES AND USES OF PETRODOLLARS

TABLE 1

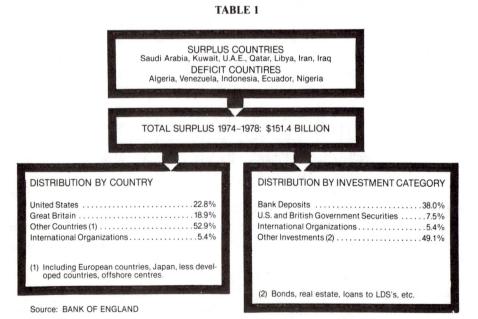

| SURPLUS COUNTRIES |
| Saudi Arabia, Kuwait, U.A.E., Qatar, Libya, Iran, Iraq |
| DEFICIT COUNTIRES |
| Algeria, Venezuela, Indonesia, Ecuador, Nigeria |

TOTAL SURPLUS 1974–1978: $151.4 BILLION

DISTRIBUTION BY COUNTRY	
United States	22.8%
Great Britain	18.9%
Other Countries (1)	52.9%
International Organizations	5.4%

(1) Including European countries, Japan, less developed countries, offshore centres.

DISTRIBUTION BY INVESTMENT CATEGORY	
Bank Deposits	38.0%
U.S. and British Government Securities	7.5%
International Organizations	5.4%
Other Investments (2)	49.1%

(2) Bonds, real estate, loans to LDS's, etc.

Source: BANK OF ENGLAND

low-risk investment outlets for their surpluses. Secondly, it allowed industrialized countries (such as Italy), major corporations and, especially, LDC's (Less Developed Countries) to finance their requirements. The banks simply took the oil producers' deposits and used them to make loans to deficit countries. Thus, for example, Brazil, by borrowing huge amounts and allowing its external debt to soar, managed to avoid any slowdown in economic growth between 1974 and 1978. At

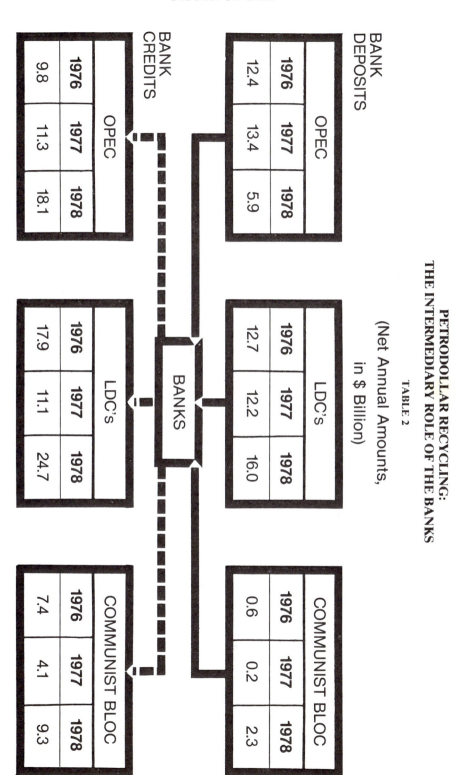

PETRODOLLAR RECYCLING:
THE INTERMEDIARY ROLE OF THE BANKS

TABLE 2

(Net Annual Amounts,
in $ Billion)

BANK DEPOSITS

OPEC

1976	1977	1978
12.4	13.4	5.9

BANK CREDITS

OPEC

1976	1977	1978
9.8	11.3	18.1

LDC's

1976	1977	1978
12.7	12.2	16.0

BANKS

LDC's

1976	1977	1978
17.9	11.1	24.7

COMMUNIST BLOC

1976	1977	1978
0.6	0.2	2.3

COMMUNIST BLOC

1976	1977	1978
7.4	4.1	9.3

17

first, OPEC countries had the money but no banks. Today, as we shall see, they have both.

Table 2 clearly illustrates the intermediary role played by the banks in the years 1976–1978. Note that OPEC does not constitute a homogeneous financial group. Some OPEC members are surplus countries while others are in deficit, and were themselves borrowers on international capital markets during the three-year period. Considered together, OPEC countries were obviously gross lenders on the markets. But they were not alone. Industrialized countries (omitted from the table for statistical reasons) were also gross lenders, as were the LDC's (which borrowed and received capital in excess of their financing requirements and put the surplus back onto the markets). Until 1977, OPEC was a net depositor, but the situation turned around in 1978 and it became a large net borrower. The LDC's (with the exception of 1977) and the Socialist Bloc countries were net borrowers throughout the period.

The Trade Response

As an immediate result of the oil crisis, OPEC accumulated a 1974 current account balance of payments surplus of close to $60 billion dollars, while industrialized countries and the LDC's rapidly built up huge payments deficits. Four years later, the OPEC surplus had shrunk to only seven billion dollars. The industrialized countries[1] had swung back into surplus, while the position of the LDC's continued to deteriorate (See Table 3). What had happened was that the industrialized countries had managed to transfer the oil deficit to the rest of the world. They boosted their exports to the LDC's, to the Socialist Bloc countries and, especially, to OPEC, while reducing their imports from all three. In the process, they maintained their surplus position vis-a-vis the LDC's, increased their surpluses vis-a-vis the Socialist Bloc countries, and cut by a huge margin their deficits vis-a-vis OPEC.

Inside OPEC, Saudi Arabia, Kuwait and the Emirates continued to register sizable payments surpluses, but other oil producers were showing substantial deficits before 1978. Iran, for example, returned to borrowing on the Eurodollar market in 1977. This spectacular turnaround was an indirect cause of the second oil crisis in 1979.

The Conjuring Trick

The success of the industrialized nations in lightening their oil payment burden was due in large part to their manipulation of price and foreign exchange developments. In effect, the West performed an elaborate conjuring trick. On the one hand, the industrialized countries responded to the OPEC oil price rise with price hikes of their own for their manufactured exports. Thus OPEC countries were forced to pay more to import the Western goods they wanted, and the terms of trade index of OPEC members plunged to 81 in 1978 from 100 in 1974, a drop of one fifth in five years.

On the other hand, industrialized nations managed to reduce the real price of OPEC oil through the steady depreciation of the means of payment for oil—the dollar—against other major currencies.

---

[1]The countries of the Organization for Economic Cooperation and Development (OECD), including the U.S., Japan, and major West European nations.

Between January 1974 and December 1978, the price of oil fell 15 percent in terms of Japanese Yen, 19 percent in German Marks and 36 percent in Swiss Francs. All industrialized countries were able to benefit, in differing degrees, from the dollar's decline. The depreciation of the dollar has often been interpreted as a form of monetary aggression by the U.S. against Europe and Japan; more realistically, it should be seen as a deliberate, collective response of the industrialized West to the actions of the oil producers.

CURRENT ACCOUNT BALANCE OF PAYMENTS
(in billions of dollars)

TABLE 3

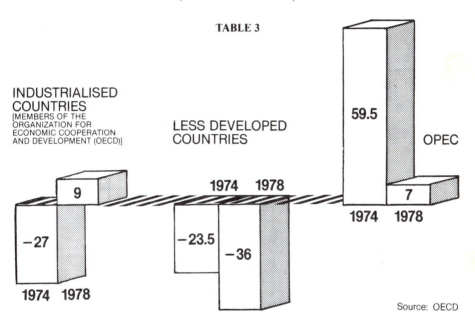

Source: OECD

The case of the U.S. deserves special comment. Because of privileges granted at the Bretton Woods conference of 1944, and later reinforced by the 1976 Jamaica accords, the U.S. has the right to print international currency and thus is able to finance trade deficits by the simple expedient of creating more dollars. Now compare the total amount paid by the U.S. for oil imports between 1974 and 1978, which was $125 billion, with the U.S. trade deficit over the same period, which was $96 billion. The comparison suggests that the oil purchases were only partly paid for in real terms. Of course, other factors have to be taken into consideration, including payments for services and movements of long-term capital. Nonetheless, the figures indicate that the oil bill in real terms was never fully paid. This is all the more true when you consider that the dollar balances accumulated by OPEC members in the U.S. can never be recovered; of course, they continue to yield interest, but because of their colossal size, OPEC can never hope to get them back.

It is clear that the U.S. did even better than Europe and Japan. The Europeans and the Japanese succeeded in reducing their oil bills in real terms; the Americans, in a sense, never had to pay for their oil at all. This explains why imports and consumption of oil actually increased in the U.S. from 1974, and why the U.S. did not have to suffer deflation; in fact, after the oil crisis the U.S. launched into the strongest and longest economic expansion in its history.

The Effort to Conserve

The industrialized countries also made an effort to respond to the oil crisis by reducing their consumption of imported oil and by searching for new, non-OPEC oil supplies. In general, however, the conservation plans had almost no effect before 1978. The performances of different countries and areas varied considerably. Between 1972 and 1978, oil consumption dropped 5.2 percent in Europe, rose two percent in Japan and increased 12.6 percent in the U.S. But overall, the degree of dependence of industrialized nations on imports from OPEC changed little. In 1973, the OECD countries as a group imported 66 percent of their oil. This figure actually rose to 68 percent in 1977. It then fell to 61 percent in 1978, but this was less the result of reduced consumption than of new oil supplies from the North Sea.

The search for non-OPEC oil was no more successful than the conservation effort. In the past six years, the rise in non-OPEC oil supplies has come very largely from increased production by just three countries—Britain, Norway and Mexico. In the U.S., exploitation of the Alaskan oilfields has not prevented an overall decline in national production. In 1979, more than five years after the oil crisis, OPEC still accounted for a little less than half of total world oil production, compared to a little more than half in 1973.

A Crisis Without Solution

The industrialized world failed to comprehend the gravity of the oil crisis at the time it occurred. This is obvious from the reactions of both governments and public opinion. After the great oil shortage scare of 1974 and fears of depression in 1975, memories of the crisis quickly grew blurred. By 1976, everyone had calmed down. There was a tendency to make light of what had happened, combined with a yearning for a return to normality. In reality, nothing had been resolved, as became obvious several years later.

A False Sense of Security

From 1976, politicians and others tried to convince themselves that the oil cartel must sooner or later collapse. The media watched closely for the slightest signs of an OPEC breakup. Disagreements among OPEC members at their annual meetings were closely scrutinized. After 1978, as the oil payment burden was temporarily reduced and as economies began to recover, many people came to believe that the oil crisis was a thing of the past. Their conviction was strengthened by the temporary oil glut of 1978, when supply exceeded demand. (In fact, the glut was due very largely to purely technical factors.) The media were full of reassuring news. Oil storage tanks at service stations in the U.S. were full to overflowing; at seaports, oil tankers were forced to line up to unload. We witnessed the blossoming of a kind of collective euphoria, just at the time when we were about to be plunged into the second oil crisis.[1]

Energy problems showed how fragile was the solidarity of the West. The International Energy Agency (IEA), set up under the auspices of the OECD, never became much more than an oil data bank, and one more forum for lackadaisical discussion. Most Western countries simply followed the old rule of every man for himself. France gleefully signed special oil supply contracts with certain Middle East countries. The U.S. stuck to establishing special, discreet ties with Saudi Arabia. The European Economic Community demonstrated its inability to draw up a common energy policy. The belief that the oil crisis was over was deeply rooted in people's minds. The Vice President of the World Bank, for example, told me in all seriousness that a second oil crisis was out of the question because "the Third World could not endure it." To a large extent, this false sense of security was based on the conviction that development of new energy sources was within reach.

The Mirage of Alternative Energy Sources

Possible substitutes for oil as an energy source include nuclear energy, solar energy, geothermic energy and gasification of coal. New sources of oil itself could come from exploitation of oilsand, oil shale and heavy oils, and from exploration for oil and natural gas at great depths under land and sea. For a long time, illusions about the potential of all these sources persisted. The lead times required for bringing new energy sources to fruition were hugely underestimated. In most cases, the technology was not up to the task (the water-fueled engine will not be with us for a while), or projects did not prove economical, despite the higher oil price. Generally, production costs for substitute energy sources were dramatically higher than had been expected. As one analyst put it, the cost of substitution was always close to the market price for oil, but always above it. Today, with the exception of nuclear energy, which costs between $7 and $11 for the equivalent of a barrel of oil (in 1979 dollars), production costs of energy from substitute sources range from $35 per barrel of oil equivalent to at least $62. Furthermore, some of the new procedures, such as exploitation of oil shale and surface coal mining, pose almost insurmountable environmental problems.

The fact is that seven years after the first oil crisis the roles played by the world's various energy sources have hardly changed at all. One exception is nuclear energy in France. Unlike the U.S. and West Germany, France after 1975 did not fundamentally modify its nuclear energy program, with the result that by 1985 close to half of French electricity production will come from nuclear power.[2] But the French exception only serves to confirm the general rule, which is that between the two oil crises, alternative energy sources did not keep their promise, either because of inadequate technology or because of insufficient financing.

---

[1] The same kind of euphoria is evident again today during the 1981 oil glut, which has been caused by world recession. I predict that within a year and a half, the glut will be over and new tensions will break out.

[2] This is as forecast before the socialists came to power in France in May 1981.

The Wastage of Resources

The first oil crisis led to a series of economic dilemmas which cast a dark shadow over prospects for the 1980's. The crisis introduced severe distortions into both national economies and international economic relationships. A major example is the current wastage of world savings.

Up to 1973, capital investment decisions were dictated very largely by the criteria of profit maximization and optimal use of resources. Capital had a tendency to be invested wherever profits appeared highest. It also tended to be employed for productive purposes. Thanks to currency convertibility and freedom from foreign exchange controls, capital was able to flow throughout the world unimpeded by official barriers. This was one of the main reasons for the persistent U.S. balance of payments deficit: profit-seeking U.S. investors moved long-term investment capital all around the globe. It was also a major reason for the rapid rate of world economic growth for 30 years.

The first oil crisis caused a radical change in the situation. The oil producers' petrodollars tend to be invested according to nationalistic criteria. This means less than optimal use of available capital resources, i.e., they are no longer being used in the most efficient or useful way. From a world point of view, construction of desalination plants in Middle Eastern deserts or of steel plants far away from the areas where steel is used is obviously not the best way to employ resources. Petrodollars also tend sometimes to be used for prestige investments, such as deluxe real estate, or for buying arms. The Shah of Iran spent $36 billion to equip his armed forces—and look at them today. (The Saudis are now following the Iranian arms-buying example) In other instances, the oil producers make short-term speculative investments instead of long-term productive ones (such as in plant and equipment or long-term financial placements). Arab speculators lost heavily in the silver market collapse of March 1980, triggered by the activities of the Hunt brothers. The surge in the gold price reflected a growing Arab appetite for the yellow metal. But their investments in gold represent hoarding, pure and simple, and sterilization of resources. Thus a major portion of world savings, which could be used to productive ends, is being diverted from the international financial system and rendered sterile.

As long as the drop in returns on capital affected only a relatively small proportion of available world capital resources, the consequences were not serious. But the tens or hundreds of billions of dollars being used by oil producers for unproductive imports or in other less-than-optimal ways represent perhaps between one-ninth and one-sixth of total world savings. The prospect of a drop in the productivity of such a huge amount of capital has serious implications for world economic growth. And remember that the population of the world is going to more than double in the next 20 years; economic growth is more necessary than ever in order to welcome these extra billions of people.

The rise in the oil price also caused a fall in the marginal profitability of capital, i.e. a rise in the capital-output ratio. The price of capital is largely conditioned by the price of energy; in fact, capital incorporates energy in various forms. Every rise in the price of energy thus causes a rise in the price of capital and a fall in its marginal profitability. That means an increased quantity of capital becomes necessary to produce the same amount of goods. It is possible that the huge petrodollar surpluses to be recycled in the years ahead will not even cover the capital surplus required just to maintain economic growth at current levels. The search for new oil and non-oil energy sources is going to require huge capital resources. Under the circumstances, it is doubtful that the volume of world savings will be large enough to provide those resources.

The Petrodollar Investment Problem

For some years now, the investment outlets which absorbed petrodollars without too much trouble after the first oil crisis have steadily become clogged up. On the one hand, the ability of oil producers to spend their money on durable goods imports has certain limits: even arms purchases cannot go on increasing forever. As for real estate purchases, resistance to such investments is already showing up in a number of countries, for economic, political and social reasons. Finally, even short-term deposits in the international banking system cannot be increased indefinitely. In the 1980's, new investment outlet solutions will have to be found. The problem concerns especially Saudi Arabia, Kuwait and the three Emirates, which, with a combined population of slightly less than 12 million, had accumulated assets of about $300 billion at the end of 1980. These countries are well aware of the difficulties presented by the concentration of too much wealth in too few hands. They have already encountered almost insurmountable problems in finding safe outlets for their constantly expanding riches. Domestically, they face threats of disruption. (The example of Iran is fresh in everyone's mind.) Externally, they are threatened by the greed of other nations.

The "Noose Effect"

The oil crisis had the effect of placing the world economy in a noose, which is being progressively tightened to choke the life out of economic expansion whenever it begins. It's step-by-step strangulation. Economic behavior has many times been forcibly altered by such things as higher taxation, the closing of supply routes, even the loss of an empire. But now we are dealing with a totally unprecedented situation. The adjustments we must make in our economic behavior are required of us not just once, but repeatedly. The price of oil has not been fixed once and for all. It is perpetually subject to being raised further. The more the oil consuming countries succeed in creating surpluses or savings, the more the producers are tempted to give another turn of the oil price screw, if necessary by reducing their production levels. The consumers are thus threatened by a constant skimming of their resources, which are whisked abroad as soon as they are produced. There is no limit to the turning of the screw, which causes, in principle, a never-ending process of impoverishment. This process is apt to cause widespread lassitude, even despair, among the people of industrialized nations, as they watch the fruits of all their labors repeatedly disappear. Each time the industrialized economies adjust to a new oil price level and achieve a balance among investment, savings and consumption, along comes another oil price rise to destroy the balance by creating a new deflationary gap.

Thus the world economy staggers from crisis to crisis. Successive oil price hikes repeatedly prevent creation of the conditions required for lasting economic expansion. Inevitably, the gap between the developed and the less developed countries widens, sowing the seeds for a world crisis of unprecedented proportions.[1]

---

[1]This widening gap illustrates how false were the analyses made five years ago according to which the oil price rise represented the revenge of the Third World.

CHAPTER 2
The Recession of
1974/1975

A New Kind of Crisis

The world recession of 1974/1975 began in the U.S. in March 1974 and was transmitted to European countries and Japan with delays of between 10 and 12 months. Transmission mechanisms included international trade, capital movements and a contagious spreading of recessionary psychology. The crisis took Europe by surprise, and Europeans did not fully understand at the time what was going on. Europe had been enjoying the longest period of economic expansion in its history, dating back to the end of World War II. It was hard for European people to comprehend that that period was finally drawing to a close.

There were some good reasons for this lack of comprehension. For some time, in France for example, recession meant nothing more than a slowdown in the rate of economic growth, from the previous four to five percent a year. This helped make people complacent. Furthermore, in 1975, Europeans saw that the U.S. economy was already recovering swiftly, and they confidently expected the same thing to happen in Europe. However, as we shall see, the nature of the 1974/1975 crisis was very much different in the U.S. than it was in Europe and Japan.

Forced Deflation in Europe

The U.S. suffered a classic recession resulting from a capital spending boom and excessive accumulation of inventories. Industrial production plunged 15 percent between June 1974 and March 1975. Afterwards, adjustments having been made, economic recovery was rapid.

In Europe and Japan, it was a very different story. Their recessions also displayed some classic symptoms. Like the U.S. economy, the economies of Europe also suffered from an excessive inventory buildup and subsequent liquidation. But there the comparison ends. For the problems afflicting European economies proved to be structural in nature, and thus extremely difficult to solve. What triggered these problems, of course, was the oil crisis, which was both deflationary, because it reduced national incomes, and inflationary, because it sharply raised costs. Inevitably, it caused a slowdown in European economic growth, by imposing both balance of payments and anti-inflation constraints on economic policy-making.

The oil price rise caused huge increases in the import bills of European countries and Japan. French payments for imported oil, for example, surged to 43 billion francs in 1974 from just eight billion two years earlier. Thus, to prevent an unacceptable rise in their external debt, these countries were forced to adopt tough deflationary fiscal and monetary policies, designed to achieve an export surplus and restore their balance of payments positions to health. It goes without saying that such deflation implies a sharp contraction of domestic demand, resulting in a slowdown in economic growth.

At the same time, these countries were forced to take deflationary steps to control imported cost inflation caused by the higher oil prices. Germany managed to overcome these handicaps, but only, as is too often forgotten, at the price of very slow economic growth for several years.

Italy and France also prevailed, but only in a very incomplete way, and their success remains fragile. Britain was a case apart. The British were eventually freed from external constraints by North Sea oil, which made them self-sufficient in energy; but in the meantime, the British government was still forced to impose extremely severe wage restraints, which led to reduced buying power and a very weak economic growth rate. (The situation was made worse, of course, by the decaying of British industrial plant, which would have condemned Britain to very moderate growth whatever happened.)

The U.S. escaped the European and Japanese problems because it was able to refuse to submit to external constraints; U.S. oil imports increased more rapidly than ever, and the U.S. trade deficit rose to an all-time high. This refusal very largely explains the exceptional performance of the U.S. economy from 1976 to 1978. As we have said, the surge in energy costs was clearly the main cause of the 1974/1975 recessionary crisis in Europe and Japan. It is worth adding however that the general rise in world inflation which had become apparent from the beginning of the 1970's also played a significant role.

The recessionary crisis was accompanied by sharp growth in social welfare payments. Reflecting this, national budget deficits rose to record highs in many countries, including Britain, Germany and Italy.

It is clear that governments were helpless to find remedies for their countries' new economic ailments. In France, the government tried anti-inflation policies in 1974, then switched to reflation in 1975, then changed course again in 1976 to adopt the economic program of Prime Minister Raymond Barre. Three radically different policy approaches in as many years, and all equally unsuccessful. The bottom line is that in Europe the recession was not followed by a rapid recovery as in the U.S. There has only been a weak, indecisive improvement in economic activity. Growth rates, varying of course from country to country, are certainly better than the performance during the recession itself, but are still far below pre-recession levels. It is a lifeless, directionless recovery, of a kind not seen before.

The "L" Curve

Every economist worth his salt owes it to himself to invent a "Curve" or an "Effect". We already have the "V" curve to describe a sharp fall in economic activity followed by a rapid recovery, and the "U" curve, which describes a more gradual version of the same thing. Now the time is ripe for invention of the "L" curve, to describe a situation in which, after a recession, economic activity remains flat for an extended period.

Like most men, economists are strongly conditioned by experience. Based on what they have seen and learned, they expect recessions to be followed by recovery as surely as night follows day or winter leads to spring. It is always important, of course, to understand exactly what is meant by *recovery*. Everything depends on the point of departure. If you take as a reference point the very bottom of the curve, then there is always a recovery of sorts, however limited it may be. But this time around, the real problem is not which reference point to take. Rather, it is to discover whether, after the 1973 oil crisis and the subsequent recession, the old recovery rules still apply.

Did the events of that crucial period fundamentally alter the old patterns of production, consumption and world trade? Or were the upheavals of that period simply transitory and superficial in nature? Did everything change, or did everything remain the same?

The example of West Germany is significant. The German economy fell into recession well ahead of other economies; expansion began to falter as early as the first quarter of 1973, and then stopped. Subsequently, despite the introduction of revival programs, the growth curve of the German economy remained obstinately flat and recession or delayed recovery continued for almost three years. Recovery always seemed to be just around the corner, but repeatedly proved elusive.

The same pattern was evident in Italy, where recovery did not get underway until the second quarter of 1975. In Britain and France, it did not begin until the third quarter of that year.

The explanation lies in the oil crisis. The quadrupling of oil prices caused virulent cost inflation, which proved resistant to traditional remedies. It continued long after demand inflation had disappeared. Thus governments were forced to continue deflationary policies for longer than usual—or to delay recovery programs, which comes to the same thing. The oil crisis, in fact, created a permanent deflationary effect. Real national incomes have been reduced by higher oil prices not just once, but repeatedly. This has frustrated efforts at economic revival, and made increases in economic activity limited and uncertain.

Even the U.S., which managed for a long time to finesse its way through the energy crisis thanks to the Dollar Exchange Standard, cannot escape the iron laws of higher oil prices. It is no coincidence that the majority of U.S. economists are predicting only a weak recovery from the 1980 U.S. recession, similar to what happened in Europe and Japan after 1974. Everywhere, we are dealing with a new type of economic crisis, a direct result of the oil problem.

Economic Distortions: Productivity, Unemployment and Black Market Labor

The oil crisis and the economic crisis interacted to produce profound distortions in all elements of economic life, from prices to the relationships among savings, investment and consumption, to patterns of foreign trade. Three elements merit special attention because of their importance in socio-political terms: unemployment, the effect of higher oil prices on the productivity of capital and labor, and the rise of black market labor practices.

An Historical Regression: The Substitution of Man for the Machine

Curiously, this phenomenon has received very little attention from most economists, except in the United States. And yet, it is of profound significance. The phenomenon can be briefly explained in the following terms: less productive but cheap human labor now has a tendency to replace more productive but expensive machine power. What has been happening throughout the world during the past six years can be interpreted as an interruption of the process of substituting mechanical power for human labor. This process dates back to the industrial revolution of the 19th century and was accelerating sharply in the postwar decades before the oil crisis. Fortunately, the interruption should prove temporary. In theory, it is surprising that the phenomenon should have become particularly evident in the country which was the last to feel the effects of the oil crisis: the United States.

The U.S. economic recovery from 1975 was accompanied by a sharp rise in job creation. The number of employed people rose by close to 14.8 million, or 16.4 percent, between April 1975 and February 1980. The unemployment rate fell from nine percent in May 1975 to less than six percent in 1979. Never has the number of employed Americans been so high as a proportion of the total population. The explanation is that human labor was being substituted for capital investment. From 1967 to 1973, employment in the U.S. rose 13.5 percent while Gross National Product (GNP) increased 22.6 percent. But from 1974 to 1979, employment rose 14.8 percent, almost matching the GNP expansion of 15.9 percent. Almost all European countries displayed a similar pattern.

The substitution of men for machines explains the striking growth of black market labor. In France, the underground economy now accounts for an estimated 10 to 15 percent of GNP; in Italy, the figure is 15 to 20 percent. As the price of capital rose, employment of capital was replaced by clandestine—and therefore cheap—employment of manpower. Employers forced to pay more for their equipment and machinery have a natural tendency to make use of cheap black market labor, which allows them to pay less than the minimum wage without making social welfare contributions. Black market labor is of course not a new phenomenon; but since the oil crisis it has assumed unprecedented proportions in industrialized economies. The workers involved include women, retired people, unscrupulous unemployed people and students; the activities involved range from construction to manufacturing, from accountancy to agriculture.

The pause in the process of substituting machine power for manpower resulted from the sharp fall in the marginal productivity of capital which followed the oil crisis. The most obvious result of this fall was a weakening of demand for capital and a consequent drop in capital investment. Areas of economic activity which had previously been profitable were suddenly obsolete and fell into stagnation. For a long time, the rising cost of capital made it more economical to continue using existing plant—old and inefficient but fully depreciated—than to invest in new facilities. (On top of this, plants were operating at way below capacity because of generally low levels of economic activity).

But the biggest problem arising from the drop in the productivity of capital was the growth of competition between capital and labor. This slowed down, and then reversed, the process of substituting capital for labor. Now this reversal, in favor of employment, would seem to suggest a fall in unemployment. And yet, unemployment rates rose in almost all industrialized countries. Why? The answer is that employers were seeking the cheapest possible labor to replace increasingly costly capital, and so overall demand for qualified, expensive workers fell, while demand for unqualified, poorly-paid workers rose. This explains why graduates fresh from colleges and universities often have a hard time finding appropriate employment, while immigrants have no difficulty finding poorly-paid menial work. In the U.S., many of the new jobs created have benefited *wetback* illegal immigrants, now estimated to total 10 million.

There are two possible reactions to such circumstances. The West German-style response was to offset rising energy costs through further improvements in labor productivity, achieved by investments designed to modernize plant and equipment. This allowed Germany to maintain and improve the international competitiveness of its products, even while paying its highly qualified work force wages among the highest in the world. The German approach involved a reduction in job offers, a relatively high level of unemployment, and a subdued rate of economic growth. But this approach enabled the Germans for a long time to keep inflation at very low levels and to produce comfortable balance of payments surpluses. The American response was almost directly the opposite of the German one. The U.S. faced a much less critical energy problem than the Europeans, since the rise in U.S. energy costs was limited and delayed. Still, the Americans reacted with a relative reduction in labor costs and rapid economic growth which allowed for the creation of many new jobs. Today (thanks partly to the depreciation of the dollar) U.S. labor costs are below those of several European countries, including Germany, Sweden and the Netherlands.

The substitution of man for machine is a regressive and profoundly unhealthy process. Clearly, it goes against the historical trend which has permitted industrialization and improvements in living standards. However, it is a process which is likely to continue until a new balance is found between the price and the productivity of capital. Such a balance could be found either through a relative fall in the price of energy or through a rapid rise in labor productivity. Unfortunately, in the present circumstances, improved labor productivity can only be achieved to the detriment of employment levels. Which brings us to the contemporary unemployment dilemma.

Can Unemployment be Reduced?

Roughly speaking, unemployment has doubled in most industrialized countries since the 1973 oil crisis. The United States is a major exception. Also in West Germany unemployment has dipped, thanks to the forced return by the German government of immigrant workers to their own countries. But overall, it is clear that unemployment has become a constant concern in most industrial societies.

First, a comment on the much-discussed question of the links between unemployment and inflation. According to the famous Philips curve, inflation falls when unemployment rises, and vice versa. However, since the beginning of the 1970's, there has been no such trade-off. It has been clear for a long time that inflation can rise together with unemployment. It is even possible that inflation creates unemployment through the uncertainties which it generates and the misallocation of resources which it causes. The unemployment problem can also be approached in terms of which sectors of the economy are creating jobs, and which are not. Between 1973 and 1980, the number of actively employed people rose sharply in the U.S., increased somewhat in Japan, France and Italy, and fell in Britain and West Germany. The interesting point is that in all these countries the industrial and non-industrial sectors of the economy performed similarly in employment terms. In the U.S., Japan, France and Italy, the increases in employment were largely or entirely due to jobs created outside the industrial sector. In Britain and Germany, the declines in employment were much sharper in the industrial sector than outside it. The facts indicate that throughout the industrialized world, industry has ceased to be a creator of new jobs.

Historically, the existence of unemployment has been the norm rather than the exception. In fact, unemployment has been endemic, with the exception of a brief period of European history—the 30 years following World War II. And even that period of full employment did not affect the whole of Europe, but only the northern, most industrialized part. To the south, in Turkey, Greece, Portugal and southern Italy, for example, it never did prove possible to create enough jobs for the available labor force. In developing countries, of course, unemployment is built into the structure of the economy. Even in the U.S., average postwar unemployment has been much higher than in northern European countries. It is obvious that a prolonged period of slow economic growth or of economic stagnation means continued under-employment. The industrialized countries may thus be forced to adapt themselves for a long time to come to endemic unemployment of a new kind. Contemporary unemployment in industrialized countries is a result both of the economic crisis and of a cultural crisis; it is a phenomenon of rich, advanced societies with well-developed social welfare systems. In theory, even at times of slow economic growth, there is no reason why the unemployment problem could not be solved with appropriate policies. Unemployment only exists as a function of a certain structure of salaries and incomes. To abolish it, in principle, would require nothing more than an across-the-board drop in incomes, creating a financial surplus which could be used to finance useful work which at present is not economic.

In reality, of course, such simple-sounding solutions are not practical because of social and cultural factors. It is also worth pointing out, on a fundamental level, that unemployment statistics can vary considerably. Governments have often tinkered with the definitions to reduce the official unemployment rate, which is a little like changing the scale on a thermometer to reduce the patient's fever. Factors behind rising unemployment certainly include the entry of women into the labor market on a massive scale. There are many cultural reasons for this, including higher levels of education, the women's liberation movement, the drop in the birth rate and the increased role played by the services sector in developed economies; but the biggest single reason is probably inflation, which has pitilessly eroded the buying power of single-income families.

Another major factor is the social welfare systems developed by industrialized nations. Any rise in unemployment benefits, for example, is enough by itself to cause an increase in the official unemployment rate.

Youth unemployment is a contemporary phenomenon with a variety of complex causes. These include the refusal to accept certain jobs considered degrading or too poorly paid, a fall in the level of educational qualifications caused by the democratization of education systems, and the fall in the birth rate which makes it possible for families to support unemployed adolescents at home. Finally, there is the increase of black market labor which helps to swell official unemployment figures. But however much of the unemployment problem can be explained by cultural factors, the fact remains that the hard core of more or less identifiable unemployment has grown markedly in industrialized countries in the past six years, showing that there is a clear link between unemployment and the oil crisis.

Must we conclude that our capitalist economies have been condemned to languish forever, and that unemployment will remain a blemish on modern societies, like cancer or industrial pollution? Some analysts appear to feel this way, and to have resigned themselves to their fate.

Whatever happens, it seems certain that unemployment will remain endemic until a fall in the price of energy allows economic growth rates to rise, and a strong burst of productive, job-creating investment to begin. That amounts to an iron law of economics, from which it is not possible to escape, no matter how subtle the arguments or ingenious the proposed solutions.

CHAPTER 3
The Monetary Crisis

The Failures of the Monetary System

There is no such thing as perfect order in international monetary affairs. There never has been and there never will be. Only academics in ivory towers could suppose otherwise. The world's central bankers know only too well that the idea of an orderly international monetary system is a myth. Any system must be analyzed not in terms of order but of disorder, not in terms of balance but of imbalance. All economic and monetary systems are built around political systems; they are always dominated by one nation or group of nations, which try to use them for their own political ends. The Comecon system is designed to further the growth and power of the Soviet Union and the Socialist bloc. The Americans used the Dollar Exchange Standard system to increase their power throughout the world. The present world monetary system is variously described these days as absurd, ailing and in a state of collapse. All of these descriptions are only partly true. The fact is that since August 1971, when the end of dollar convertibility into gold marked the offical death of the Dollar Exchange Standard, the international monetary system has functioned quite well. It prevented a collapse of the world economy after the first oil crisis, which was no minor achievement.

But the system does have one huge flaw: it operates essentially to the benefit of the United States and to the detriment of other countries. An even more fundamental problem is that the system is inexorably fueling world inflation. It could lead, sooner or later, to an explosion. Many experts have pointed out, and rightly so, that the Dollar Exchange Standard worked to the benefit exclusively of American power. So far, however no one has provided a convincing explanation of why the rest of the world put up with the system for so long. There were obviously powerful reasons why the majority of the international community tolerated a state of affairs so prejudicial to its interests. I shall attempt to explain these reasons in the pages which follow. I will also explain how the countries of the European Economic Community tried to escape from the yoke of the dollar, and why they failed for a long time to do so. Finally, I shall try to show how permanent depreciation of the dollar is leading inevitably towards remonetization of gold, even though this is still being vigorously opposed by the American authorities.

The Inflationary Spiral

The world monetary system is steadily fueling global inflation. Since World War II, there have been a series of plateau periods, when prices were relatively stable, separated by periods during which inflation accelerated abruptly. Between 1950 and 1965, the average rate of inflation was around three percent. A strong inflationary trend then prevailed from 1965 to 1973, taking the world inflation rate to a new plateau where it ranged between five and seven percent. The first oil crisis then propelled the rate up to the eight to ten percent range. Each time the inflation rate has reached a new plateau, the high point has been at least three percentage points above the high point of the previous plateau period; similarly, the low point has been above the previous low.

It is obvious that the huge amounts of liquidity injected into the world economy played a major role in this world inflationary process. A rough method of estimating the liquidity creation is to calculate the total size of the Eurodollar market.[1]

Unfortunately, no one knows the exact size, either in gross or net terms; even the Bank for International Settlements (BIS), which in a way is the Eurodollar market's bookkeeper, admits that the available figures are only approximations. This reflects the huge number of different kinds of operations conducted in the market, as well as *double counting* and quite simply a lack of systematic records.

A major reason for the huge growth in liquidity was the postwar U.S. balance of payments deficit: quite simply, the U.S. created money which found its way overseas through the balance of payments mechanism.

Another reason, after the oil crisis, was the investment of petrodollar surpluses through the recycling process discussed earlier. This was not strictly speaking money creation, but rather a transfer of liquidity, notably in the form of short-term bank deposits, which swelled international liquidity. These deposits were used as the basis for Eurodollar loans which helped to offset the drain on resources caused by higher oil prices.

A third reason, although there is no agreement among experts on this, was probably that the extension of credit through the Eurodollar market has the same kind of multiplier effect that it has within national economies. Whatever the process of its formation, the mass of international liquidity did not cease to expand. This expansion was clearly in response to a need—the need to struggle against the permanent deflation resulting from the oil payment burden.

The result was that the American privilege of borrowing without ever repaying—the secret of the "deficit without tears", in the famous phrase of economist Jacques Rueff, was extended to practically all countries of the world. Rich or poor, Eastern or Western, all countries acquired liberal access to the horn of plenty of international credits, which freed them from the unpleasant disciplines of economic stabilization programs.

---

[1] A more precise term is "Xeno-currency market" (from the Greek "Xenos", meaning "foreign"): this description recognizes that besides the dollar, the German mark, the Japanese yen and other currencies are also being used more and more often in international settlements.

An obvious illustration of the process was the surge in international debt, particularly the debt of developing countries. Another was the decline in the role played by the International Monetary Fund (IMF) in the international payments system.

I still remember, when I was an economist at the IMF, how the media in certain countries, for example in Latin America, heaped opprobrium on the IMF. This was because the "vultures" of the IMF almost always insisted, in return for loans, that countries adopt tough economic stabilization programs to restore their economies to health. Today the IMF in some respects is little more than a forum for advice and discussion. It still plays a major role as a lender to small countries with shaky international credit ratings. But the powerful lords of the Third World, such as Argentina and Brazil, hardly take the trouble any longer to seek the assistance of the IMF. They much prefer to borrow without constraints from major international banks, such as Citibank or Chase Manhattan Bank, even if the terms are burdensome. Ever-rising world inflation is a natural result of the international lending system which has been developed.

What remains to be explained is why, long before the oil crisis, such a flagrantly risky system was ever established in the first place, and how it has endured for so long. To understand the reasons, we have to leave the field of economics for a moment to consider a few geopolitical realities.

The U.S. Money-Printing Privilege

The U.S. was granted the privilege of printing international currency at the 44-nation Bretton Woods conference of 1944. It was a truly extraordinary privilege, which was only tolerated by the world for so long because of an implicit consensus among the Bretton Woods participants. In effect, the privilege was based on an exchange. The U.S. won the right to finance its permanent balance of payments deficit with depreciating dollars; in return, the U.S. allies got the chance to acquire cut-price U.S. military protection through the Atlantic alliance. It should be stressed that the true nature of this exchange—military security in return for dollar accumulation—was never publicly articulated by any politician, or formulated in any official or unofficial document.

The most precise formulation was provided by President Nixon, who showed himself to be either the most cynical or the most candid of U.S. presidents by declaring outright to astonished U.S. allies at the Ottawa conference of March 1973 that it was impossible to separate military solidarity (meaning the protection which the U.S. provided for the allies) from economic solidarity (meaning advantageous terms for exports to Europe of U.S. agricultural products, and European support for the value of the dollar).

General de Gaulle wanted to free France from its reliance on U.S. military protection, and so he also tried to break loose from the protection of the dollar in the monetary arena. But as events showed, it was easier to withdraw from a military alliance than to extricate oneself from the international monetary game.

For a long time, the Dollar Exchange Standard was considered by many to be a godsend, because its facilities provided an almost inexhaustible source of liquidity which was essential to the smooth functioning of the international monetary system. Although it looked so unfair, the system was accepted because it proved to be to everyone's advantage. Today, the terms of the original exchange have been so radically altered that the implicit consensus is in danger of breaking down.

The Crisis within NATO

Almost since its inception in 1947, the NATO alliance has been plagued by a variety of problems. There has been permanent disagreement over the contributions of individual members of the alliance to the common defense effort, with the U.S. arguing that the Europeans do not pull their weight. Another bone of contention has been reimbursement of the costs of stationing U.S. troops in West Germany. This problem became acute at the beginning of the 1970's, when the U.S. balance of payments deficit became a subject of controversy and the Jackson-Nunn amendment was adopted, making the maintenance of troops conditional on the size of German compensation payments.

In the Nixon-Kissinger period, trade problems erupted within the alliance, notably the conflict between the U.S. and the European Economic Community over trade in agricultural products, illustrated by the famous *chicken war*. But up until recently, all the alliance's problems remained peripheral, regional or sectoral in nature; today, they have assumed the proportions of a fundamental crisis. In the past few years, Washington has been repeatedly at loggerheads with its allies over such issues as the installation of medium-range missiles on European soil and use of the neutron bomb. The crises over Iran and Afghanistan revealed profound disagreements between the U.S. and key European allies. France and West Germany were both reluctant to show solidarity with Washington by imposing economic sanctions against Iran or by boycotting the Olympic Games; on the other hand, both countries showed themselves very eager to resume the interrupted dialogue with Moscow.

For the first time in 30 years, it seems that not just one isolated ally, but the European allies as a group, no longer share the U.S. view of the Soviet danger and of how it should be met. The allies no longer appear willing to accept American suzerainty as submissively as before. The whole balance of power within NATO is being called into question.

The Implicit Consensus

The implicit consensus reached among the countries of the Atlantic alliance can be interpreted in terms of a trade-off between economic advantages and political or military advantages. For almost thirty years, the U.S. provided military protection for its allies, who in turn agreed to finance the chronic U.S. balance of payments deficit by absorbing increasing amounts of constantly depreciating dollars. The depreciation losses, more or less voluntarily accepted by the allies, represented in a sense the price tag for U.S. protection. This protection allowed the Europeans to plow into growth-generating investments resources which they would otherwise have been forced to use for their own defense.

Up to the end of the 1960's, European countries were spending only between two and five percent of their Gross National Product (GNP) on defense, compared to eight to nine percent for the U.S.[1]

---

[1] The figure for the U.S. has now fallen to five percent.

According to the State Department, the U.S. between 1950 and 1970 spent around $1.3 trillion on defense and the Soviet Union about $1 trillion.[2] By comparison, European defense outlays in the same period amounted to no more than $300 to $350 billion.

The price paid by Europe and Japan for military protection can be roughly estimated by calculating the dollar reserves accumulated by European countries and Japan, and then deflating the total by the U.S. inflation rate. The difference between the nominal and the inflation-adjusted figures represents the cost to the allies of accumulating dollars.

In 1978, Japan's dollar reserves totalled $29 billion, which was about equivalent to $10 billion 1950 dollars. The loss of about $19 billion represents the support given by Japan to the dollar, i.e. the price to be paid for the benefit of U.S. protection.

As for the European Economic Community, the dollar reserves of member countries in 1978 amounted to about $80 billion, which was equivalent to $29 billion in 1950, giving a loss of about $50 billion. Now, when these loss figures are compared to the amounts which the allies would have had to invest in defense to guarantee a degree of security comparable to that provided by the U.S., the advantages to the allies of U.S. protection become obvious. The issues are not quite as simple as the figures indicate. It should be noted, for example, that U.S. defense expenditures had a beneficial effect in developing certain sectors of private industry, such as aeronautics and electronics. But overall, the fact remains that military outlays absorb funds which then become unavailable for productive investment. Indirectly, the American defense umbrella made it possible for Europe to save resources not just in the billions of dollars, but in the hundreds of billions.

This fact is implicitly recognized by those who stress that a truly autonomous Europe should spend about as much of GNP on defense as the U.S. does.

Breakdown of the Consensus

In the early 1970's, a fundamental change took place in U.S. policy, which went unnoticed for some time. Choosing among priorities, the Americans decided to reduce their defense posture and their ability to guarantee the security of their allies. The change of course was clearly indicated by the decline in the percentage of GNP spent on defense. It led to a dramatic weakening of U.S. defense capabilities, which was no doubt responsible for allowing the Soviets to enter Afghanistan, for permitting the Iran crisis to develop, and for increasing the risk of a major crisis in the Persian Gulf.

The U.S. military response capability was eroded progressively, first in the field of conventional warfare, and then in the nuclear field. As of right now, the U.S. is no longer in a position of military superiority vis-a-vis the Soviet Union; worse, it is not managing to maintain parity of forces. Thus, the European allies can no longer count on automatic U.S. intervention in case of conflict. U.S. protection, unfailingly provided for a quarter of a century, is no longer as axiomatic as it was.

Unsurprisingly then, the European allies are no longer willing to pay their dollar

---

[2]Calculated in 1970 dollars.

tribute. Why continue to pay contributions when the principal reason for them—protection—appears to be increasingly unreliable? The allies are increasingly inclined to demonstrate more independence in their relations with their principal ally, the U.S., while seeking to establish more independent diplomatic relations of their own with the Soviet Union.

Here lies the fundamental cause of the current profound crisis within the Atlantic alliance. In the circumstances, it seems doubtful whether the U.S. money-printing privilege can survive much longer. Europe failed in its attempt to free itself from the yoke of the dollar throught the creation of the European currency "snake". But what must be kept in mind is that all past crises within the Atlantic alliance had a temporary, superficial quality. None of them, not even France's withdrawal from the military wing of NATO, threatened to destroy the very principle of Atlantic solidarity. Now it is different. As the decade of the 1980's opens, the alliance is confronted with a crisis of unprecedented severity.

European Currency Reform

The Failure of the Snake

The 1972 attempt to set up the European currency snake represented an effort to establish an island of coherence and calm in a sea of international monetary chaos. The effort ended in failure. And yet it was a praiseworthy try at monetary cooperation, carried out with considerable panache. The idea was to tie the various European currencies together by establishing fixed parities among them so that they would fluctuate as a group within predetermined limits against external currencies—most importantly, of course, the dollar. The group's fluctuations would resemble the undulations of a snake when it moves.

The hope of French President Pompidou and British Prime Minister Heath was that the system would pave the way for full European Monetary Union, foreseen for 1980. The snake was to mark the beginning of the road towards a common European currency, which would demonstrate the desire of a united Europe for autonomy in the monetary arena. From its birth in April 1972, however, the unfortunate snake acted like a boa constrictor which had swallowed prey too large to digest.

After less than three months, in June 1972, the pound sterling left the snake, never to return. The Danish crown left as well, but rejoined at the end of the year. In January of 1973, the Italian lira left the system for good. The whole snake was then set free to float against the dollar. The German mark was revalued twice in 1973, first in March, then again in June; the Dutch guilder and Norwegian crown were also revalued. The French franc left the snake in January 1974, rejoined in July 1975, then left again in March 1976. The snake had become little more than a meeting place for currencies, where they quickly greeted each other before going their own separate ways.

The snake concept failed under the pressure of the tumultuous events which folowed the quadrupling of oil prices. At the time, snake member countries flung wild accusations at each other. The French accused the Germans of aligning themselves with U.S. policies, the British of trying to go it alone, and the Italians of doing both things at the same time.

But the truth of the matter was simple. The Europeans were victims of a collective illusion. The value of a currency is only maintained by economic and political efforts of the government concerned. In Europe, there is not one government, but many, each of them sensitive to the aspirations and pressures of its electorate. There is not one European policy, but many policies, varying according to the ability of different countries to control inflation, i.e. to accept a certain degree of wage and price discipline. Rates of inflation varied so widely among the snake member countries that it was impossible for the system to work.

Roughly speaking, there were three groups of countries in the world at that time, those with inflation of less than five percent—such as West Germany and Switzerland—those with inflation in the 10 percent area—France, Belgium and Japan—and those with inflation of 15 percent and more—Britain, Italy and Spain. The countries in the first group, a small minority, were very close to the U.S. model. Those in the third group were close to the Brazilian model. How could such divergent trends be contained within a single system? The snake was a long shot, which failed to pay off.

The failure made clear that the disparities among the economic policies of the snake member countries were stronger than their disparities with the policies of other non-snake countries. The Europeans decided to try to learn from their experience, and to start again, using a more flexible approach, more adapted to realities. The result was the European Monetary System (EMS), established in March 1979.

The Success of the European Monetary System

The EMS, which was the result of long and arduous negotiations, is a system of extraordinary technical complexity. It is also extremely ingenious, and takes account of inflationary realities. Britain, with its high inflation rate, remained outside the system; Italy, hardly any better off than Britain in the inflation area, joined the system, but was allowed generous fluctuation margins for the lira.

The system provides very flexible adjustment mechanisms, allowing a member country to devalue or revalue its currency against other currencies in the system painlessly and discreetly. Hardly six months after the system began operating, the German mark was revalued two percent; a few months later, the Danish crown was devalued five percent. These adjustment mechanisms have their limits, of course. Even when carried out discreetly, a series of ill-timed exchange rate adjustments would end up reducing the credibility of the system. But up to now, it must be said that the system has functioned perfectly. Above all, it rode out the storm caused by the severe dollar crisis of 1979.

The system has a number of ingenious features, such as the *divergence indicator,* which rings the alarm when there is excessive divergence of one currency from the others. Without doubt, the most important feature is the requirement for concerted action by EMS member countries. This puts the system on the right path, the path towards joint consultation on economic policy making. The lack of such joint action was the main stumbling block for all previous attempts at European monetary cooperation.

Up to now, let it be said, the EMS has been lucky, because its start-up coincided with a spectacular reversal of positions within Europe. The German mark, whose traditional strength could have put strains on the system, has gradually collapsed under the weight of its heavy burdens, while the supposedly weak currencies, such as the French franc and the Italian lira, have been riding high. The pound sterling, which was wisely kept out of the system, would have caused major problems, not, as once feared, because of its weakness, but because of its excessive strength.

The period during which the EMS has been operating is clearly atypical. It is not every day that oil is discovered in the North Sea; and the surprising reversal of the German balance of payments position is hardly illustrative of traditional German economic behavior. At some point, things are likely to get back to normal, and the moment of truth for the EMS will arrive. Only then will we be able to tell if it is really possible to frame a joint European economic policy, which is the essential precondition for a durable monetary policy. And looming over all attempts to construct regional monetary systems is the gradual remonetization of gold as a basis for international settlements.

The Permanently Depreciating Dollar

It is not easy to disentangle the threads tying together the oil crisis, the economic crisis and the geopolitical crisis. The preceding account is obviously not complete, nor is it supposed to be. The purpose has been to try to show how phenomena which are usually analyzed separately are in fact connected to each other in a variety of ways.

It remains to analyze the position of the dollar, the preeminent international currency, and its relationships with the price of oil and the price of gold, the dollar's great rival. We have seen how the depreciation of the dollar helped to limit the impact of the oil shock. But what are the implications for the world economy of the chronic dollar crisis?

External Dollars vs. Domestic Dollars

In a sense, there are now two kinds of dollars in existence—two distinct currencies—the domestic dollar, used within the United States, and the external dollar, used for international settlements. Although issued in principle by the same monetary authority, the Federal Reserve Board, these two currencies in reality are created and behave in different ways. To a degree, it can be argued that fluctuations in the value of the external dollar are beyond the control of the U.S. authorities. At current rates of exchange, the buying power of the dollar within the U.S. is far greater than in certain other countries. In West Germany, for example, the dollar may buy as much as 30 percent less than it does at home.[1]

The value of the external dollar does not always conform to economic logic. For example, in early 1975 the dollar should have strengthened on foreign exchange

---

[1]This was in 1980, since when the situation has changed dramatically.

markets. The U.S. had been suffering for several months from a severe recession, which was good for the U.S. balance of trade: despite the quadrupling of oil prices, the U.S. trade deficit remained moderate, proportionately little changed from earlier levels. And yet, the dollar continued to lose ground against the Swiss franc and German mark. The explanation lies in the fact that the quantity of dollars circulating outside the U.S. has become so great that they have assumed a life of their own, obeying their own laws, just as an inland sea has its own tides.

The Eurodollar market, which used to grow steadily by about two or three billion dollars a year because of the U.S. balance of payments deficit, is now expanding by several tens of billions annually. This has completely changed the name of the game, and explains why the external value of the dollar is so sharply divergent from its "real parity", i.e. its buying power within the U.S.

We are still a long way from the point at which the U.S. authorities become powerless to influence the value of the dollar on foreign exchange markets. But it remains to be determined whether the famous policy of *benign neglect* towards the dollar's exchange rate represented a chosen course of action, or whether it was imposed on the U.S. authorities by force of circumstances. What passed for a deliberate policy might well have been a disguised confession of impotence on the part of the authorities.

The recovery of the dollar in recent years has proved that it is still possible for the Federal Reserve, in cooperation with other major central banks, to turn foreign exchange market trends around. But what is striking is how these turnarounds up to now have been of limited extent and duration.

The implication is that the U.S. monetary authorities may no longer be able to fundamentally change the course of events, but only to change trends temporarily. One day it may be necessary to separate the fate of the domestic dollar from that of the external dollar. That would mark the end of unrestricted dollar convertibility.

The Yo-yo Principle, or Why the Dollar Fails to Recover

For more than 10 years, foreign exchange dealers and economic forecasters have been waiting in vain for the dollar finally to stage a full recovery. Sharp falls in the dollar are regularly followed by small rises, which fail to bring the currency back to where it started from. This steady depreciation is due not only to inflation differentials, but also to the persistant excess of dollar supply over demand for dollars outside the United States. The dollar is behaving like a yo-yo, which descends as far as it can go down a length of string, then climbs back, but not quite to the point it fell from.

Take the example of the dollar's exchange rate with the German mark. On February 13, 1973, the rate was 2.9003 marks per dollar. The dollar fell to 2.32 marks in July 1973, recovered as far as 2.81 in January 1974, then quickly fell back to 2.35 in May. It again recovered to 2.69 in September 1974, only to fall back to 2.31 in March 1975. By September 1975, the dollar was back up to 2.61, but fell to 2.38 in December 1976. In February 1977, the dollar rose to 2.40, before plunging to 1.96 in September 1978, and further to 1.90 in October, after some fluctuations. After President Carter's first dollar support package, the dollar recovered in 1979, only to drop again in September of that year.

With the U.S. economy in recession in the second quarter of 1980, the dollar should in principle strengthen, thanks to a reduction in the U.S. trade deficit resulting from the domestic economic slowdown.

Classical theory, and in particular the thesis of economist Gustave Cassel, explains exchange rate relationships in real terms, i.e. in terms of the buying power of the currencies concerned. The theory that exchange rates are a function of inflation differentials starts from the same buying-power principle. If prices are perfectly stable in country A while inflation is running at 10 percent in country B, the currency of country B will eventually depreciate by 10 percent against the currency of country A. In theory, floating exchange rates should allow the adjustment to be immediate. In practice, things are a bit more complicated. At any given time, currencies are either overvalued or undervalued against each other because of foreign exchange market expectations. Furthermore, adjustments do not take place progressively, but all of a sudden, producing the kind of monetary crises we have seen frequently in recent years.

Generally speaking, it is safe to say that the primary influence on exchange rates is the performance of prices in individual countries, which in turn, after a time lag of several months, determines balance of payments developments. To complete the picture, of course, we must take into account interest rates and capital movements, which on occasion play a key role. But to repeat: over the long term, prices are the prime mover of exchange rates.

The trouble in the dollar's case is that it is not a currency like other currencies. It does not fit the general pattern, because it is an international currency held overseas in the form of Eurodollars. Dollar-denominated assets held outside the U.S. are now estimated to exceed $750 billion (with some experts putting the figure as high as $1 trillion).

Thus two factors are interacting to determine the value of the dollar. The first, applying to the *domestic* dollar used within the U.S., is the U.S. inflation rate, which can cause ups or downs in the dollar depending on its performance; the second, applying to the *external* dollar, is the overabundance of dollars held around the globe, which is steadily eroding the dollar's value in terms of other currencies.

This erosion has been estimated by an econometric model at about two percent a year, assuming no inflation differentials. This suggests the dollar should fall against the currencies of countries with the same inflation rate as the U.S. by about two percent a year, and that at the end of each cyclical crisis, the dollar will recover, but only to a level slightly below the level previously attained. This mechanism worked perfectly through the 1970's. Now what about the 1980's? Some forecasters are now saying the 1980's could see the reappearance of a dollar shortage. Are we moving towards a new dollar gap, with the U.S. balance of payments in surplus and the sea of external dollars steadily shrinking? That would mean that the reversal of currency relationships in favor of the dollar in 1981 could last for some time. After the yo-yo dollar, shall we see a yo-yo German mark?

The Gold/Oil Exchange Rate

No discussion of the dollar is complete without reference to its eternal rival, gold. But the question arises, does the gold/dollar exchange rate have meaning any more?

More than five years ago, I contributed to introducing the concept of an exchange rate between gold and oil—yellow gold against black gold. Now that this idea is widely accepted, allow me to return to it for a moment.

In December 1973, the Persian Gulf oil producers quadrupled the price of a raw material owned mostly by them, and which is indispensable to the functioning of industrialized nations. In simplified terms, the price went from about $2.4 a barrel to about $10. All of a sudden, the Gulf producers were endowed with unprecedented buying power. As their reserves rose with dizzying speed, they acquired not only economic enfluence but political clout as well.

Two years later, at the end of 1975, industrialized countries came up with a get-rich-quick plan of their own: they would revalue their central bank gold holdings. The subsequent rise in the average price of gold from about $42 an ounce to $170 boosted the value of the official gold holdings of France, for example, from $4.2 billion to $17 billion—enough for the French to pay for two full years of oil imports at 1975 prices.

What was going on? Why did the gold price follow the oil price upward?

Well, let's remember that before December 1973 the price of an ounce of gold was about $42 while the price of a barrel of oil was about $2. The ratio between the two prices was thus about 20 to one. The rise in the oil price, in one fell swoop, cut the ratio to about four to one; it now took a quarter of an ounce of gold to buy a barrel of oil. But the ratio could be almost restored to the previous level immediately by the simple expedient of raising the gold price to $170 a barrel. It is hardly surprising that there was an unfavorable reaction from the oil producers, who saw revaluation of the official gold price as a ploy to eliminate the advantages they had won in December 1973. Afterwards, of course, the oil price continued to rise, paralleling the leap in the free market price of gold.

In 1980, the average price of a barrel of oil was around $30. A 1 to 20 ratio between this price and the price of an ounce of gold would require a gold price of $600—which happens to be the level around which the free market price was fluctuating. Without attributing too much significance to this ratio, we cannot fail to conclude that it provides an indication of the relative values of gold and oil. It will continue to do so until technology or luck allow us to replace our present oil supplies with cheaper forms of energy.

The oil producers, to the extent that they fail to find safety for all their funds in yellow gold or other investments, will be tempted to invest in the next best thing, which is keeping their black gold in the ground. And if oil in the ground represents a refuge from world inflation, it is logical to assume that as inflation accelerates gold will sooner or later be restored to a privileged position in the international settlements system.

Gold Emerges Victorious

The 1970's will go down in monetary history as the decade of the big battle between gold and the dollar. The United States spared no effort to demonetize the metal. Convertibility of the dollar into gold was suspended by President Nixon on August 15, 1971. Subsequently, the dollar was twice devalued, in December 1971 and February 1973, but convertibility was not restored.

Then the Jamaica conference of January 1976 ratified the second amendment to the statutes of the IMF, providing for abolition of the official gold price. The IMF also arranged to sell off one sixth of its gold stocks and to return another sixth to IMF member countries.

At first, the U.S. tactics appeared likely to succeed. The U.S. Treasury decided to allow Americans once again to hold gold and to conduct gold transactions as of January 1, 1975. This caused an advance rise in the gold price to close to $200 an ounce at the end of 1974. But the Treasury's auction of a part of its gold stocks met only limited demand and this, together with the announcement of IMF sales, caused a drop in the price to around $100 in August 1976. Then people finally woke up to realities, and the steady rise in the gold price got underway.

The Treasury announced in January 1978 its intention to restart gold sales from May of that year, but this did not reverse the upward price trend. Instead, the trend continued to accelerate, particularly after September 1979. On January 21, 1980, the price reached $850 an ounce, then fell back to $480 in April before rising again in stages to $700 in September.

The return of gold to the center of the monetary stage was confirmed by the U.S. Treasury's decision to make no more gold sales after November 1979—although that was just the time when such sales would have been most useful.

Elsewhere, other countries were taking measures which tended to help restore the *de facto* monetary role of gold. For example, the German Bundesbank made a loan to Italy in 1974 which was secured by gold. The central banks of some countries, notably France, went ahead and revalued their official gold holdings. And the European Monetary System took the process a stage further by providing an indirect role for gold in settlements among member countries.

The rise in the free market gold price and the use of gold by official institutions signify a reactivation of its role, which is the first stage towards remonetization. After the shocks of the dollar crisis and the oil crisis, gold appears to be the only reliable store of value, just as in earlier periods of monetary confusion and uncertainty. This is no doubt a prelude to its becoming a standard of value once again.

* * *

The most surprising thing about the evolution of the world system over the past six years is not the number of shocks which have been inflicted upon it, but rather its remarkable ability to absorb those shocks.

The other point to stress is that all the problems that have plagued us in the geopolitical, monetary and trade areas have been inextricably linked to each other.

World inflation paved the way for the oil crisis, which in turn triggered the economic crisis. This led to a surge in the accumulation of petrodollars, which further stimulated inflation. Inflation ate into defense budgets, seriously weakening the external security of the West at the very time when threats to supplies risked destroying the process of detente.

Following the alarm of 1973/1974, the West collapsed into a period of extraordinary inertia. Both politicians and the public chose to put off the necessary adjustments for as long as possible, thereby creating the conditions for a new crisis six years later. But there were major differences in the ways in which the world's major economic zones were affected. Inside those zones, there were also major differences in the reactions of individual countries to the new international constraints on their behavior.

These differences help to explain a spectacular reversal which took place in the relative positions of the major economic powers during the race for growth in the period between the two oil crises.

PART TWO:
The Race For Growth: America Takes the Lead

The period between the two oil crises was a major historical turning point, separating the expansionary decades of the 1950's and 1960's from the still uncertain 1980's. In just six years, a profound change took place in the relative positions of the United States and Europe. For the first time in 30 years, the U.S. was able to move to the front of the pack, as Europe and Japan faltered in the race for growth. Certain Third World countries, for their part, managed to get by surprisingly well.

The American renaissance is not easy to explain. It was hardly the result of abandoning bad habits: the U.S. balance of payments deficits continued, as did budget deficits, rising inflation and excessive consumption and household debt. U.S. economic policymakers turned their backs on all courses of action which could have served as a basis for a healthy and lasting recovery. What seems to have happened, in the period from 1974 to 1978, is that the U.S. decided to go for growth at any price, using one bad method after another—government deficit spending, credit expansion, etc. The eventual result was double digit inflation and a legacy of economic ailments which will be difficult to cure.

In the energy field, the U.S. reacted to the warning of December 1973 by allowing its dependence on imported oil to rise from 20 percent to 50 percent five years later.

In the area of defense, which was crucial, the Americans reduced substantially the defense burden which had weighed so heavily on their efforts at economic expansion for 30 years. Both as a percentage of the national budget and as a percentage of Gross National Product, defense outlays declined.

Today, the U.S. still possesses major advantages over other countries, but they only concern one of two distinct parts of the U.S. economy. The most striking development in the U.S., in the period between the two oil crises, was the emergence of a dual economy, one part technologically advanced and productive, and the other labor-intensive and backward, with some of the characteristics of underdevelopment.

Generally speaking, all the major industrialized nations reacted to the 1974/1975 recession initially by adopting Keynesian economic policies. The results were mixed. By 1976, the U.S., Japan, West Germany and France had all managed to achieve reasonable growth rates, together with reductions in unemployment (except in

France). Other countries, such as Britain and the The Netherlands, succeeded less well in finding the path back to economic growth, because of structural problems within their economies which were independent of the effects of the oil crisis.

In the subsequent stage, after the modest recovery which began in 1976, governments returned to the restrictive policies which they had abandoned after the 1973 oil crisis. Thus, on the eve of the second oil crisis, the economic policies of the major industrialized nations had three main characteristics:

* priority was given to the fight against inflation.

* emphasis was placed on monetary policy because of disappointment with the results of budgetary policies; as a result, interest rates were generally higher than before.

* each country tried to maintain or increase the strength of its currency to ward off imported inflation. Even the U.S. took this route at the end of 1978.

The period between the two oil crises saw some major changes in the relationships of industrialized countries with OPEC. Europe as a whole still imports close to 65 percent of its energy requirements, and Japan 90 percent. The figure for the U.S. is about 25 percent. But these statistics conceal some important developments. Between 1973 and 1978, the U.S. deficit with OPEC increased to about $16 billion from $12 billion, while the countries of the European Economic Community managed to reduce their OPEC deficit to $9 billion from $10.5 billion. U.S. exports to OPEC as a percentage of U.S. imports from OPEC imports fell to 49 from 74 percent; the European percentage rose to 88 from 44 percent.

Inside the European Economic Community, the performance of individual countries obviously varied. West Germany and Italy, for example, strengthened their positions vis-a-vis OPEC considerably, while France registered more modest gains.

CHAPTER 1
America's Great Leap Forward

The United States has just been through one of its longest and most dynamic periods of economic expansion since World War II. Following the savage recession of 1974, the economy began to recover in March 1975, and continued to grow without interruption for almost five years. From 1976 to 1979, the average annual growth rate of the Gross National Product was 4.5 percent, a rate of expansion rarely experienced in the U.S. since 1945. It has perhaps not been emphasized enough how exceptional a period this was in U.S. economic history. While the U.S. was rediscovering a taste and a capacity for strong growth, other industrialized countries were slowing down under the impact of the oil crisis. The growth rates of European economies were halved. Even Japan found itself on a much slower growth path than before.

The main reason for the brilliant U.S. performance was probably that the Americans were only paying a small part of their newly-increased oil bill. In the years following the oil crisis, the U.S. trade deficit was almost equal to payments for imported oil. The U.S. trade deficit, of course, is financed by the creation of dollars. That means that the U.S. was escaping from the external constraints imposed by OPEC's rise in the oil price. Another major reason for the prosperity of the U.S. in the second half of the 1970's was the sharp cutback in defense spending, which released new resources for consumption.

Energy and defense factors combined to allow the Americans to outpace their habitual rivals.

American Economic Handicaps

At the end of the Vietnam War, and just before the first oil crisis, the U.S. found itself in a relatively unfavorable economic position. After emerging from World War II as the unchallenged leader of the West, with industrial might unmatched throughout the world, the U.S. during the next 30-odd years had steadily lost most of its economic lead over Europe and Japan. The U.S. balance of payments had been in deficit almost uninterruptedly since 1949, and so had the federal budget. The worst part of the budget situation was that most government spending had become built into the structure of the economy. In 1950, one U.S. worker in 10 was employed by the government; by 1975, it was one in six. Federal budget deficits had become an almost permanent feature of U.S. economic life. Rising unemployment had also become a feature, even while inflation continued to rise. In 1974, consumer price inflation hit a high of 12 percent, and wholesale prices were up by more than 20 percent.

To complete a dark picture, household savings were singularly low by comparison with other countries. From 1966 to 1976, the U.S. household savings rate ranged from 6 to 8 percent, compared to rates of 19 percent in Japan and 12 percent in West Germany. Furthermore, there was a chronic shortage of productive investment. Gross fixed capital formation was well below that in other major industrialized countries. For example, between 1960 and 1973, private sector capital investment accounted for 14 percent of GNP, only the 11th highest percentage among the OECD countries, and compared to 29 percent in Japan and 20 percent in Germany. This factor alone is just about sufficient to explain the relative weakness of U.S. economic growth, which averaged 4.1 percent from 1960 to 1973, compared to five percent for Germany, six percent for France and close to 11 percent for Japan.

Many different explanations were offered for America's economic troubles. Marxist analysts interpreted them as a condemnation of the capitalist system. A more simple interpretation is that they were the result of bad management. The fact is that both presidents Johnson and Nixon were very lax in managing economic affairs. The economic machine was pushed to its limits. Liquidity was recklessly injected into the system, with no respect for the need to maintain a balanced economy. To encourage the public to swallow the Vietnam War pill, household consumption was stimulated as much as possible. In the circumstances, it was not surprising that the American machine broke down, taking part of the whole world system with it.

In 1971, the U.S. balance of payments deficit soared to an unprecedented high of $30.5 billion, and the Bretton Woods world monetary system was abandoned, to be followed by a system of floating exchange rates. This allowed the U.S. to get rid of the last constraint—in truth, a very limited constraint—on its freedom in the domestic economic policymaking arena. However, this bad management was only a temporary episode in U.S. economic history. By itself, it cannot explain all the shortcomings of the U.S. economy—the slow growth, the persistent balance of payments deficit, the latent inflation, etc.

What does help to explain these shortcomings is the existence of two major American handicaps. The first is defense spending, which acted as a major drag on economic growth. Between 1950 and 1970, the U.S. spent $1 trillion in current dollars on defense, the equivalent of about $2 trillion in 1977 dollars. Between 1965 and 1975, defense outlays totaled another trillion current dollars, equivalent to about $1.5 trillion in present-day dollars. At times, defense was absorbing close to 10 percent of GNP. For several decades, a major portion of national resources, which other countries were free to spend on ports, roads, railroads and production facilities, was devoted by the U.S. to non-productive defense outlays. Some specialized industries in the private sector of the economy benefitted from the technological spinoffs of investments in defense. But the fact is that military spending is for the most part economically sterile.

The second handicap is the extraordinary surge which took place in health, education and welfare spending. These outlays now account for almost 10 percent of GNP, up from 5 percent a decade ago. As a percentage of the federal budget, they are one and a half times as big as defense spending. One American in three is a beneficiary of federal aid in one form or another. The growth of these expenditures was a result of the Great Society policies inaugurated by Kennedy and continued by Johnson. It reflects the fact that the U.S. was unable to integrate into the productive economy a significant part of the active population—a very large proportion of the blacks (12 percent of the total population), a sizable proportion of the Puerto Rican and Mexican minorities, and now a growing proportion of young whites who, because of lack of qualifications or lack of motivation, either cannot or will not participate in industrial society.

The effect of the expenditures was to allow a large and growing percentage of the population, which was previously excluded from the consumer society, to become integrated into it—without producing anything. Food stamps and welfare checks have created tens of millions of new consumers who draw on the resources of the nation without putting anything back in terms of goods and services. This constitutes a millstone around the neck of American society, which is a perpetual source of inflation.

The Recovery of 1975

The second quarter of 1975 marked the end of one of the most severe recessions in U.S. history, during which unemployment hit a postwar high of 9 percent, and the Gross National Product showed its steepest fall in 30 years (a drop of 5.7 percent from the fourth quarter of 1973 to the first quarter of 1975). Because of the seriousness of the slump, some analysts thought it might be evidence of a profound crisis of capitalism itself. Such phenomena as the declining trend of corporate profits and the stagnation of the purchasing power of households were seen as possible warning signs that the U.S. economy was heading inescapably towards a final cataclysm. Even economists who did not share this view felt that the slump was of an unprecedented kind, with characteristics suggesting that difficulties would persist long after economic recovery began.

There were a number of factors to account for such pessimism. For the first time, recession was afflicting the U.S. economy and the other major industrialized economies simultaneously. The terms of trade of industrialized countries had deteriorated sharply because of the quadrupling of oil prices, and the international payments system was in decay.

Domestically, the U.S. had for the first time experienced a real price explosion, with wholesale price inflation topping 20 percent in 1974. The deterioration of key U.S. economic indicators seemed to suggest the beginning of a cumulative process capable of leading to a full-scale 1930's-style depression.

The economic recovery which followed was engineered in three main ways:

• consumption was maintained by automatic federal budget stabilizing mechanisms.

- corporate costs were reduced.
- demand inflation and cost inflation were lowered simultaneously.

The Maintenance of Consumption

Those who predicted in 1974 that the U.S. was about to enter a deflationary spiral comparable to the depression of the 1930's had failed to take fully into account the automatic stabilizers incorporated into the federal budget.

From 1929, personal consumption fell by more than a quarter in four years, and personal income by a third. Those were impressive statistics in the 1930's. Today, they would be even more so, since consumption has risen to account for more than two-thirds of GNP.

In 1974, however, personal consumption dipped by only 0.9 percent, then rose 1.8 percent in 1975. To be sure, there were some dramatic falls in certain sectors of the economy. Automobile production was down 53 percent in 1974, and production of other durable goods was off 9.2 percent. But overall, personal consumption was more or less sustained, and proceeded to signal economic recovery from April 1975. In the fourth quarter of 1975, personal consumption reached a new peak of $1 trillion at an annual rate.

The explanation for this was quite simply the performance of household disposable income. Between 1974 and 1975, the disposable income of households rose 31 percent, bringing the total back to around 1973 levels in inflation-adjusted terms. This remarkable trend in personal income during such a turbulent period was essentially due to transfers of resources through a variety of budget mechanisms. Public transfers to households rose 47 percent, and social welfare payments were up 29 percent.

In the 1975/1976 budget, the deficit of $66 billion, up $21 billion from the deficit the year before, was almost entirely due to the effects of the economic cycle. It reflected a $50 billion drop in fiscal revenues and a $15 billion rise in unemployment insurance outlays.

The automatic stabilizers worked well. But the task was not just to halt the economy's decline. It was also necessary to promote a recovery, and here a significant role was played by the lowering of corporate costs.

The Reduction of Corporate Costs

The cutting of corporate costs was the most striking phenomenon of the 1975 recovery. It was contrary to all the many forecasts of decay in the private sector of the U.S. economy, and it allowed corporate profits to rise again after a long period of decline. After-tax net profits, which had fallen from $64 billion in 1974 to $47 billion at an annual rate in the first quarter of 1975, rose to an annual rate of $50 billion in the second quarter and then to $60 billion in the third quarter (all figures in constant 1972 dollar terms).

Leaving aside profits on inventories, the improvement in net profits was even more dramatic—a leap from $19 billion (1972 dollars) in the third quarter of 1974 to $42 billion in the third quarter of 1975. The result was that the share of net profits in corporate value added, which had plunged from 13 percent in 1965 to 3.2 percent in 1974, recovered to 6.3 percent at the end of 1975.

This improvement in liquidity led rapidly to a significant stabilization of corporate balance sheets, as a few statistics will indicate:

• the ratio of short-term debt to total non-mortgage debt fell from 50 percent at the end of 1974 to 45 percent at the end of 1975.

• short-term bank loans outstanding fell $16 billion (after rising $41 billion in 1974), and liquid assets also rose $16 billion.

• the liquidity ratio, which had fallen to 0.52 at the start of 1975, recovered to 0.57 at the end of the year.

The climb in corporate profits reflected a spectacular improvement in productivity, after a long period of falling productivity which had fed speculation that the U.S. economy was in decline. After falling at an annual rate of seven percent in the first quarter of 1975, productivity in industry rose at an annual rate of 2.3 percent in the second quarter, 9.9 percent in the third quarter and 6.5 percent in the fourth quarter. For 1975 as a whole, productivity was up 4.9 percent. This was followed by a further 4.4 percent improvement in 1976. The productivity gains owed a lot to rising retail sales, but even more to falling corporate costs. In the first place, inventory liquidation was spectacular, totaling $25 billion in the first quarter of 1975 and $30 billion in the second.

Furthermore, other costs, including depreciation, rent and interest charges, which had risen strongly in 1974 and early 1975, began to stabilize. But perhaps the most remarkable factor was the drop in labor costs. After rising 12.5 percent in 1974, wage costs per unit of production increased only 7.7 percent in 1975. This was caused less by wage restraint—wages continued to rise at an eight to nine percent rate—than by the fact that companies reduced considerably the number of their employees. Between 1974 and 1975, employment in industry fell 8.5 percent.

The result of all this was that as the U.S. emerged from recession, U.S. companies—and through them, the economy as a whole—were in a more favorable position than their counterparts in Europe and Japan.

The Reduction of Inflation

In February 1976, U.S. consumer prices rose 0.1 percent, after increases of 0.4 percent in January and 0.6 percent in December 1975. In the 12 months to end-February, the inflation rate was 6.3 percent.

At the wholesale level, prices rose 0.3 percent in March 1976, after increases of 0.3 percent in February, 0.2 percent in January, 0.1 percent in December 1975 and zero in November. The wholesale price inflation rate in the 12 months to end-March was 5.6 percent. These figures represented a dramatic reduction in inflation from a year or so earlier. From December 1973 to December 1974, the consumer price increase was 12.2 percent, while the wholesale price rise was 21 percent.

Stable food prices played an important role in the overall lowering of inflation: from July 1975 to July 1976, agricultural prices rose only 0.4 percent, thanks to excellent harvests the year before. But more important still was a slowdown in the rate of increase of industrial prices, which advanced by only 5.3 percent from February 1975 to February 1976. Unit labor costs, which rose 12.2 percent in 1974, increased only 9 percent in 1975. This was still far above the 2.7 percent recorded in 1972, but a marked deceleration nonetheless. Unemployment reduced wage claims sharply in 1975, and probably in 1976 as well.

It is clear, in summary, that economic recovery mechanisms functioned at three levels—household consumption, corporate profitability and price stabilization.

The recession of 1974 and the subsequent 1975 recovery left the U.S. economic landscape significantly changed in a variety of ways.

Defense spending continued to be reduced throughout the period, contributing to further changes in the East-West balance of power, in favor of the Soviet Union. But that is a separate story, which we will take up again later.

Elsewhere, the recession contributed to stabilization of certain sectors of the economy. Household finances were improved as debt was reduced. People's expectations for the future were brought back to within reasonable proportions, and the psychological climate underwent a perceptible change. The recession also taught a lesson to the corporate sector, which reacted by increasing working capital and sharply reducing short-term debt.

Overall, the approximately two-year administration of President Ford, and in particular the actions of William Simon as Treasury Secretary, succeeded in bringing about a progressive return to stability. Inflation was brought back to German levels, and remained under five percent in 1976. The Ford team displayed exemplary wisdom in the area of bank credit, which was all the more praiseworthy with a presidential election campaign underway. As it turned out, the Ford team's tight control of money supply growth ended up costing Ford the election, as economist Paul Samuelson remarked somewhat bitterly when the results were announced. The policies which helped to restore balance to the economy proved fatal to the Republican cause in the political arena.

The Ford administration was able to leave office with heads held high, and not only because of monetary policies. The budgetary performance had also been remarkable. For the first time ever in an election campaign period, government spending had been below forecasts. The Ford administration had largely kept its promise to strangle inflation and to reduce the trade deficit to reasonable proportions—and all in a period of economic recovery. Unquestionably, Ford left the economy in a better general state of health than when he took office.

In the energy field, however, Ford was clearly a failure, allowing U.S. dependence on Arab oil to continue rising. In February 1976, for the first time in its history, the U.S. imported more oil than it produced itself. After a brief lull, the craze for gas-guzzling autos began again. Energy savings in industry remained extremely limited. The U.S. had failed to learn the lessons of the oil crisis.

By the end of 1976, the U.S. economy was in a state of fragile stability. The fever was down but that did not mean all the ailments had been cured. The fundamental problems—the excessive defense burden, the crushing weight of transfer payments to non-productive sectors of the economy, and the excessive consumption of energy at abnormally low prices—remained to be solved.

This became all too obvious during the Carter administration.

The Carter Administration

Keynes with Carter Sauce

During the 1976 election campaign, anyone trying to explain Jimmy Carter's economic program in simple terms would not have had an easy task. While he was a candidate, Carter's ideas reflected above all the wishes and aspirations of voters he had to have on his side—blacks who comprised a major portion of the non-productive population, and workers threatened by unemployment. It was not surprising that he was in favor of job creation and an expansion of federal aid. At the same time he made the traditional election campaign promises concerning fiscal reform, while vowing repeatedly to put the economy back on the road to expansion.

It must be recognized that Carter faced difficult and contradictory tasks: to reduce unemployment and boost economic growth, while lowering inflation and balancing the budget, all in four years. But the men he chose to attack these problems had hardly distinguished themselves in the field of economics up to that time.

The three key players were the Chairman of the Council of Economic Advisors, Charles Schultze, Treasury Secretary W. Michael Blumenthal, and Budget Director Bert Lance. Lance was a provincial banker whose main claim to fame was to have lent a helping hand at the right moment to a presidential candidate with whom he had a natural affinity as a fellow Georgian and neighbor. Blumenthal had hardly distinguished himself by outstanding competence, having little experience in government. Of the three, Schultze was unquestionably the most prominent. His dominant characteristic was what might be called "disillusioned liberalism." He was one of those men nourished by the noble ideas of the Kennedy era, who believed early on that social problems could be solved by recourse to massive federal programs, but were forced by experience to recognize the difficulties involved. The doctrinal attitudes of such men were thus marked by a certain skepticism.

It was Schultze who presented to Congress the long-term aims of the new Carter administration. These can be roughly summed up as follows:

• Gross National Product was to grow during the first Carter term by 22 percent—annual growth of 5.2 percent—which would raise the number of people employed to 100 million and cut unemployment to 4.75 percent.

• Inflation would be progressively reduced to 4 percent from 6 percent, and disposable income of households per head would rise by 17 percent.

• The savings rate of households would be 6.5 to 7 percent.

• Capital spending would rise 10 percent a year. At the same time the federal budget would be restored to balance, while being reduced as a proportion of GNP to 21 percent from 23 percent.

In sum, the new administration was seeking what former German central bank Governor Otmar Emminger once called the "magic triangle"—growth with full employment and price stability. As Carter was soon to discover, it was a lot easier to state such goals during an election campaign than to translate them into economic reality. As it turned out, he reached and even surpassed his goals in the economic growth and employment areas, but failed in other equally critical areas, most notably the area of inflation.

A Mixed Performance

The Carter administration can rightly pride itself on its economic growth achievements: under Carter, the U.S. enjoyed one of its longest-ever periods of economic expansion. Unfortunately, the price to be paid was an unacceptable rise in inflation. From 1976 to 1979, annual average GNP growth was 4.5 percent. Growth remained strong until the end of 1978, after which the economy slipped into semi-stagnation from early 1979. From March 1975 to March 1979, industrial production rose about 37 percent.

In the employment area, Jimmy Carter's success was undeniable. From May 1975 to December 1979, the number of people employed rose by about 13.8 million. Never had the number of employed Americans been so high as a proportion of the total population. The creation of new jobs was largely in the areas of commerce, the services sector and the public sector. In manufacturing industry, the number of jobs rose only slightly above the level prevailing before the 1974 recession. The overall effect was a sharp drop in the unemployment rate from nine percent in May 1975 to slightly less than six percent in 1979. It is worth pointing out that according to official estimates, the structural unemployment rate in the U.S. economy is slightly above five percent.

Reflation at the Wrong Time

As we have said, Carter inherited from the Ford administration a fairly satisfactory U.S. inflation performance. Consumer price inflation was down to 4.9 percent at the end of 1976, from 12.2 percent at the end of 1974—and the economy had been expanding during almost all of that two-year period. By March 1980, however, consumer prices were rising at a record year-on-year rate of 14.7 percent, and some monthly figures had approached an annualized rate of 18 percent. The subject of inflation under Carter is so important that it will be discussed separately later in this chapter.

The Carter administration never had an unchallenged chief of economic policy making. There were frequent territorial disputes among presidential advisors and cabinet officers. Contradictory statements from officials several times had disastrous effects on the dollar. But more serious still was the fact that there was a basic inconsistency in the policies which the Carter team adopted: they chose to stimulate the economy at a time when it was expanding. Their policies were a phony version of Keynesianism. Keynes advocated stimulation of demand to put the economy back on its feet; but the U.S. economy under Carter was already *on* its feet. Despite rapid economic expansion, the budget remained constantly in deficit: from 1977 to 1980, the cumulative deficit totaled about $160 billion. Likewise, monetary policy remained expansionist until fairly recently: taking into account the inflation rate, interest rates under Carter were hardly ever high enough to act as a deterrent to borrowing, with the exception of the spring of 1980.

In many respects, the flight from paper currency was provoked by the authorities. Housing starts, for example, remained stable at around two million in

1978. Despite rising interest rates, they only began to fall seriously around the end of 1979. The fact is that the authorities were trying to defy fate by preventing a contraction of the construction industry, the usual harbinger of general economic recession. In the past, rising interest rates had led to a drain on the resources of savings and loans associations, as the ceiling on the interest they could offer on deposits caused funds to be diverted from them to higher-yielding investments. In this way, the volume of mortgage lending declined sharply and rapidly.

In 1978, however, the authorities acted to maintain mortgage lending by giving Savings and Loans permission to issue savings certificates indexed to the return on Treasury Bills. They also raised the interest rate ceiling on mortgage loans—above which rates are considered usurious—on several occasions.

Finally, the low return on traditional savings deposits caused an acceleration in the velocity of circulation of money. Since inflation does not benefit lenders, many Americans drew heavily on their savings to exchange them for tangible goods.

Carter's economic policies lacked coherence and overall direction. Specific goals were targeted, without any understanding of the big picture. Often, decisions were taken in response to the pressure of events. This was particularly true in the areas of energy policy and monetary policy.

A Hesitant Energy Policy

The U.S. did not really take its first important energy policy decisions until June 1979, when controls on prices of domestically-produced oil began to be lifted. After that, Congress passed the windfall profits tax bill, but only after seven months of wrangling. The new tax should raise from the oil companies a total of $227.3 billion up to 1990, compared to $296 billion sought by Carter. A part of this government income will be used for development of alternative energy sources, and another part will be distributed among the underprivileged in compensation for the oil price rise. However, the fact remains that the U.S. still has no overall energy policy designed to achieve major energy savings. This lack is undoubtedly a result of the Carter administration's constant tendency to hesitate and change its mind.

In three years, Carter went from a quest for energy conservation to a policy of promoting domestic production. In April 1977, he proposed to Congress an energy program designed to restrict consumption by levying taxes on oil and ending price controls. But Congress, which must share a considerable part of the blame for the long delay in implementing a real energy policy, only approved those parts of the Carter program which freed prices of newly-discovered natural gas and imposed future taxes on energy-wasting vehicles. The Congressional debate lasted until November 1978. It was only with the second oil crisis that Carter was able to win approval for the program which was finally adopted. The income to be received from the windfall profits tax was one of the reasons Carter was able to present a 1981 budget showing a slight surplus. The other reason was anticipated income from a $4.62 per barrel levy on imported oil. But this measure was subsequently rejected by Congress.

An Uncertain Monetary Policy

Carter administration monetary policy remained hesitant and uncertain for a long time. The monetary authorities delayed adopting a more restrictive policy stance for fear of provoking a recession in the run-up to the next presidential election. They were finally forced by necessity to act—often too late—in several stages.

First, the fall of the dollar in 1978 forced Carter to mount a dollar support package, announced on November 1, which involved raising the Federal Reserve discount rate and, above all, mobilizing the equivalent of about $30 billion for foreign exchange market intervention. In October 1979, the worsening of inflation and another fall in the dollar forced the new Federal Reserve Board chairman, Paul Volcker, to take measures designed to restrict bank liquidity by raising reserve requirements, while allowing money market interest rates to fluctuate more widely.

The relative failure of these measures, due partly to the fact that the recession was late in arriving, and partly to accelerating inflation, forced Carter, in mid-March 1980, to tighten monetary policy further, using the novel approach of quantitative restrictions. But the flight from the currency continued, triggering higher interest rates and chaos on the bond market.

Carter's program also provided for presentation of a 1981 budget showing a slight surplus. But the toughest measures were those taken in the monetary policy area: the Federal Reserve Board seized its opportunity to strengthen its control over credit flows. Faced with very strong demand for credit, the Fed endeavored to limit supply by raising the cost of resources of banking and financial institutions. The Fed increased the reserve requirement rate on banks' managed liabilities. Furthermore, and above all, it extended the same requirements to banks not affiliated with the Federal Reserve system. Finally, it forced all institutions granting unsecured personal loans to make special deposits equal to 15 percent of the increase in their outstanding loans. These measures soon led to a sharp slowdown in economic activity. It is certainly regrettable that they were not taken much earlier. Because they were not, inflation became more and more embedded in the structure of the U.S. economy.

The Carter Inflation

The serious inflation problem now afflicting the United States is to a large extent attributable to President Carter. Right from the start, the Carter administration embarked on a long series of actions which, considered individually, would not have had a major inflationary effect, but considered together contributed very largely to making inflation one of America's major problems. In 1979, a group of experts, at a meeting chaired by the chief economist of a major U.S. bank, tried to take stock of the measures taken by the Carter administration which had an inflationary component. It was decided that out of 47 measures analyzed, 43 could be considered to contain germs of inflation.

Among these 43 were the decisions to increase the minimum wage, restore farm price supports and subsidies to limit production, increase social security contributions and settle the miners' strike. The stage-by-stage increase in the minimum wage came to 9.4 percent by 1979, and benefitted more than five million people. Social security contributions, split equally between employers and employed, were increased strongly several times. The extra cost to the economy has been estimated at $4.5 billion in 1979 alone. And all the time, the budget was constantly showing a huge deficit. Not since 1929 had an administration deliberately pursued a budget deficit policy during a period of economic expansion. Classical orthodoxy, of course, requires budget deficits during recessions and budget balance or budget surpluses during periods of economic growth.

Part of the reason for all this was Carter's choice of men to fill key positions within his administration. Say what you like about Bert Lance and his hasty methods of financing personal expenses, but his resignation as Budget Director was a hard blow for Carter. Lance's replacement, Mr. MacIntyre, an affable and courteous man, succeeded only very partially in filling the gap left by Lance's departure. Elsewhere, men such as Council of Economic Advisors Chairman Schultze, Treasury Secretary Blumenthal and presidential economic advisor Nordhaus demonstrated neither competence nor mastery of their briefs. They were men who were still fervently practicing an ancient religion, a kind of antiquated neo-Keynesianism which offered constantly increasing injections of liquidity into the economy as a panacea for all problems.

According to some analysts, economic models employed during Carter's term in office were also responsible for some of the damage. The argument is that these models, based on revenue flows, failed to account fully for trends in business activities and were not able to provide for management of self-sustaining growth. They thus provided intellectual justification for perpetual stimulation of the economy.

Whatever the explanation, the results are there for all to see. Up to May 1977, the budget deficit was falling from quarter to quarter; after that time, this trend was sharply reversed. Thus, the economy did not fall into recession because of a fundamental change in American psychology. The economy enjoyed a 12 to 24 month reprieve, which was of course only delaying the inevitable. Following in the footsteps of so many other countries, the U.S. became a country with inflation embedded in the structure of its economy. The first victims of this world sickness were in Europe and Latin America. American consumers and businessmen became like their counterparts in the rest of the world. They got used to inflation, and took account of it when making decisions. Inflation became a feature of the American economic landscape. Today, each interest rate increase and each price rise has the opposite effect of what was intended.

Rising prices, far from discouraging consumers, cause them to rush to make purchases to beat inflation. In this way, price increases artificially boost consumer demand. For this process to be possible, credit must be plentiful—as it has been, until recently. Individuals must also be ready to draw on their savings—as they have been, causing the household savings rate to sink to three percent (from six to eight percent a few years ago). The core inflation rate, the rate of underlying inflation which is very hard to reduce without causing a savage and prolonged economic slowdown, was around six percent when Carter took office. By 1980, it was around 10 percent.

Towards a Dual Economy

The U.S. economy presents some bizarre anomalies. How do we reconcile declining productivity with a remarkable rise in industrial investment? How do we explain sharp increases in employment in an economy which has long provided the model of highly capital-intensive industry? The explanation for these apparent inconsistencies appears to lie in the fact that the U.S. economy is in the process of developing a dual aspect. Analysis suggests that a strongly labor-intensive economy is now developing side-by-side with the traditional economy, in which productivity continues to grow.

Developing towards Under-Development

Is the United States, the country where mass production was invented, going to retrogress to a state of economic under-development? The question is worth asking. Consider the question of U.S. productivity, which is the measure of the efficiency of industry. The image of the U.S. has long been that of the capitalist country *par excellence,* with advanced technology industries and workers earning twice what their counterparts in Europe and Japan earn—all thanks to a level of productivity unequaled throughout the world.

However, for some years already, wages in certain European countries, notably the Netherlands but also Sweden, have been well above American levels. This is accounted for to a great extent by exchange rate developments. But even when exchange rate effects are taken out of the calculations, the fact is that certain European workers are better paid than equally qualified American opposite numbers. Here lies one challenge to preconceived ideas about the United States.

Some analysts believe that the very mediocre U.S. productivity performance has resulted from changes in the composition of the labor force, which has come to include more women and young people, with limited job qualifications at the time of employment. These new entrants into the labor force typically prefer employment in the services sector (which now accounts for two thirds of GNP, compared to slightly more than 50 percent in European economies), and productivity increases in certain services areas have been very small, for obvious reasons: hairdressers still use methods similar to those employed by our great-grandparents.

To understand more clearly what has been going on it is helpful to break down overall productivity figures by sectors of the economy. In the private sector as a whole, annual productivity growth was 2.2 percent in the 1960-1978 period, compared to 2.6 percent for 1950-1978. This fall appears to support the view that the overall competitiveness of the U.S. economy is declining.

But in the sector of manufacturing industry alone, productivity growth remained at 2.6 percent throughout the two periods. In the economic recovery year of 1975, productivity growth in manufacturing industry reached almost 5 percent, and continued at 4.4 percent in 1976. Furthermore, the first effects of huge capital investments made in 1977-1978 will only begin to appear in the years ahead. Thus we may be about to witness a significant rise in U.S. productivity, at least in the industrial sector.

In four years, close to 14 million new jobs were created in the U.S., causing the unemployment rate to drop in 1978 below the six percent barrier. This extraordinary leap in employment makes it appear that the U.S. economy is *developing towards under-development,* by becoming more and more oriented towards labor-intensive activities. To an extent, this observation is accurate. Unquestionably, as we have seen, the oil crisis and higher oil prices led in the U.S. to a reversal of the historical trend towards substitution of capital for manpower. This explains the importance of black market labor, much of it done by illegal immigrants from Mexico, who are now estimated to total 10 million.

But the fact is that the industrial sector of the economy has not increased employment. It has largely limited itself to rehiring employees laid off during the recession of 1974. The new job-seekers have turned to the services area, and the tertiary sector of the economy has developed strongly, partly as a result of the natural evolution of a consumer society, and partly because of the social welfare system and the enormous transfers of wealth which began with Lyndon Johnson's Great Society. The surge in employment in the tertiary sector has in no way prevented a fundamental overhaul of the industrial manufacturing sector.

The Highly Capital-Intensive Sectors of the Economy

Too little attention has been paid to the industrial restructuring effort which has been undertaken in the U.S. during the past few years. This effort may turn the U.S. once again into a fearsome competitor, when it awakes from its slumber. Perhaps the sleeping giant will be goaded into action by the effects of the 1980 recession. The restructuring of U.S. industry already accomplished has, in fact, been remarkable, involving modernization of plant and equipment and reduction in rates of energy consumption. It could open the way for a new surge of American industrial power in the coming decade. For some time after economic recovery began in March 1975, capital investment remained relatively weak. But then there was a remarkable pick-up, with corporate investment increasing 9.2 percent in 1977 and 7.8 percent in 1978. In the final quarter of 1979, investments rose to a record of $143.5 billion in constant dollar terms, even as most economists were predicting an economic slowdown.[1]

The sharpest increases in investment were in the area of durable goods, which may be considered the nucleus of industrial logistics. In current dollar terms, while industrial prices were rising 8 percent, investment in durable goods production rose 17.3 percent in 1977 and 14.3 percent in 1978; in the auto industry, the rates of increase were 65.4 percent in 1977 and 14.7 percent in 1978.

Investments generally rose much more slowly outside the durable goods area, but in 1977 were up 32.7 percent in the rubber industry, 19.4 percent in the oil industry and 24.3 percent in the airline industry (which boosted the rate of increase to 46.2 percent in 1978).

The capital investments are impressive simply in volume terms. But the really important point is that most of the money went into modernizing facilities rather than expanding production capacity. In 1977, 71 percent of investment outlays in the steel industry went towards modernization. The comparable percentage was 74 percent in the aerospace industry, 87 percent in textiles, and 60 percent in the auto industry. This trend continued in 1978.

---

[1]It should be pointed out that a significant proportion of these investments went towards antipollution equipment to comply with new federal law requirements.

The investment surge has brought about a remarkable renovation of the American industrial machine. At the end of 1978, for example, in the durable goods area, only 12 percent of plant and equipment was considered obsolete, compared to 20 percent at the end of 1976.

The auto industry merits special attention. Few Europeans have yet understood that in the years to come the main danger to their auto industries will come not from Japan, and not from newly-industrialized countries, but from the United States. Within a few years, Detroit is going to be reborn. Between now and 1985, the U.S. auto industry will invest $70 billion. Under pressure from the federal government, which wants U.S. autos to get 27.5 miles to the gallon by 1985, the industry is rapidly adapting to the new environment of international competition. Once over its present difficulties, it will be in a position to manufacture autos just as eye-catching, economical and profitable as Japanese or European competitors. And the Americans will have the advantage of production on an international scale, which will allow them to market their products throughout the world at highly competitive prices. Right now, Detroit is maneuvering into position first to reconquer the domestic American market, then to cross swords with foreign competitors in third markets, and perhaps in the competitors' own markets as well.

Energy Savings

The energy policies adopted in Washington since the first oil crisis have generally been considered a relative failure, and with good reason. After President Nixon's Project Independence, various energy policy efforts by his successors ran into Congressional opposition and skepticism among the public. A 1978 poll showed that more than 50 percent of Americans were still unaware that the U.S. must import oil to satisfy its energy requirements.

But the relative inefficiency of the government in the energy policy area stands in striking contrast to the efficiency of American industry, which managed all on its own to put itself in a position to adapt to the new realities. In 1978, U.S. oil imports dropped to 8.1 million barrels per day from 8.7 million in 1977, and the ratio of imports to total U.S. consumption fell to 43 percent from 48 percent (although this was partly due to the rise of Alaskan production). The growth in total consumption of oil also began to slow down. In 1978, consumption increased only 1.9 percent (to 18.7 million barrels per day), compared to increases of 6.9 percent in 1976 and 5 percent in 1975.

The trend towards energy conservation did not result from an economic slowdown: the economy grew four percent in 1978. Rather, it resulted from structural changes in the economy. For a long time, it was generally accepted that a one percent rise in United States GNP meant an identical one percent increase in energy consumption. But this energy/GNP ratio dropped to 0.85 in the 1975-1977 period, and has fallen further since. In fact, the quantity of energy necessary to produce one dollar of GNP in the U.S. has been declining since the beginning of the 1970's. In 1970, one dollar of GNP required 62,400 British Thermal Units. This fell nine percent to 56,900 in 1977, and then dropped to 56,000 in 1978.

The U.S. economy has long had the reputation of being a wasteful devourer of energy. But it is now in a position to reduce energy consumption, and efforts to strengthen that position are likely as the oil price rises further.

This brief overview of the U.S. economy has left some areas unexplored, while revealing many uncertainties in the areas discussed. What is clear is that the Americans have only just begun the massive restructuring process which is required by today's realities. This is especially true in the area of energy. It is also clear that the surge in capital investment has still hardly touched several sectors of the economy which are badly in need of modernization, such as railroads, electricity production and some public services. Nonetheless, contrary to many forecasts, U.S. industry has proved itself remarkably capable of adapting to change, using the considerable profits accumulated during recent years of expansion to begin a reorganization of its production potential.

The Recession of 1980

The United States is an economist's paradise. It's like a bazaar. The visitor passing through from abroad can take his pick among economic forecasts of all kinds. The U.S. is a huge machine churning out economic analysts, who in turn churn out estimates and predictions. There are daily dissections of the movements in M1 or M2 money supply, and of the real or imagined intentions of the Chairman of the Federal Reserve and the advisors to the President. In recent times, the forecasters have been repeatedly caught out.

Within two years after the U.S. economic recovery began in March 1975, some economists began to predict a new recession. A year or so later, not at all discouraged, the same economists again forecast an economic slowdown. The forecasters' crystal ball was especially dim in 1978, when the great majority of U.S. economists was predicting a fall into recession in 1979, by the end of the year at the latest. The forecasts were contradicted by events as regularly as they were made. As it was, the much-awaited recession finally began in early 1980.

Until February 1980, economic activity was sustained by the flight from paper currency. The household savings rate dropped to around three percent, an unprecedented low. But signs of a change in the trend were multiplying. For several months, the auto and construction industries had been slowing down. In March, auto production was off 25 percent from a year earlier. March housing starts were only slightly above one million at an annual rate, and were down 42.2 percent from March 1979. In the spring, the slowdown spread to all sectors of the economy. Industrial production in March fell 0.6 percent, after a 0.2 percent decline in February. The utilization rate of productive capacity fell to 83 percent in March from 83.9 percent in February, and the number of hours worked and the volume of industrial orders also declined. Retail sales in March fell 1.9 percent, matching the February fall. The economic slowdown was accompanied by a rapid rise in unemployment, to seven percent in April from six percent in February; in two months, the total number of unemployed rose by 950,000 to 7.3 million.

Before the recession, the creation of new jobs had allowed many American families to cope with worsening inflation. Despite the loss of purchasing power of their income, more and more households had actually improved their living standards through the addition of a second wage earner: 53.5 percent of American families included at least two wage-earners in 1979, compared to 51.5 percent in 1978 and only 44 percent in 1970. But many newly-created jobs are unstable, and quickly disappear when the economy slows. Thus, as the recession began to bite, unemployment rose sharply and the buying power of households deteriorated rapidly.

Some analysts have suggested that economic activity could be sustained by an increased U.S. military effort. However, there are limits to the stimulus that can be expected from military spending. It would take additional outlays of $25 billion in real terms to raise by one percentage point the amount of GNP spent on defense (4.5 percent in 1979, down from 8.1 percent in 1969). In the draft 1981 budget, defense outlays are slated to rise by less than $10 billion.

There are good reasons to believe that the 1980 recession will be different from past U.S. recessions, which mainly affected the business world without having a serious impact on consumers. This time around, inventories remained at normal levels up to the time the recession began. Corporate executives had learned from experience not to gamble on rising demand by building up stocks.

The consumer, on the other hand, is in trouble. As we have seen, American households are over-indebted, having borrowed heavily to make their purchases, and especially to buy their homes. Their liquid savings have been reduced to a minimum. Now they are suddenly faced with an erosion of their buying power caused by rising prices and a fall in their income. This is a consumption recession, which is especially serious because consumption accounts for almost three-quarters of final demand in the U.S. economy.

Traditionally, U.S. recessions have been "V"-shaped, with a sharp economic decline followed by a vigorous recovery, as in 1974/1975. This time, the pattern promises to be different. The economic growth rate can be expected to fluctuate around zero for some time. The recovery, when it arrives, will be much less decisive than in the past, somewhat along the lines of what we have been experiencing in Europe.

Security and defense issues will once again become critical economic problems in the decade of the 1980's. The U.S. will have to find a way to reconcile the cost of maintaining global power with domestic economic policy requirements—the eternal conflict between guns and butter.

The price to be paid for U.S. rearmament may be depreciation of the dollar. It will be difficult to significantly reduce social welfare spending, given the existence of a dual economy, one part full of dynamism and the other labor-intensive and heading for a state of under-development. Finally, there is the energy problem, which the U.S. will have to confront in all its ramifications.

The easiest response for the government to the nation's economic troubles could be a rush for growth. That would lead to still higher levels of inflation, with incalculable consequences for the U.S. and for the world.

CHAPTER 2
The Slowdown in
Europe & Japan

Vicious Circles, Virtuous Circles

From 1960 to 1973, rapid economic growth allowed European countries and Japan gradually to close gaps in their economies between demand and production. As a result of the first oil crisis, those gaps widened once again. All the countries concerned experienced sharp slowdowns in growth, accompanied by a general rise in unemployment and accelerating inflation. In many countries, household consumption rose, while exports increased sharply, helping to sustain economic activity.

However, there were profound differences in the ways individual countries reacted to the crisis. Investment levels were maintained in some countries, but fell in Britain and Italy. In West Germany, the Netherlands, Belgium and Denmark, productivity rose much faster than the average European rate of increase—but only at the price of falling employment levels. The countries in the German mark zone, the leaders of the European pack, followed the Germans in making structural adjustments within their economies, although the adjustment process was slow and full of difficulties, especially for Belgium.

Until 1973, economic growth had to a considerable extent hidden the disparities within industrialized Europe. The oil crisis brought them to light, and increased the risks of a breakup of the European community. Judged by their reactions to the oil crisis, European countries and Japan can be divided into two groups—foolish countries and sensible countries. France, which is considered separately in the next chapter, falls between the two extremes.

Foolish Countries

Some countries, notably Italy and Britain, sought their salvation after the oil crisis through a doubling of inflation accompanied by accelerated currency depreciation. This allowed them, for a time, to safeguard employment. Excessive employment and falling investment then led to a collapse of productivity, which further stimulated inflation and caused more currency depreciation.

These countries thus became locked in a vicious circle, for lack of a sufficiently strong social consensus on how to proceed. Monetarism then appeared as a substitute for the actions which a strong consensus might have produced. Credit controls and higher interest rates became the magic wand which would control inflation. For a time, these countries managed to keep unemployment in check, but only at the price of economic stagnation characterized by sharp falls in investment. From 1977, the full extent of the pernicious effects of the vicious circle became apparent. Only then did Italy and Britain begin to adopt more realistic economic recovery policies. To this day, however, these countries have still not managed to initiate a real restructuring of industry. As a result, they are in an unstable condition to face the challenges of the coming decade.

The Italian Example

First, a few caveats. Analysis of the Italian economy is difficult because there is a lack of reliable statistics. In 1978, for example, the government's central statistics institute revalued the Gross National Product by 10 percent without providing clear justification. Furthermore, Italy is a country which does not operate according to standard patterns of behavior. Its actions and reactions are frequently unpredictable. After being close to national bankruptcy in 1976, Italy staged a spectacular recovery the following year by running up a substantial current account balance of payments surplus. Another characteristic is the marked lack of a social consensus, resulting from an ill-defined concept of the role of the state which makes economic adjustments more difficult. Following the oil crisis, weak Italian economic growth was accompanied by distortions in the structure of demand. In four years, the share of total resources going to consumption held steady at around 65 percent of GNP, while the exports share rose from 15 percent to 20 percent, and the investments share dropped from 20 percent to 15 percent. Like Britain, Italy was paying its oil bill by sacrificing investment, i.e. by sacrificing the country's future.

But before making too severe a judgment on the Italians, it should be remembered that Italy remains the sixth largest industrial power in the world, and continues to show a surplus in trade with the redoubtable West Germans.

At first, Italy simply absorbed the oil shock. The trade deficit was financed by borrowings from abroad, mainly by state-owned enterprises. Inflation took off, reaching 19 percent in 1974 and 17 percent in 1975, while the lira depreciated rapidly, falling to 653 per dollar in 1975 and then to 832 per dollar in 1976. In 1975, Gross National Product shrank 3.5 percent, a sharper economic decline than in any other major country. On the other hand, unemployment increased only slightly (it was already very high by comparison with neighboring countries). Italy was caught in the vicious circle, a race between prices, wages and the exchange rate.

In 1976, the lira fell faster for a time than Italian prices rose. In the spring of 1976, Italy's credit on international capital markets finally dried up. Italian borrowers could no longer find foreign lenders. Italy then turned to the Bundesbank, the German central bank, which renewed a $2 billion 1974 loan secured by Italian central bank gold holdings. In the spring of 1977, Italy was granted two further loans of $500 million each from the IMF and from Italy's fellow members of the European Economic Community. These loans were conditional on Italy adopting an economic stabilization program.

In 1978 and 1979, the Italian economy grew by 1.9 percent and 2.6 percent respectively, one of the weakest growth performances in Europe. Then in 1979, growth accelerated to five percent. The weak growth rate up to 1979 helps to explain how Italy managed to put its balance of payments back in order. Exports were encouraged by feeble domestic demand connected with a fall in public and private sector investment. The currency depreciation policy also helped on the balance of payments front, by providing exporters with a new competitive advantage. But at the same time, it broadened the effect of the oil crisis by boosting imported inflation. Italy's terms of trade deteriorated, signifying a steady impoverishment of the Italian economy. After its plunge in 1976, the lira stabilized somewhat, with the effective exchange rate slipping by about six percent a year (by the spring of 1980, large Italian corporations were saying that the lira was overvalued, damaging their competitiveness on overseas markets).

In 1977, the current account balance of payments registered a surplus of $2 billion, a spectacular turnaround from a deficit of several billion dollars the year before. In 1978, the surplus increased to $6.3 billion, and continued at $6 billion in 1979, making Italy's balance of payments performance comparable to that of Germany.

On the other hand, inflation remained rampant, at 18 percent in 1977, then 12 percent in 1978, then back up to 16 percent in 1979. As in France, inflation was acting as a social lubricant. It reflected indexation of salaries and wages, and a colossal public sector deficit. After 1977, the rise in both prices and salaries and wages remained consistently above 11 percent a year, higher than in most of the countries with which Italy must compete, while the public sector deficit reached 13 percent of Italian GNP.

By contrast, unemployment rose less than in other leading industrialized nations, and today stands at around seven percent of the active population. The inflexibility of employment levels, which is partly a result of a high rate of endemic unemployment built into the economy, and partly a result of excessive social welfare protection, helps to explain Italy's weak productivity performance, one of the worst in Europe.

In summary, Italy's adjustment to the oil shock can be understood in terms of three reactions: currency depreciation, a fall in investment (according to some analyses, private sector productive investment today is only about two-thirds of what it was eight years ago), and expansion of the already existing underground economy. The distinction has often been made between two separate economies in Italy—an official economy, in which the large corporations operate, and a clandestine or underground economy. In the official arena, there are two different kinds of corporations. On the one hand are the big public corporations, which are suffering from huge deficits resulting from abnormally weak productivity and excessive numbers of employees. On the other hand are the private sector corporate giants, such as Fiat and Montedison, which are going through hard times, and which can only improve their international competitiveness through further depreciation of the lira.

By contrast, the underground economy contains large numbers of prosperous small companies, unknown to the tax authorities, and free to hire and fire at will.

These companies are estimated to account for 20 percent of Italian exports. Their structure, and the structure of the clandestine world in which they operate, tends to be liberal rather than capitalistic. In their chosen fields, whether it be textiles, shoes or engineering, these small entrepreneurs are often unbeatable. They have an admirable ability to spot opportunities on overseas markets, and they exploit them energetically. Their huge contribution is to provide work and a livelihood for many workers unable to find suitable employment in the official economy.

This fragmented economic structure is clearly in need of a fundamental overhaul. But the Italians have no Mrs. Thatcher to help them out. Ever since the oil crisis, Italy has simply been muddling through on a day-to-day basis. A few years ago, Finance Minister Pandolfi came up with a plan for structural reform of the economy to be implemented over three years (1978-1981), but the plan was shelved as soon as it was presented. Some economists believe Italy is destined to retrogress to a state of under-development, as small companies proliferate, characterized by low rates of productivity growth and limited spending on research and development. Re-deployment of Italian resources has been confined to the sectors of the economy where it is easiest, i.e. those sectors where capital intensity is low and techniques employed are the least capitalistic. This has left the economy as a whole highly exposed to competition from newly-industrialized countries. Italy risks being squeezed between those countries on the one hand and the most technologically advanced countries, such as Germany, on the other. This is the measure of the fragility of Italy's post-oil crisis recovery, and of the vulnerability of its economy in the medium and long term.

The British Example

Like Italy, Great Britain was addicted for a long time to the poisoned delights of the vicious circle which begins with currency depreciation. While West Germany was winning awards for economic excellence, Britain received consistently bad marks.

From 1974 to 1978, British Gross National Product growth averaged less than one percent a year, one of the worst performances in all of Europe. Over the five-year period, inflation totaled more than 80 percent, after reaching a record annual rate of 23.5 percent in 1975, higher than any other industrialized country. The worldwide recession of 1974/1975 affected Britain more seriously than other countries: GNP shrank in both years, and the subsequent recovery was weaker than elsewhere. This dismal performance was accompanied by a strong rise in unemployment, which reached 5.6 percent of the active population in 1978. In 1980, British GNP (excluding the effects of North Sea oil) was just about back to the level of 1973, since when output of the OECD nations as a whole has expanded 20 percent.

Britain had a number of things in common with Italy: an initial post-oil crisis strategy based on currency depreciation, an overwhelming preoccupation with job security and a lack of a strong social consensus. However, the British experience was profoundly different from the Italian one, partly because Britain was undergoing a steady process of de-industrialization, which began about 15 years ago, and which was in striking contrast to the industrial dynamism of Italy at the start of the 1970's. In 1975/1976, inflation in Britain accelerated dramatically, fueled by a drop in the pound sterling. Between the beginning and the end of 1976, the pound lost almost 20 percent of its value against the dollar. In April 1976, with the arrival of James Callaghan as Prime Minister, new policies were adopted, designed to stabilize the value of the pound and get a better grip on wage inflation. At the end of the year, Britain was the recipient of a $3.9 billion loan from the IMF, the biggest loan ever made by the Fund to any country. Under the terms of the loan, Britain undertook an economic stabilization program which soon made itself felt.

From 1977, the economy began a tentative recovery with the arrival of North Sea oil income. The current account balance of payments swung from a deficit to a slight surplus. Private sector investment began rising again. Foreign exchange reserves increased sharply to $21 billion from $4 billion, while the value of the pound stabilized. British inflation was brought down to 8.5 percent, its lowest point of the decade, following a slowdown in the rate of increase of wages and salaries.

In 1978, private sector consumption was up six percent, as real household income rose significantly, and private sector industrial investment spurted following an improvement in corporate profits. In 1979, GNP rose 3.3 percent, but wage increases won by labor pushed inflation back above 13 percent. The current account balance of payments deficit reached the equivalent of one percent of GNP, while combined public and private investment dropped five percent to its lowest level as a percentage of GNP since 1964.

In May 1979, Mrs. Thatcher took office as Prime Minister and began to implement economic policies radically different from those tried in the past, policies designed finally to attack the fundamental problems of the British economy.

Britain's two major economic handicaps date back to well before the first oil crisis. They are an inadequate industrial performance and an extreme susceptibility to inflationary pressures. After 1974, Britain's inflation rate was far above the average for the OECD countries. The policies of the Labor party, in power at the time, were pragmatic, day-to-day policies, dominated by the desire to safeguard employment. The main aim was to win time, in the hope that things would improve when income started to flow from North Sea oil production. The government never dared, or cared, to tackle the problem of restructuring industry and adjusting the economy to the realities of international competition. Successive drops in the value of the pound caused only temporary improvements in Britain's international competitiveness, lasting for no more than six or nine months at a time.

At the most fundamental level, the problems sprang from extremely weak productivity growth. Between 1973 and 1978, British productivity rose only 0.5 percent a year, compared to 1.7 percent in Italy, 3.7 percent in France and 5.9 percent in Japan.

A characteristic of the British situation has been extremely sharp fluctuations in the inflation rate, resulting partly from frequent reversals of economic policy—the notorious Stop-Go syndrome. Over the years, this syndrome has sown uncertainty in the minds of industrialists, and helped create a steady process of deindustrialization, illustrated by declining industrial employment, low industrial profits and low levels of capital investment. In 1974, the share of industry in the British economy was down to 28 percent from 34 percent a decade earlier. In 1978, imports captured 18 percent of the British market, up from only 6.7 percent 15 years before, as Britain's trade balance in manufactured goods deteriorated sharply.

Mrs. Thatcher is trying to attack the country's fundamental economic problems with free market policies based on monetarism. Her medium-term aim is to give Britain back its industrial dynamism, to strengthen the structure of the economy and put a definitive end to Stop-Go. The Thatcher approach is not without merit, but her task is a tough one. The first oil shock was one more blow to an already badly shaken economy. Since structural adjustments were never made, the second oil crisis caught the country in an extremely precarious position, even though it was self-sufficient in oil by that time, thanks to the North Sea. North Sea oil could turn out to be a double-edged sword for the British. The strong rise in the pound which it has helped to provoke is seriously hurting Britain's international competitiveness, given the continuing high rate of inflation. Thatcher's policies came with impeccable credentials. It would be a great pity if her remedies proved too potent and ended up killing off the patient.

Sensible Countries

The German Model

Between 1975 and 1979, West Germany managed to achieve excellent economic growth of 13.7 percent. This was the fastest rate of expansion of any European country, and compared to growth of 18.6 percent in the United States and 26.1 percent in Japan. Today, calculated in dollars, German Gross National Product is twice the size of Britain's and one-third bigger than that of France. As Germany's economic growth continued, inflation dropped from year to year, reaching a low point of 2.7 percent in 1978, when inflation in France, for example, was running at 9.1 percent.

The German balance of payments performance was just as remarkable. The current account produced large surpluses, including a surplus of close to $9 billion in 1978, before finally plunging into deficit in 1979. Germany's reserves are the biggest of any country in the world. In the autumn of 1979 they reached 98 billion marks, more than three times French reserves at the time. (Today they have fallen back to 77.4 billion marks). And that is not all. In the 1975-1979 period, German unemployment was reduced to 800,000, the lowest figure in Europe.

How was all this possible, given that Germany was struck by the oil crisis just as other European countries were?

Generally speaking, Germany's success was due to the fact that it reacted to the crisis better and faster than its rivals. Like the United States—but for different reasons—Germany managed to free itself from the external constraints imposed by the quadrupling of oil prices in December 1973. The price for this freedom was subjection to a powerful domestic constraint—the compelling need to control inflation. Germany was the first country to react against inflation, at the end of 1972, even before the oil crisis. Nonetheless, in 1973, the German inflation rate was still close to that of France and above that in the U.S. Because of an economic stabilization program adopted in February 1973, Germany became the only country not to suffer from accelerating inflation in 1974, which was no small achievement. In effect,

Germany went into the oil crisis with its economy already cooling off, which put it in a better position than neighboring countries to absorb the shock of higher oil prices. The Germans suffered economic stagnation in 1974, and recession in 1975; over the two-year period, GNP shrank more than two percent. But then, they was rewarded for their sensible policies with four years of good growth.

The first, relatively moderate, recovery plan was launched in 1975. Then in 1977, the desire to put the German economy back onto the road to strong expansion, which eventually turned Germany into Europe's "locomotive," led to a second plan which involved a multi-year program of investments and two separate programs of fiscal reform. In 1975, the budget deficit equaled six percent of GNP, then dropped to stabilize at around three percent from 1977. But the deficit was largely covered by long-term savings, and so was not inflationary. A part of government outlays were covered by increased revenues resulting from economic growth.

From the end of 1976, investment, which had dropped sharply in 1974/1975, took off again and returned to earlier levels. The results were remarkable, and represented a success for Chancellor Schmidt, whose strategy could be summed up as follows: "Today's profits are tomorrow's investments, and tomorrow's investments create jobs the day after tomorrow."

As a result of measures taken to strengthen the financial position of corporations, which included steps to reduce employment levels,[1] the self-financing ratio of German companies today is over 80 percent.

Germany's success was best illustrated in the external payments area. Despite constant appreciation of the mark, the trade balance produced huge surpluses—33 billion marks in 1973, a record 51 billion in 1974, and 41 billion in 1978. Today, Germany sells more machine tools than all other industrialized countries put together. It registered a surplus in trade with the oil producers up until 1978, before falling into deficit with them in 1979.

Germany's financial muscle is also reflected in the fact that the mark is now the second international currency after the dollar, accounting for 11 percent of central bank reserve holdings. Unlike its neighbors, Germany opted consistently for a strategy based on inflation control and constant currency appreciation. Between 1960 and 1979, the mark rose 95 percent against the French franc, and 211 percent against the pound sterling. Between 1973 and 1979, the mark went through six distinct phases of appreciation, for a total gain of 34 percent against the French currency and 33 percent against the dollar.

The German strategy was only made possible by the smooth functioning of a series of mechanisms which constitute Germany's *virtuous circle.* In this circle, currency appreciation leads to a reduction in imported inflation, lightening the burden of payments for oil and limiting increases in prices of other essential raw materials. At the same time, currency appreciation strengthens the foreign competition facing German companies, which are thus forced to make efforts to modernize production facilities and increase productivity. Labor unions play their part by moderating wage demands, thanks to an exceptionally strong social consensus. The *virtuous cir-*

---

[1]This reduction was made easier by the return of immigrant workers to their own countries. The number of these workers in Germany has dropped to 2 million from 2.5 million in 1974.

cle functioned unfailingly in Germany up to and including 1978. German exports constantly rose faster than the average rate of increase for OECD countries. In 1978, Germany caught up with the U.S. as the world's number one exporter. In 1979, however, the pattern of consistent success was broken, and the current account balance of payments swung into a deficit of six billion dollars.

The turnaround was attributable to external factors, notably a change in the international environment. For one thing, other countries were also becoming more virtuous, including France, Britain, Italy and the U.S. Furthermore, the German authorities had become concerned about the dangers inherent in an excessively strong currency, and were trying to limit appreciation of the mark to preserve order on domestic markets. Because this new strategy was being launched just at the time of the second oil crisis, the burden of oil import payments began to weigh very heavily on the German economy. Payments for imported oil now account for 5.4 percent of German GNP, more than double 2.5 percent just two years ago. The mark began to weaken, and in March 1980 Germany arranged borrowings from Saudi Arabia, Kuwait and the Emirates. Now, even the U.S. is being called to Germany's rescue.

The break in Germany's *virtuous circle* will no doubt prove to be temporary. The ingredients of German success are well known. For a long time they have included extremely moderate consumption and the ability to accumulate long-term savings. They also include alert and efficient management of the economy, and an exceptionally high degree of public support for government economic policy decisions. German productivity growth has been remarkable. From 1974 to 1977, productivity in German industry increased by close to 20 percent (although the price paid was a sharp fall in employment levels). Investments designed to improve productivity accounted for 75 percent of all investments in 1978, up from 50 percent in 1970.

This means that the restructuring of German industry has become a permanent, ongoing process. It is worth recalling that when the Germans began rebuilding their industrial machine more than 30 years ago, they immediately chose the areas of activity—chemicals and heavy industry—best suited to satisfy emerging world demand. Also, Germany and Japan are the two countries which succeeded best in exploiting new OPEC demand. For a period up to 1976, German industry marked time. But from 1977, when investment took off again, there was a new advance in the country's productive power. Modernization efforts were directed to acquiring new techniques or new products in areas such as computers, auto manufacturing, electronics, plastics, etc. Concern about the need to save energy led to investment in developing new energy sources. As a result, Germany entered the 1980's with an up-to-date and highly sophisticated industrial machine, largely immune to competition from newly-industrialized countries.

The Japanese Recovery

Japan's strategy following the oil crisis was different from Germany's, especially in the area of exchange rate policy. However, the results were comparable, thanks to an overhaul of the Japanese economy undertaken with incomparable efficiency and energy.

The Japanese economy was hit hard by the first oil shock, and the adjustment process was full of difficulties for a long time. Japan's oil import bill in 1974 rose $13 billion, equal to 3 percent of the country's GNP. At the time, the economy was in an overheated state, with inflation high and widespread, and so the impact of the crisis on wages and prices was especially severe. There followed the deepest recession Japan had experienced in more than 20 years. The economy shrank 2.2 percent and only began to show signs of recovery in the first quarter of 1975. Subsequently, in the four years up to 1979, the average annual economic growth rate was only about five percent, less than half Japan's earlier rate of expansion. Nonetheless, the Japanese performance was remarkable. After the recession of 1974, the trade balance returned to strong surplus through 1978. Consumer price inflation declined steadily to a low point of six percent in 1978, and by the end of that year the yen had risen to around 180 per dollar, compared to 300 per dollar in 1975.

What was Japan's secret?

As we have said, the oil crisis came at a very unfavorable moment in the Japanese economic cycle. Industrial production was up 15 percent in 1973, and inflation was roaring ahead, with wholesale prices increasing by 20.3 percent in the year and consumer prices by 14.2 percent. Wages increased 20 percent. The government had been trying to take some of the steam out of this overheated economy since early in the year. Between March and December 1973, the Bank of Japan's official discount rate was raised from 4.75 percent to nine percent. Money supply growth was slashed from 25 percent in 1973 to 10 percent in July 1974, and national budget policy was kept very tight.

The recession that followed was extremely broadly based. However, inflation continued to accelerate, reaching 24.5 percent at the wholesale price level in 1974, both because of higher import prices and a 40 percent leap in wages. On foreign exchange markets, the yen fell sharply to around 300 per dollar in 1974, from 265 per dollar in September 1973. The trade balance registered a 1974 deficit of $2.3 billion while the current account of the balance of payments was $4.6 billion in the red. In 1975, however, thanks to the deflationary measures taken by the authorities, inflation began to cool off and the trade balance was restored to health.

The government then began to employ an economic recovery strategy based on an increased budget deficit (government debt rose from 8 percent of GNP in 1974 to 23 percent in 1978), and on export promotion. Corporate investment, which had fallen sharply during the recession, began to recover. The yen was held by the Japanese authorities at around 300 per dollar during 1975 and 1976, then began to rise strongly to a high of about 170 per dollar in October 1978, thanks to huge trade surpluses (the 1978 surplus was $18 billion), and pressure from the United States. Unemployment during all this time doubled to two percent from one percent before 1973.

The 1973 oil crisis caused fundamental changes in the structure of prices in Japan, and the government responded in a number of ways. Under the aegis of the Ministry of International Trade and Industry (MITI), which acquired extensive new powers over industry under a law of May 15, 1978, industries which had become unprofitable, such as steel and textiles, were either scaled back or liquidated. Simultaneously, also under the aegis of MITI, key industries of the future, such as electronics, were rapidly developed with budgetary and fiscal aid from the government. The government also promoted energy-saving investments with remarkable results: oil consumption per unit of production dropped 30 percent in the steel industry, 23 percent in the chemical industry, 14 percent in the cement industry and 37 percent in the auto industry. Last but not least, the government promoted exports by keeping the yen artificially undervalued in 1975 and 1976 (and again in 1979).

By aiding profitable industries and organizing the disappearance of lame ducks, MITI succeeded in completely transforming Japanese industry and adapting it to the new realities of international competition. The share in total Japanese exports of heavy industry—steel, petrochemicals and shipbuilding—declined, while the share of mechanical engineering industries rose. Geographically, the export emphasis also shifted, in favor of sales to China, South-East Asia, OPEC and medium-income developing countries.

Between 1975 and 1979, Japanese leaders managed the economy with great efficiency. They did not hesitate to change course very rapidly when required, and thanks to the Japanese social consensus they were free to implement their decisions. The result is that the Japanese economy today is in a better position than any other to face the competition of the 1980's.

At the time of the first oil crisis, some people questioned the ability of Japan to overcome the shock, given the fact of its near-total dependence on imports to supply its energy requirements. By contrast, the second oil crisis—which ate up another three percent of Japanese GNP—was greeted with little fuss as far as Japan was concerned. The second time around, in fact, Japan's adjustments were more gradual, with better control of inflation than after the first oil crisis, and a more balanced distribution of the burden of lost revenue between households and companies. Monetary and fiscal policies were only lightly restrictive. As a result, economic growth hardly slowed down at all. On the inflation front, wholesale prices rose at rates comparable to 1974, but consumer price rises were more restrained. The healthy financial position of corporations allowed them to absorb part of the shock by reducing profit margins in some cases, while yen weakness allowed them to raise export prices. Finally, wage settlements remained very moderate (up seven percent in 1980, compared to 40 percent in 1974). The bad news was a serious and lasting deterioration in the balance of payments situation.

Discussion of Japan's performance is not complete without mention of the extraordinary cohesion of Japanese society, and the social discipline based on a consensus of incomparable strength. This allowed, among other things, a degree of labor mobility unparalleled anywhere in the world. The Japanese authorities were able to move literally hundreds of thousands of workers out of industries such as steel and shipbuilding into the newer industries considered crucial to the country's economic future. And all this was achieved without protests, without tears, without strikes and without demonstrations.

* * *

For many industrialized countries, the transition period after the first oil crisis is ending pretty badly. The fragility of the Italian economic recovery, the grave difficulties of Mrs. Thatcher's Britain, and the spectacular turnaround in the German balance of payments are cause for some concern about the ability of Europe to absorb the second oil shock. The crumbling of the industrial structure in some countries is also worrying; in Italy, the expansion of the underground economy is a sure sign of industrial regression. Everywhere, social welfare systems inherited from the pre-oil crisis period of prosperity are weighing heavily on weakened economic structures. Finally, there is a process of de-industrialization underway in some countries, reflected in falling levels of private sector investment. It is almost as if these countries, faced with external pressures, had decided to devour themselves in order to survive.

CHAPTER 3
The French Experience

1974-1976: Groping for Solutions

For more than two years after the oil crisis, France groped unsuccessfully for solutions to its new-found economic problems. The leap in oil prices at the end of 1973 tripled France's oil import bill from 14.6 billion francs in 1973 to 43 billion in 1974, causing the trade balance to swing from a 1973 surplus of seven billion francs to a 1974 deficit of 16 billion. Inflation, which was already being fueled by rapidly rising raw material prices and strong overall demand, went through the roof. In May 1974, consumer price inflation hit an annual rate of 17.5 percent. For 1974 as a whole, consumer prices were up 15.2 percent, almost double the 1973 rate of increase of 8.5 percent. Clearly, action was urgently needed to restore the economy to balance.

Accordingly, in June 1974, following the election of Valery Giscard d'Estaing as President, the new government announced a major anti-inflation program, tightening both monetary and fiscal policies. However, because of delays in implementation, the impact of this program coincided with the effects of a slowdown in overall demand and heavy inventory liquidation already underway. The result was that industrial production nosedived, and the economy spiraled downwards into recession in 1975, causing a sharp rise in unemployment. Gross Domestic Product (GDP) growth for the year was down to 0.2 percent, from 3.2 percent in 1974. Consumer price inflation also declined, but only to 9.6 percent. The most spectacular result of the recession was the turnaround in the trade balance, which showed a 1975 surplus of 5.6 billion francs, as imports dropped almost 10 percent. This led to a strong rise in the franc on foreign exchange markets, allowing it to return in July to the European currency snake—which it had been forced to leave in January 1974.

Somewhat belatedly, the government realized how serious the recession was and gradually relaxed monetary policy in 1975 while taking budgetary policy steps to bolster consumption, housing, exports and investment. But when the actions taken appeared insufficient to stimulate overall economic recovery, the government of Prime Minister Jacques Chirac over-reacted in September with a 30.5 billion franc "program for the development of the French economy," incorporating strong measures to stimulate both personal consumption and investment.

As demand quickly expanded and inventories were built up again, growth in industrial production soared to an annual rate of 21 percent at the end of 1975 and the start of 1976. Consumer price inflation picked up again, to an annual rate of 10 percent between April and October 1976, mainly because of strongly rising wages, and the trade balance plunged back into a 20.5 billion franc deficit for the year, as imports surged and export growth slowed. This created heavy foreign exchange market pressure on the franc, which was forced to leave the currency snake again in mid-March 1976. Monetary policy was tightened again, while fiscal policies remained expansionist until the autumn—to the extent that the effects of the September 1975 reflationary package were still being felt.

Overall, the effect of government actions from the outbreak of the oil crisis until September 1976 was to contribute to violent upheavals in the economy without solving the underlying problems which had been created. The government did confront the energy problem in 1975 by approving a program of nuclear power station construction and by taking measures to cut oil consumption.

But both the anti-inflation program of June 1974 and the recovery program of September 1975 were heavy-handed and, above all, badly timed. The government always seemed to be one step behind developments within the economy. After this prolonged period of fumbling, a new government led by Prime Minister Raymond Barre was installed in September 1976 and proceeded to employ a radically different and much more flexible economic policy approach.

1976-1980: Facing Realities

The new government of Raymond Barre, who was named both Prime Minister and Minister of Finance and Economics, recognized the need to finally start adapting the French economy to the realities of the post-oil crisis international environment. It then managed, against all the odds, to win both the time and the political support needed to implement its economic program. For an economic policy chief to stay in power for over four years is rare in French history. For him to rule as Prime Minister and enjoy widespread support for so long—from the President, from the parliamentary majority and even from public opinion—is almost unheard of. The result was a period of domestic social stability, deriving from an implicit social consensus rarely achieved in France. From the outset, the economic program of the Barre government was based on a doctrine of liberalism combined with healthy pragmatism.

The approach of the government to solving its problems was essentially empirical and pragmatic, rather than doctrinaire. It practiced what might be called "the politics of the possible." Barre did not manipulate the levers of power too quickly or too violently. He took a gradualist approach, adopting measures designed to modify the course of events over time, rather than suddenly and drastically. His pragmatic instincts led him to alter or abandon altogether some of the government's original economic targets, either because they appeared impossible to attain, or more likely because the price for attaining them appeared too high. Thus policies of wage restraint were implemented very flexibly, monetary policy was sometimes loosened, and budgetary policies were much less restrictive than might have been expected. Over the years, the government gradually came to rely on foreign exchange and monetary policy disciplines, rather than on more direct and coercive policy methods: it was monetarism French-style.

The results were mixed. Household consumption and exports continued to be the main engines of economic growth, while private sector investment remained weak. Inflation remained stubbornly between 9 and 10 percent, and then accelerated to almost 12 percent in 1979 under the impact of the second oil crisis. The trade balance improved through 1978, but then plunged back into heavy deficit in 1979—again as a result of the oil crisis. Overall economic growth did not match pre-oil crisis levels of over five percent, but it still continued at an average annual rate of more than three percent, and real disposable income and personal consumption continued to rise. At most, the French suffered only relative austerity.

TABLE 4

% changes

	1974	1975	1976	1977	1978	1979
Real growth in gross domestic product....................	3.2	0.2	5.2	2.8	3.6	3.1
Real growth in buying power of household disposable income ..	2.8	4.4	3.0	3.1	4.8	1.6
Real growth in personal consumption	3.0	3.0	5.4	2.8	4.4	3.2

Two fundamental objectives of the government when it took office were to restore price stability and return the trade balance to surplus.

The Trade Performance

From 1976 through 1978, French exports in volume terms rose 14.1 percent, while imports in volume terms increased by only 6.1 percent, and the terms of trade improved by 1.9 percent. (This improvement measures the increase in income resulting from the fact that French export prices rose faster than import prices.) This produced a trade surplus of 2.5 billion francs in 1978, compared to a deficit of 11.1 billion in 1977. It is difficult to say whether the improved export performance was the result of specific government actions or simply a nationwide export drive; export sales of some products, in particular capital goods, had already begun to improve before the new government took office.

But on the import side, the effect of government policies was evident: sharp declines in the growth rates of imports of consumer goods were clearly the indirect result of government actions to limit increases in household disposable income. At all events, the improvement in the trade balance proved short-lived.

In 1979, following the surge in oil prices which began early in the year, the trade balance plunged back into a deficit of 10.1 billion francs. Then, in the first eight months of 1980, the deficit soared to a whopping 40.5 billion francs, as export growth slumped to 1.6 percent, import growth continued at 5.1 percent and the terms of trade worsened by 7.4 percent as a result of the higher oil prices. Over 80 percent of the deterioration of the trade balance in the first eight months of 1980, as compared with the same period of 1979, can be accounted for by oil imports; the remainder was attributable mainly to a loss of certain export market shares and a rise in non-oil imports caused by an upturn in domestic consumption and investment.

Overall, the trade performance in recent years has provided clear proof of the extreme vulnerability of the French trade balance to domestic and external economic developments; any rise in French personal consumption or investment activity has an almost immediate negative impact on the trade balance. However, the fact remains that by international standards, France has not fared too badly. For example, the French deficit of $8.5 billion in the first half of 1980 was not much bigger than the West German deficit of $5.6 billion and the Italian deficit of $7.7 billion, and was smaller than the Japanese deficit of $10 billion.

Furthermore, and this is extremely important, France has benefited from a spectacular improvement in its balance of services—the non-trade component of a country's current account balance of payments.[1] Because of this improvement, the overall current account balance remained in surplus in 1979 by about five billion francs, despite the big trade deficit. The surplus on services has been rising constantly in recent years because of a number of factors, including a sharp increase in the surplus on tourism resulting from improvements made in tourist facilities, and above all a leap in income from technical cooperation agreements and other overseas contracts. As a result, the services balance is financing a growing part of French goods imports, and causing the French current account balance of payments to outperform the balance of payments of other key nations, including West Germany and Japan.

The anticipated French current account deficit of about $7 billion in 1980 compares to an expected German deficit of $16 billion. The performance of the current account is clearly one of the main reasons for the continuing strength of the franc on foreign exchange markets in 1980.

The Battle Against Inflation

The battle against inflation was described by Barre himself as the cornerstone of his government's economic program. With consumer price inflation running at an annual rate of 10 percent when he took office, one of his first actions was to freeze most prices until December. Subsequently, there were several factors favoring a slowdown in inflation, including a sharp decline in imported raw material prices in 1977, a fall in energy prices (resulting from a sharp rise in the franc against the dollar in 1978 and stable energy prices in dollar terms), and relatively slow growth in prices of agricultural products from mid-1978 onwards. Nonetheless, French consumer prices continued to rise at close to 1975-1976 rates, and then began to accelerate in early 1979, mainly because of the surge in the oil price.

---

[1]The services balance includes such things as tourism, transportation, insurance, income from technical cooperation agreements abroad, etc.

The original inflation target, implicit in the government's program announced in September 1976, was to reduce consumer price inflation to 6.5 percent. Later, the government stopped aiming for a reduction in inflation and limited itself to trying

CONSUMER PRICES 1974–1979

(December to December)

TABLE 5

%

	1974	1975	1976	1977	1978	1979
Overall	15.2	9.6	9.9	9.0	9.7	11.8
Industrial products .	18.6	7.8	7.9	7.4	9.9	13.4
Food products	12.1	10.7	11.4	11.9	7.9	9.6
Services.............	13.4	11.4	11.7	8.6	11.3	11.5

to prevent it from accelerating. Seen in this light, the government's policies were successful—until 1979. But overall, the performance of prices was disappointing, and compared unfavorably with some other industrialized countries, where inflation slowed sharply in the period concerned.

There were three main reasons for this.

In the first place, fiscal and monetary policies were not sufficiently supportive of the anti-inflation struggle. The government succeeded in its major aim of slowing the rate of wage increases. Annual average increases in hourly wages in 1977, 1978 and 1979 were 12.7 percent, 12.5 percent and 13 percent respectively, compared to increases of 19.1 percent in 1976 and 17.3 percent in 1975. However, the anti-inflation effect was partly offset by a rise in *indirect* income of households—i.e., a sharp rise in total social welfare payments.

The national budget deficit, after falling from 38 billion francs in 1975 to 20 billion in 1976 and 18 billion in 1977, leaped again to 34 billion in 1978 and 38 billion in 1979. As a percentage of Gross Domestic Product, the French deficit remained between 1 and 1.6 percent in the 1976-1979 period, compared to much higher rates reached in other countries—for example 11 percent in Italy, 4 percent in Britain and 3 percent in Germany.

But in France budget deficits have traditionally been financed by money creation while in Germany, for example, they are financed out of long-term savings. The savings habits of households in Germany largely offset the inflationary effects of budget deficits, while in France the high degree of public sensitivity to inflation tends to maximize those effects. To push its anti-inflation strategy to its logical conclusion, the government should have stuck to its original aim of eliminating the budget deficit altogether, rather than trying only to keep the deficit within limits considered reasonable. But of course, there were non-economic factors involved here. As Barre has rightly said: "Politics is sometimes the art of knowing how far you can overstep the mark." As for monetary policy, the government's aim was to keep the rate of money supply growth below the expected rate of real growth in Gross Domestic Product. However, as Table 6 shows, money supply growth exceeded nominal GDP growth in 1977 and 1979.

A second factor limiting success in the fight against inflation was the decision to defend the franc at the relatively weak level of slightly less than five francs per dollar at the end of 1976 and early in 1977. If the government had instead chosen to

TABLE 6

%

	1974	1975	1976	1977	1978	1979	July 1980[1]
Annual money supply growth (M2).........	18.1	16.1	12.8	13.9	12.2	14.4	11.1
Annual GDP growth (nominal)..........	14.7	13.6	15.5	12.1	13.5	13.9	

(1): Forecast

support the franc for example at the 4.60-4.80 level—the level which had prevailed until shortly before the government took office—it could probably have shaved more than half a percentage point off consumer price inflation in 1977.

Keeping the franc strong, and thus limiting imported inflation, was always an integral part of the government's anti-inflation strategy, but in its first months in office it seems to have chosen the wrong point at which to dig in its heels to defend the currency. The lessons of this mistake were taken to heart later, when the government pursued a vigorous strong-currency policy.

The third factor, and probably the most important, was the government's failure to carry out fundamental reforms to lower the core rate of underlying inflation built into the structure of the French economy. The main causes of structural inflation in France include the importance of the agricultural sector, heavy operating costs in the public sector, indexation of incomes and lack of competition in the services and distribution areas. In line with its free market philosophy, the government lifted controls on industrial prices from mid-1978, and controls on prices of services from the beginning of 1980. This helped introduce now elements of price competition, but in the absence of an all-out attack on the causes of structural inflation it seems to have worsened the overall inflation performance. The new surge in inflation which began in 1979 was very largely the result of higher oil prices, but it can also be attributed to some extent to the lifting of price controls, as well as to increases in public utility prices, which had remained for a long time below cost.

In retrospect, it seems that the battle against inflation may have been fatally compromised in 1977, the new government's first full year in office, when it failed to establish firmly enough the credibility of its anti-inflation strategy. After that, political factors, including elections in 1978, intervened to provide fuel for inflation, and widespread inflationary expectations persisted, making it impossible to consolidate small early gains made in the anti-inflation struggle.

Despite the limited success of the government's anti-inflation policies, however, two positive notes should be struck. In the first place, the government managed to prevent prices from flying out of control as a result of the second oil crisis. Secondly, the anti-inflationary strategy employed had the virtue of helping the government to implement its industrial policies—which represent, without any doubt, the most unequivocal success of its term in office.

The Restructuring of Industry

While lower inflation and a healthier trade balance were the most widely publicized objectives of the Barre government, both aims were in fact subordinate to the overriding need to strengthen French industry and adapt it to the harsh realities of international competition in the post-oil crisis world. This Number One priority was always implicit rather than explicit in the government's economic program. But it is the key to understanding the logic behind the Barre government's actions. To help French corporations strengthen their financial positions, the government employed various methods, all supported by vigorous jawboning from Barre—which in itself had considerable effect in pushing corporations in the desired direction.

In the first place, the government sought to re-direct savings flows towards productive purposes, to ensure that industry and the economy as a whole had the funds required for a full-scale restructuring effort. Major steps were taken to strengthen the bond market, encourage long-term financial placements, and discourage speculative investment in real estate. A savings law of July 1978, providing fiscal incentives for French share purchases, was very successful in allowing companies to raise funds through the stock market rather than through increasing bank debt, as they were being forced to do up to that time. Savings which were previously being channeled into housing were re-directed to corporations. In 1978, corporate funds raised through capital increases tripled from 1977 to 12.8 billion francs; in 1979, the figure rose further to 13.5 billion. Also in 1979, the stock market index of French shares rose 17 percent, while stock markets elsewhere in the world stagnated or declined.

Secondly, as we have seen, the government lifted price controls, first those on industrial prices in 1978, and later those on prices of services. This represented conscious but careful use of inflation to help companies rebuild finances badly weakened by the recession of 1975. The strategy may sound surprising in view of the importance attached to the battle against inflation. However, although the freeing of prices does seem to have been a factor in rising inflation in late 1979 and early 1980, there is every reason to believe that the flexibility achieved in the prices structure will in future work in both directions—pushing prices up at times but causing them to decline sharply at others. Furthermore, given the time required in France to eliminate certain structural cost elements, freeing prices was the only realistic way to restore corporate profit margins. By employing inflation as it did, the government was simply facing realities and demonstrating that inflation is not an absolute evil but a relative evil, one which must not be allowed to get out of control.

The policy of defending the franc on foreign exchange markets also became an element in the government's strategy for adapting French industry to post-oil crisis competitive conditions. Apart from limiting the inflationary impact of higher prices for imported oil, a strong currency—or at least a stable one—should force exporting companies to modernize their operations and cut costs, and thus enter the *virtuous circle* described earlier. When it first took office, the government may not have recognized the vital importance of a strong currency as clearly as it should have done. But that soon changed. The strength of the franc from early 1978 onwards has been as much the result of government support for the currency—notably interest rate support—as it has been the result of improvements in French economic fundamentals. Since March 1979, when the European Monetary System was established with the franc as a member, French interest rates have moved solely as a function of external constraints in general and German interest rate movements in particular.

THE GERMAN MARK AGAINST THE FRENCH FRANC
(average monthly rates on Paris Foreign Exchange Market, in francs per mark)

CHART 1

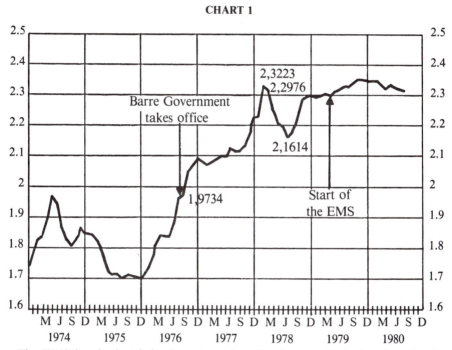

The EMS has in fact helped to strengthen the degree of priority given by the authorities to a strong franc, and has also increased the credibility of the strong franc policy in the eyes of foreign exchange market operators, to the extent that they have become convinced EMS parities can and will be defended. The restoration of confidence in the franc among foreign investors has led to major capital inflows.

Since the first realignment of EMS parities in September 1979, the franc has actually outperformed the German mark, despite the fact that inflation in France has been running about seven percentage points higher than in Germany.

Overall, the government's industrial policies have had considerable success in strengthening the performance of French corporations and in rebuilding their finances. Productivity has been rising at an ever faster pace—3.1 percent in 1977, 4.6 percent in 1978 and 7 percent in 1979. Corporate profits have improved and, above all, the self-financing ratio of corporations has risen steadily from a low of 64 percent in 1976 to 79 percent in 1979—which was not far from the pre-oil crisis level of 82 percent in 1970.

However, the bad news is that private sector capital investment has not picked up, despite repeated incentives to investment provided by the government. While productive investments by public sector corporations rose by an annual average of

THE DOLLAR AGAINST THE FRENCH FRANC
(average monthly rates on Paris Foreign Exchange Market, in francs per dollar)

CHART 2

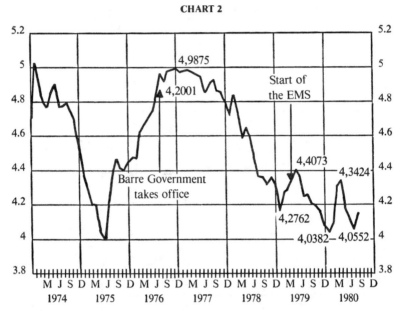

more than 10 percent from 1977 through 1979, private sector outlays stagnated.

It has become obvious that the rebuilding of corporate financial resources is only the first stage of the battle to increase investment in France. The other half of the battle is to remove uncertainties in corporate minds about future levels of demand. Perhaps there is an implicit contradiction in France between the aim of lower inflation and a surplus in international trade on the one hand, and the aim of stimulating

PRODUCTIVE INVESTMENT[1]

TABLE 7

%

	1973	1974	1975	1976	1977	1978	1979
Private sector	+ 4.6	− 2.9	− 12.1	+ 8.3	− 3.3	+ 1.0	+ 0.7
Major public sector corporations	+ 6.7	+ 5.0	+ 22.5	+ 3.4	+ 11.5	+ 10.6	+ 9.3

(1) Includes investments in the industrial sector, plus the sectors of commerce, services, transport, energy, construction, and public works.

Source: INSEE

a lasting recovery in investment on the other. At all events, how to strengthen the investment results so far achieved is clearly one of the problems remaining in France's economic future.

Facing the Future

The second oil crisis has further tightened the external constraints on the French economy. Problems which appeared solved have returned to haunt us. Progress made in some areas remains to be consolidated in new and more difficult conditions.

Unemployment

One of the most pressing problems outstanding is unemployment. From September 1976 to September 1980 the seasonally adjusted total of unsuccessful job applicants increased 57 percent from 930,000 to 1,460,000, the biggest increases occurring in 1977 (+22 percent) and 1979 (+12 percent).

There were a host of different reasons for this leap in unemployment, including demographic factors, the slowdown in economic growth, the rise in productivity, layoffs resulting from industrial restructuring, a slowdown in the trend towards shorter working hours and the increase in the number of women seeking work. It is unfair to charge—as some analysts have—that the Barre government ignored the unemployment problem. But it is true that the government's actions to combat unemployment were indirect rather than direct: job creation was to result from the government's measures to increase exports and investment. It was the application in France of German Chancellor Schmidt's theory that can be stated as follows: "Today's profits are tomorrow's investments, and tomorrow's industrial investments create jobs the day after tomorrow."

However, after four years, it is clear that this chain of logic has broken down in France. The rise in profits has not been capable of increasing investment sufficiently, and the investment which has taken place has not created enough jobs. In France, as in other industrialized countries, including Japan, Italy and the U.S., the vast majority of new jobs created have been outside the industrial sector.

In a review of his term in office,[1] Barre described the rise in unemployment as "unavoidable," and attributed it partly to the inclusion in the unemployment figures of people who are actually working (in the underground economy), and to the increased number of women seeking work. There is no doubt that his interpretation explains at least part of the rise in unemployment. But it does not alter the fundamental problem, which is one of formidable complexity. So far, no long-term plan to solve the problem has been drawn up, and according to some analyses the number of unemployed could rise to 2.5 million by 1985. At some point, solutions will have to be found, even if they compromise economic policy in other areas.

The Social Security System

In his review of the past four years, referred to above, Barre explicitly condemned "the collectivization . . . of our economy" and "the growth in revenue transfers." The best illustration of these phenomena is the rise in expenditures of

---

Raymond Barre: The French Economy Four Years Later, in "Revue des Deux-Mondes," September 1980.

the social security system, and the deficit of that system. In the 1975-1979 period, expenditures for sickness benefits, old-age benefits and family allowances increased 28.9 percent in real terms, compared to real growth of 15.5 percent in Gross Domestic Product. After outstripping receipts by 10.8 billion francs in 1978, spending was estimated to be in balance with receipts in 1979, partly because of government measures to increase contributions and tighten control over benefit payments. But the deficit will probably soon reappear, as contributions to the system, which are based on wage payments, are depressed by wage restraint and unemployment, while outlays continue to rise rapidly.

The unemployed make no contributions, but still have the right to receive payments from the system. The fact is that current expenditures are based on a benefits program inherited from an earlier, more prosperous period. A real solution to the deficit problem would require cutting expenditures through changes in the program itself. Such changes could obviously trigger violent reactions from the public. But at some point it will be up to the government to adapt the system to the new economic realities in France.

Import Penetration.

While growth of the French economy has slowed markedly since the first oil crisis, the ratio of import penetration of the French industrial sector has continued to grow about as rapidly as before the crisis. This is a very troubling phenomenon, signifying both increasing dependence on abroad and a reduction in domestic sales outlets available to French producers.

IMPORT PENETRATION RATE OF THE INDUSTRIAL SECTOR[1]

TABLE 8

%

1965	1970	1974	1975	1976	1977	1978	1979
13.0	19.5	24.1	22.0	24.7	25.4	25.8	27.3

(1) Imports as a percentage of total production plus imports minus exports.

Source: INSEE

In the capital goods sector, which is considered a key area for the future development of French industry, the ratio of import penetration has been rising even faster than in the industrial sector as a whole, and reached 32.8 percent in 1979. French capital goods manufacturers have been able to offset their loss of part of the domestic market by finding new export markets, but this could make them vulnerable to future world crises. The trend towards higher rates of import penetration may be making the French trade balance excessively sensitive to the ups and downs of the economic cycle, as any rise in investment triggers an almost immediate rise in capital goods imports. The trend indicates a certain loss of vitality in French industry, which may have its origins in the lackluster investment performance of recent years.

Investment: The Missing Link

As we have seen, private sector investment growth has remained weak, despite healthier corporate profits; it seems that in many cases corporations have preferred to use increases in financial resources for such purposes as debt repayment and higher dividend payouts, rather than for productive investments. This trend, if it continues, poses two major risks for French industry.

The first is that French industry will fall behind competition in other advanced countries, particularly West Germany, where private sector investment growth has been much faster than in France.

The second risk is a shrinking of the French industrial base, resulting from a combination of stagnant overall investment volume and investment emphasis on modernizing existing production facilities. Statistics show that capital stock has already been reduced in some sectors of industry, such as steel, metalworking, base chemicals and construction materials. Overall, from 1974 to 1979, the share of industry in total value-added held steady at about 36 percent. But in the same period the number of employees in industry fell by about 500,000, and declined as a proportion of the working population from 28.6 percent to 26.2 percent. From 1970 to 1979, the share of industry in gross fixed capital formation fell from 20 percent to 14.9 percent.

What remains to be seen is the extent to which the emphasis of French industry will shift towards advanced technology areas, and the extent to which modernization of facilities will improve productivity. Government analyses indicate that the bulk of investment in capital goods production is now being devoted to improving productivity of capital stock, which is a favorable sign for competitiveness (although it hardly augurs well for job creation.)

Will the healthy shock treatment which has been applied to some areas of French industry lead to a blossoming of new activities? Will French industry reconquer at least part of the domestic market share it has lost? The answers to these questions may hold the key to the industrial future of France.

Towards a More Forceful Government Role in Industry

The government role in aiding the restructuring of industry is still far from complete.

In the energy field, which was given official priority, government actions were forceful and the results were largely positive: from 1973 to 1979, oil consumption dropped 7.5 percent, and the share of oil in total energy consumption fell to 57 percent from 67 percent.

But elsewhere, intervention in industry by the Barre government was often hesitant and defensive in nature. In its so-called industrial *slum clearance* program, designed to aid and rationalize the weakest and most-threatened industries, such as steel and textiles, the government used public funds above all to alleviate unemployment and other social problems, rather than to promote new industrial activities. In effect, the government's policies were social rather than industrial. This was a logical result of the government's liberal philosophy. To the maximum extent possible, it wanted to release corporations from the guardianship of the state and let them stand on their own feet. But the policies were insufficient to solve the problems of some industrial sectors, as was illustrated by continuing difficulties in the textile industry, and the new crisis in the steel industry in 1980 (although it should be pointed out that the steel industry crisis affected all of Europe and the U.S. as well).

Having seen what strong government action was capable of achieving in the energy industry, through the promotion of nuclear energy and other policies, the government has begun to go on the offensive elsewhere. Rather than simply trying to plug industrial holes as they occur, the government is now actively seeking to strengthen advanced-technology industries such as the arms industry, aeronautics, computers, telecommunications, electronics, micro-electronics, energy-saving equipment and, of course, nuclear energy. The government also seems to want to develop the food industry, which has not yet lived up to its full potential.

These government initiatives, including clear definition of industrial priorities and the creation of a government body to support private sector projects, are welcome ones. But overall, they may still fall short of what is required. So far, government actions have remained concentrated on the two extremes of French industry—i.e. on the industries of the future and those of the past which are suffering the worst difficulties. In between, there are a large number of other industries which also need to be adapted to the new realities of international competition.

Conclusion[1]

There can be little doubt that the French economy has emerged strengthened from the experience of the past four years. The franc is bursting with health, the balance of payments has withstood the second oil crisis well, and foreign confidence in the French economy has been restored. Net external indebtedness at the end of 1979 was negligible (although it should be noted that France's external liabilities concern mainly strong-currency countries, while its assets are for the most part in countries generally considered weak, such as Third World countries and Communist countries of the Eastern bloc). France's international credit rating is excellent, as illustrated by the fact that the margin applied to loans to French borrowers is almost half the world average. France thus has a financial safety valve which could come in very useful in times of trouble.

However, it is not easy to make an overall judgment of the economic policy performance of the Barre government. There are a number of paradoxes. Wage growth has eased, while *indirect* household income—from the social security system —has risen quickly. Public sector investment has grown rapidly, while private sector investment has stagnated. Such developments suggest a socialist rather than a liberal economic philosophy. No doubt the explanation lies in what Somerset Maugham called "the force of circumstances."

The counterpart of the Barre government's empirical, pragmatic approach is the lack of a medium-term vision of the future, which perhaps results from a highly developed sense of fatalism among government leaders, combined with their conservative instincts. Since the economic situation of France is largely controlled by exter-

---

[1]Like the rest of this chapter, this was written before the Presidential elections of May 1981, since when, among other things, the franc has plummeted.

nal developments, there is a natural resistance to believing that problems can be solved through direct and forceful government action. The willingness to operate in a short-term context, to proceed on a day-to-day basis, has the advantage of reducing forecasting errors. But it also means that the government has no fixed point of reference, and is tempted simply to follow a middle path under the pressure of conflicting demands from different interest groups. This spirit of compromise helps to explain the limited success of government policies in certain areas, particularly the area of inflation. It also explains why there have not been structural economic reforms—with the exception of the lifting of price controls, which was certainly a significant reform, but hardly altered economic behavior in a major way.

In international terms, the French economic performance over the past four years or so has been an average one, better than the performances of Britain and Italy, but not as good as those of some other countries, particularly West Germany. France has benefited from four years of social peace, and has regained some of the economic ground lost earlier, but the recovery remains to be completed. It is possible that the tightening of external constraints caused by the second oil crisis—and perhaps soon by the third oil crisis—will mark the end of the kind of economic liberalism which France has been experiencing, and the start of stronger government interventionism, which may alone be capable of resolving conflicts among economic requirements.

* * *

Towards A Stalinist Model of Consumption

In the industrialized West, there is too strong a tendency to identify overall economic growth with growth in consumption. It is taken for granted that consumption should grow proportionately with Gross National Product, as it has usually done in the past in most industrialized countries with free-market economies.

However, it is worth pointing out that the trend has been very different in countries with authoritarian regimes. In the Soviet Union, disposable income per head did not regain 1928 levels until 1952, even though GNP more than doubled during that period of more than 20 years. Subsequently, while the Soviet Union's GNP grew at an average rate of four to five percent a year, personal consumption—even after Khrushchev came to power—rose by only about two percent a year. The Stalinist model of consumption, pushed to its extremes, involved treating consumption as a residual element of demand, while emphasizing the allocation of available resources to investment in heavy industry and defense, which were considered the top priority areas.

This is not the place to discuss the extreme methods employed in the Soviet Union. It is sufficient to say that those methods allowed the Soviet Union to release the resources required to achieve its goals, and to arrive in record time at the very front rank of world economic and military powers. There is obviously no suggestion here that Western industrialized countries should be subjected to the rigors of a Stalinist approach to consumption. But it is worth bearing in mind that for some time to come it may well be necessary for GNP and consumption to grow at very different rates, to allow more resources to be allocated to non-consumption purposes.

Take the case of France. In coming years, it appears indispensable for GNP growth to be high, since economic stagnation would mean rising unemployment. Government calculations have shown that it will be practically impossible to provide jobs for all the young people entering the labor market in the years ahead without economic growth of at least five percent a year.

Of course, lots of solutions have been proposed for the unemployment problem, such as shortening working hours, lowering the retirement age, and offering return tickets to immigrant workers to encourage them to go home. But it should be obvious that these "solutions" are merely illusions: most immigrant workers are in France to stay; there are limits to how far working hours can be shortened without excessive reductions in disposable incomes; and lowering the retirement age simply means sending into the labor market lots of pension-receiving job seekers. The fact is that France is condemned to achieving sustained or accelerating economic growth just to solve the unemployment problem.

However, the French economy is now subject to harsh new constraints, both external and domestic, so the economic growth will have to be of a new kind. Externally, it is obvious that for some years to come a part of national resources will have to be exported to pay for imports of raw materials, in particular oil; it is also obvious that the resources concerned will have to come out of consumption. Domestically, long-term savings will have to be increased to finance investments to restructure French industry, and investments to improve such things as the quality of housing and the quality of the urban environment. Again, increased savings imply restrictions on personal consumption.

The bottom line is that there will have to be a shift in the relative weight of the components of GNP: consumption will have to suffer to allow for increases in savings and investment.

This requirement applies not only to France, but in general terms to other free-market industrialized countries. It is a requirement which is easy to state, but much less easy to meet. Controls on consumption have been imposed in the past, for example in wartime, or during battles against inflation. But this time around, it is not simply a matter of a brief slowdown in consumption, after which expansion starts all over again. It is a matter of embarking on a new course, and sticking to it for a long time.

In its extreme form, the choice is between encouraging voluntary savings, in line with what might be called the liberal Victorian model, or resorting to forced savings policies, in line with the Stalinist model, which means forced limitations on consumption. In our advanced free-market societies, it should be possible to find a middle path appropriate to current circumstances, which would combine voluntary restrictions on consumption with increased savings—which are the only guarantee of a return to balanced economic growth.

But how can this middle path be found without creating a new sense of responsibility among the public, to serve as the basis for a new social consensus? The issue cannot be ignored. If present patterns of consumption are not changed, we shall have to resign ourselves to the decline of our industrial civilizations.

CHAPTER 4
The Non-Oil
Developing Countries

It has become by now commonplace to speak of Third Worlds, in the plural, rather than the Third World, in the singular.[1] According to World Bank classifications of Third World countries (excluding OPEC), there are now about 40 *Medium-Income Developing Countries,* including such star performers as South Korea, Brazil, Iraq and the Ivory Coast. Below them there is another category, the *Low-Income Developing Countries,* totaling about 60 and including a number of tiny nation-states with populations of less than one million, and in some cases even less than 100,000. The last 25 countries on this list depend on international aid for their survival. In the delicate language of the United Nations, they are the *Least Developed Countries.*

It is obviously impossible to make a single judgment of such a disparate group of nations. But what seems clear right now is that while raw material-producing countries in Africa and Asia have been suffering from the backlash of the economic crises of the 1970's, a small group of developing countries in South East Asia and Latin America have been thriving. These are the "Newly-Industrialized Countries," the so-called NIC's, for which the oil crisis seems if anything to have been a help rather than a handicap. Their growing competitiveness has caused much fear and trembling in the established industrial countries on both sides of the Atlantic. Before analyzing their surprising success and its causes, it is worth pausing a moment to take a look at a concept which has now had its hour of glory, the concept of a new "world economic order."

World Economic Order: A Seductive Notion

Out of the confusion created in people's minds by the first oil shock came a new expression to enrich the vocabulary of economics: world economic order. The speed with which it won acceptance should have been enough to raise some doubts.

The Birth of a Myth

Is there not something illusory in talking about setting up a new economic order of things, or conversely about eliminating current disorder? What it seems to imply

---

[1]I drew this distinction in my book, *The Third World and the Environmental Crisis,* published by P.U.F. in 1974.

is that international economic order previously existed, just as order exists in the ecclesiastical world or in the world of logic. But the fact is that there never has been any such order—if by order we mean a body of rules or of law governing monetary and trade relationships among nations. What we have experienced has been simply a succession of precariously balanced relationships among nations, or, to be more precise, a succession of temporary power-based relationships, in which the strong dominated the weak. To the extent that it implies a stable, if not unalterable, system, the notion of world economic order is a myth; in reality, the situation is fluid and constantly evolving.

The notion itself seems to be a descendent of various intellectual concepts, some of them explicit and some not. The idea of setting up a stabilizing world order implies a search for ways to avoid the upheavals caused by sudden change. In this sense, it represents a transfer into the area of international economic relations of the concept of countercyclical economic policies, which was one of the main themes of economic thought both before and after World War II. The aim would be to control the international economic cycle, considered to be the origin of the turbulence which has plagued world economic activity.

In another sense, world economic order recalls the concept of balance, so dear to the French school of mathematics of the second half of the 19th century. Transferred to the field of international economics, the idea becomes that of achieving a balance among developments in the areas of trade, business affairs, currencies and revenues. In yet another sense, world economic order represents an implicit condemnation of the free market concept which, rightly or wrongly, has come to be held responsible for the disorders in international trade. The idea would be to eliminate such disorder through well-thought out government measures. Whatever the theoretical value of these ideas, and whatever the strength of conviction behind them, it must be said that they are based very largely on pure logic and reason. They take little or no account of human irrationality, the human lust for power, and the calculations of self-interest—in short, all the realities which economic research had previously been trying to re-integrate into pure economics. However praiseworthy it may be at a conceptual level, the idea of constructing a new world economic order is in reality little more than a formal intellectual exercise in defining the theoretical conditions required for drawing up more harmonious rules of conduct among nations.

The Failure of the North-South Dialogue

The idea of world economic order, although seductive at first sight, has the grave flaw of being out of touch with reality. The same can be said for the North-South dialogue, which was conceived as the means for putting the idea into practice. The dialogue was no sooner launched than it became bogged down in the sands of procedure. It began at the Paris Conference of December 1975, which brought together 27 nations from the North and the South of the globe. It was then continued in a variety of forums, including the United Nations Industrial Development Organization, the General Agreement on Tariffs and Trade (GATT), and especially the Group of 77 of the United Nations Conference on Trade and Development (UNCTAD).

The dialogue concentrated especially on defining a global strategy for Third World industrial development. The aim was to increase the Third World share of total world industrial output from 7 percent to 25 percent by the year 2000. The concrete results of the negotiations were mediocre, no doubt because the very principle of holding global talks simultaneously on prices, protectionism, international aid, world economic order, etc., was simply too ambitious.

Furthermore, the United Nations was clearly an inappropriate forum for trade and financial negotiations, to the extent that such negotiations are generally highly politicized. The countries of the Soviet bloc showed almost no interest in the negotiations, which in their view had nothing to do with the real confrontation, which remained that between East and West. From the beginning, the dialogue was plagued by inconsistencies. For example, it included OPEC countries, which had fundamentally different concerns and ambitions from the rest of the participants. In fact, the real antagonism is less between the North and the South than between OPEC and the non-oil developing countries. This is obvious from analysis of trade balances, which are the real measure of world power relationships. All the rest is rhetoric. However, it took until 1980, after the second oil crisis, before the realities were recognized.

As regards achieving the aims of the North-South dialogue, the share of Third World countries in total world industrial output rose to 10 percent at the end of 1979, while their share of world exports climbed to 30 percent. The 25 percent goal for Third World industrial production is still a long way from being reached, which is only normal. But progress has already been substantial, and everyone agrees that the future growth rates of Third World countries, or some of them at least, will remain faster than growth rates of already industrialized countries. But the real point is that the Third World countries did not do as well as they did because of international conferences. They did it by themselves, by increasing their industrial and commercial capabilities, and exploiting market opportunities. This is the lesson to be drawn. International conferences have their merits, but also their limits.

In some cases they can play a useful catalytic role, notably in increasing international aid flows. But by themselves, they are incapable of changing significantly the economic framework within which the industrial power game among nations is played out. Only the market can do that. This fact represents the revenge of pragmatism over abstract thought, the revenge of the man with the sword over the man with the pen.

The North-South dialogue had some offspring. There is talk now of a *trialogue,* negotiations among Europe, the Arab world and African nations. First launched at a conference in Kigali, the capital of Rwanda, in 1979, this idea also is a seductive one at first sight. Perhaps it will prove more fruitful than the ill-fated North-South dialogue. The *trialogue* might even serve as a prototype for future worldwide cooperation.

Coping with the Oil Crisis

A Good Start

In 1974, as a result of the first oil crisis, the oil import bill of non-oil developing countries more than trebled to $20 billion from $6.3 billion in 1973. It rose subsequently to $28 billion in 1978. Oil import payments account for about 2 to 2.5 percent of these countries' GNP, and for 10 to 13 percent of their total imports. Clearly, the oil crisis had a major effect on these countries. And yet, from 1974 to 1978, they constantly achieved faster growth rates than the industrialized nations. Overall their economic growth averaged about six percent a year, down about one percentage point from the 1967-1972 period. Of course, the performances of individual countries varied enormously. For some of them, six percent growth meant they were standing still, given rapid population growth. Latin American countries were little affected by the crisis, while African nations suffered marked slowdowns in growth. Certain South East Asian countries actually managed to increase their growth rates.

Overall, the developing countries succeeded in boosting exports, which helps to explain the rise in the total reserves of non-oil developing countries from $26 billion in 1974 to about $53 billion four years later (although another reason for this increase, as we shall see, was massive borrowing on international capital markets).

So much for the good news. Now for the other side of the coin. First of all, there was a surge in inflation. Roughly speaking, inflation rates in the non-oil developing countries trebled (while those of industrialized nations more or less doubled). Latin American countries fared worse than those in Asia: Singapore actually managed in 1976 to outperform Switzerland, with a negative inflation rate of minus two percent. Furthermore, there was a sharp increase in the overall trade deficit of the non-oil developing countries, from $18 billion in 1973, to $33 billion in 1974, and $42 billion in 1978. Their current account deficit narrowed in 1977, thanks to a rise in income from services and transfers, then soared again to $33 billion in 1978.

On balance, however, the performance of these countries was positive. It may prove to be only temporary, but so far they have done well in negotiating the post-oil crisis obstacle course.

The Invasion of the NIC's

In the second half of the 1970's, the industrialized West became more and more terrified by the threat of competition from certain Third World countries, specifically the Newly-Industrialized Nations, the NIC's, which were envisioned invading Western markets like so many little green men from Mars. The idea of competition from countries in South East Asia, most notably Hong Kong, Singapore, Taiwan and Malaysia, small but highly industrialized countries, with small populations—inspired the same kind of exaggerated fear as the "yellow peril" before the Second World War. Since then, the West has calmed down a little, as studies have shown that, with the exception of some industries such as textiles and leather, Third World competition is not such a huge threat as had been supposed. According to recent analyses, even France can now hope to hang onto sectors of industry earlier thought irretrievably lost.

The real problem lies less in South West Asia than in "heavyweight" countries such as Brazil, Colombia, Argentina and India, which are rarely mentioned, but which are rapidly and dramatically strengthening their industrial power. These countries are not threatening the West with direct competition, at least not in our own markets. But they are becoming less and less dependent on imports of manufactured goods, and so the West risks losing export markets. Furthermore, some of these countries are tending more and more to cooperate among themselves, through a kind of South-South dialogue which was quite unexpected.

Colombia today has the industrial power of Spain 10 years ago. In the last decade, the Colombian economy has grown constantly at eight percent a year or more. Industry still represents only 21 percent of GNP, but is expanding rapidly. Similar things can be said for Argentina and Chile.

An even more striking example is Brazil, which has almost caught up with Italy in terms of GNP. Brazil is now producing one million vehicles a year. It is the world's third biggest shipbuilder, after the United States and Japan, and is in sixth place in aeronautics.

India is displaying similar characteristics. Of course, there are the slums of Calcutta and the unimaginable misery of the rural masses. But India now represents the tenth biggest industrial nation in the world. It has the world's third largest reservoir of qualified labor. It was only a few years ago that the Indians launched the first frigate entirely "made in India." Then came the first Indian nuclear test explosion. Now, the first Indian satellite has been put in orbit, by a three-stage rocket. But the most remarkable development is that India, traditionally half-starved by periodic famines, has become practically self-sufficient in grain production. Apart from China, there is another Asiatic giant awakening from its slumbers.

In Africa, Nigeria and the Ivory Coast are doing the same thing. What is the secret of these countries' success? It is hardly a result of the noble schemes drawn up over the past 30-odd years, such as the "world tax" or the more recent "world economic order." The reasons lie elsewhere. Loans and aid programs have played their part, but more important has been a dazzling trade performance.

The Trade Performance

The Rise in Raw Materials Prices

The impact of the oil crisis on non-oil developing countries was partially offset by a surge in prices of raw materials which began at the end of 1972. In 1973, agricultural prices rose 72 percent, and mineral prices were up 32 percent. Prices dipped during the 1974/1975 recession, then took off again in 1976 and 1977, when agricultural prices rose by more than 30 percent. Of course, the price performances of individual products varied greatly, and individual countries benefited accordingly. Coffee, cocoa, tea and tin registered record price increases, while increases were more moderate for copper, rubber, lead and peanuts, and prices of zinc, sugar and phosphate actually declined.

Price increases in 1976 and 1977 were like a gulp of badly-needed oxygen for countries such as the Ivory Coast (coffee and cocoa), Colombia (coffee) and Bolivia (tin), while a fall in the price of phosphate was a hard blow for Morocco and Tunisia. At the same time, the 1976 rise in the price of copper was not enough to allow Zaire to escape serious payments problems. Overall, however, by the end of 1977, the terms of trade of the non-oil developing countries had shown a slight improvement.

A second factor in their overall trade performance was the industrialization policies implemented by some countries.

Import Substitution

Import substitution—the development of domestic industries able to produce goods which can be substituted for imports—has a long history in Latin America. Countries such as Argentina, Brazil and Mexico all began to employ import substitution policies straight after the Second World War. More recently, however, they were also adopted in South East Asia, by South Korea, Malaysia, Taiwan, Hong Kong, Singapore and the Philippines, and have helped those countries to cut their combined trade deficit from $18 billion in 1974 to $8 billion in 1978. Like Latin American countries, they reduced their imports of capital goods significantly.

Today, Latin America alone accounts for more than half of the industrial production of developing countries, but only one-quarter of those countries' capital goods imports, down from a third only five years ago. By contrast, the share in total capital goods imports of African and Middle Eastern countries has risen sharply. In Latin America, the slowdown in capital goods imports attributable to increased domestic production has been particularly marked in Venezuela, Brazil and Mexico. But India's performance has been even more striking. Since 1974, India's share of total Asian imports of capital goods has fallen to 7 percent from 28 percent in the middle of the 1960's. While pushing ahead with import substitution, of course, many developing countries have also been building strong export industries, based on low labor costs.

The Leap in Exports

This is the phenomenon which has caused the most ink to flow, because of the real or imagined threat which it poses to certain industrial sectors in the established industrialized countries. The exports of developing countries are concentrated to a large extent in the hands of just four leading countries, Hong Kong, Singapore, Taiwan and South Korea, which together account for $18 billion out of total Third World exports of $30 billion.

The overall figures are spectacular. From 1976 to 1978, total exports of non-oil developing countries increased nine percent a year, compared to growth of only five percent a year from 1973 to 1975, and compared to a 1976-1978 growth rate of 6.8 percent a year for industrialized countries' exports. According to OECD statistics, exports of non-oil developing countries to the industrialized world rose from $86.7 billion in 1974 to $136.7 billion in 1978, while their exports to OPEC more than doubled from $5.5 billion to $12.7 billion. In the same period, the developing countries also boosted intra-regional trade among themselves from $5.2 billion to $14.4 billion, with the help of regional associations set up on the European model, such as the Association of South East Asian Nations (ASEAN) and the Andean Pact.

There are two points to emphasize: on the one hand, the successful penetration of Western markets by non-oil developing countries, and on the other, the remarkable growth of South-South trade.

With regard to the first point, the figures speak for themselves. From 1973 to 1977, the share of NIC exports in the total imports of OECD countries rose from 19 to 30 percent for shoes, from 0.7 percent to 1.1 percent for autos, from 9 percent to more than 12 percent for electrical appliances, and from 6.8 percent to about 15 percent for iron and steel. These statistics should be interpreted with care. For the time being, the rate of penetration of industrialized countries' markets comes to no more than one or two percent. But from 1973 onwards, the penetration rate rose sharply in certain sectors. For example, developing countries won six percent of the cotton textiles market in the United States, 25 percent in the Netherlands, and 27 percent in Britain. It was figures such as these that caused outcries.

In reality, competition from the NIC's is felt less in the markets of industrialized nations than in Third World markets. India is already competing with industrialized countries to sell capital goods in Africa and the Middle East. Brazil sells more to the Third World than to the United States. This phenomenon, the sharp growth of South-South trade since 1973, is the new development which deserves the most attention. In 1978, this trade totaled $22.3 billion, equal to one third of total developing country exports, and it was growing much faster than trade flows elsewhere. This means that the chances for a successful South-South dialogue are much more alive and much more realistic than those for a hypothetical North-South dialogue, with diplomats exchanging empty rhetoric.

A final point is the change in the composition of developing countries' exports. Of their total industrial product exports to OECD countries, 43 percent are now consumer goods and 22 percent capital goods. The proportion of semi-finished products has fallen significantly. However, the export effort still remains concentrated on a very small range of capital goods, electrical appliances and clothing.

International Aid and Capital Market Borrowings

Here also, the figures speak for themselves. According to the World Bank, government and government-guaranteed debt of Third World countries rose from $160 billion in terms of commitments in 1974, to around $350 billion in 1978 and close to $400 billion in 1979. In terms of the loan amounts actually drawn down, of course, the figures are considerably lower. Thanks to the major international banks, Third World countries were able to benefit from broad access to international capital markets. As we have seen, this access was crucial to the petrodollar recycling process. Furthermore, in 1978, certain developing countries managed to arrange some very profitable refinancings, consolidating their short and medium-term borrowings into long-term debt on much more favorable terms, especially as regards lower interest rates.[1] Brazil and Mexico became famous in banking circles for such refinancing operations—which, it is safe to assume, hardly brought smiles to bankers' faces. In nominal terms, total financings arranged for Third World countries rose from $20 billion in 1970 to $80 billion in 1978. In real, inflation-adjusted terms, financings grew at an average annual rate of seven percent, and almost doubled in the course of eight years. In 1978, they represented 6 percent of the GNP of developing countries, up from 3.7 percent at the beginning of the

---

[1]The refinancing process involves raising new loans in order to pay back earlier loans carrying stiffer terms.

1970's. To a very large extent, these enormous capital flows explain how the developing countries were able to advance economically despite the effects of the oil crisis.

Of the 1978 total of $80 billion, $56 billion represented borrowings on international capital markets and international aid accounted for the remaining $24 billion. The aid total was up from only $9 billion in 1970. OPEC countries supplied about $3.7 billion and Soviet bloc countries about $800 million. The rest, almost $20 billion was channeled through the Development Assistance Committee (DAC) of the OECD.

The international aid contributions of the OECD industrialized countries have been routinely criticized as insufficient. However, even though aid flows have remained well below the target levels which industrialized countries set for themselves a decade ago, they have still increased as percentages of the industrialized countries' GNP. Taking into account the effects of the oil crisis and of recession, it is a performance which cannot be judged too severely.

From 1974 to 1978, aid granted by Arab countries and OPEC as a whole averaged $4.4 billion a year, for a total of $22 billion, which compares to a total of $61.7 billion granted during the same period by industrialized countries. Direct investment by Arab countries in the Third World also remained limited, hardly exceeding $10 billion, of which about half was in the form of contributions to various IMF and World Bank funds.

The overall total of international direct investments in the world increased from $39 billion in 1974 to $64 billion in 1978, and will reach $80 billion in 1980. Much of this increase was due to investments by major international corporations, which reacted to the rise in energy costs by investing in third world countries to reduce the cost of transporting raw materials, and to take advantage of low Third World labor costs. The multinationals, too often abused, clearly played a valuable role as distributors of capital.

A dynamic role was also played by the World Bank, under the vigorous leadership of President McNamara. Annual lending by the Bank jumped from $2 billion in 1973 to $6 billion in 1978, and $7 billion in 1979. McNamara brought as much energy to the task of raining dollars on the Third World as was once brought to the task of raining bombs on Vietnam.

A number of international compensation agreements also had a modest but significant effect.

The Lome Agreement, signed in 1974 and renewed in October 1979, provided 57 countries in Africa, the Caribbean and the Pacific with free access for almost all their export products to the markets of the European Economic Community—without any reciprocity arrangements.

There was also the Stabex Fund agreement, which required the E.E.C. member countries to make compensation payments, in the form of loans or outright gifts, to cover unexpected falls in the 57 countries' income from 44 basic export products. Stabex has paid out 310 million European Units of Account since 1975—which is admittedly a very modest amount, equaling only 1 percent of the 57 countries' combined current account deficit in 1977.

Compensatory financing by the IMF has also been of modest proportions, totaling about 5 billion Special Drawing Rights since 1963 (including 3.7 billion since

1974): this was equal to only 6 percent of the current account deficit of recipient nations in 1976.

Even though the total amounts have been limited, however, these payments have sometimes been vital for small countries, or for countries whose income depends on a very small number of export products.

So far then, the non-oil developing countries have managed to rise above the obstacles placed in their path by the oil crisis of 1973. It remains to be seen if the mechanisms which saved them the first time around will work as well in the wake of the second oil crisis of 1979-1980. Up to now, analysts of the transfer of resources from rich countries to the Third World do not seem to have taken into account the effect of inflation, which can be likened to a tax on the rich nations.

The Real "World Tax"

Since the early 1960's, the problem of Third World development has given rise to a series of proposals aimed at promoting a transfer of resources from the "Have" countries to the "Have-Nots." In particular, the idea of a "world tax" in favor of Third World countries has been put forward several times.[1]

The only agreement currently in force on the transfer of resources is the one reached 10 years ago under which OECD countries promised to try to raise aid to one percent of their GNP, including 0.7 percent in the form of Official Development Aid (ODA), which is granted on very easy terms. Even though the objective is very limited, it is still far from being achieved by most countries. In 1977, the ODA of the OECD member countries equaled only 0.31 percent of their GNP, less than half the target level. However, despite their apparent failure to live up to their promises, the industrialized countries have in fact been paying a heavy resource-transfer tax in recent years, with the proceeds going to the developing nations. These tax payments take a variety of different forms, as we shall see.

Table 9 shows the components of the ODA granted by the member countries of the OECD's Development Assistance Committee (DAC). The DAC members are: Australia, Austria, Belgium, Canada, Denmark, Finland, France, Great Britain, Italy, Japan, the Netherlands, New Zealand, Norway, Sweden, Switzerland, the United States, West Germany and the E.E.C. Commission.

In 1977, the total of their bilateral donations, including debt cancellations and contributions to multilateral agencies, came to $11.8 billion. To that must be added $1.8 billion, representing the *gift element* of development loans granted at below-market rates of interest, bringing the ODA total to $13.6 billion. Further contributions of $800 million towards private sector export credits, and $400 million towards private investments raised the total of contributions to $14.8 billion. To help fill in the picture, it should be noted that in the following year, 1978, cancellation of developing country debts by DAC members leapt to $6.2 billion, following a resolution of UNCTAD.

---

[1]For example, in his book *Proletarian Nations* published in 1960, Pierre Moussa proposed a tax on rich nations in proportion to their national revenues. More recently, in October 1976, the Club of Rome, meeting in Algiers with Third World representatives, suggested international taxes managed by a World Treasury as a means towards establishing a new world order.

OFFICIAL DEVELOPMENT AID (O.D.A.)
AND OTHER CONTRIBUTIONS BY D.A.C. MEMBER COUNTRIES
(in billions of dollars)

TABLE 9

	66–68	1970	1974	1975	1976	1977
1. Net bilateral donations ..	3.5	3.3	5.3	6.3	6.5	7.2
Debt cancellations	—	—	—	—	(0.1)	(0.2)
2. Net contributions to multilateral agencies	0.6	1.1	3	3.8	4.1	4.6
3. Net development loans ..	2.1	2.3	2.9	3.5	3	2.9
Estimated gift element of these loans	62.5%	62.5%	62.5%	62.7%	62.3%	61.5%
4. Value of gift element	*1.3*	*1.4*	*1.8*	*2.2*	*1.9*	*1.8*
Sub-total: 1+2+4=ODA	5.4	5.8	10.1	12.3	12.5	13.6
Other Contributions:						
5. Support for private sector export credits	—	—	—	0.1	0.4	0.8
6. Support for private sector investments	—	—	—	—	0.8	0.4
Total: 1+2+4+5+6 ..	**5.4**	**5.8**	**10.1**	**12.4**	**13.7**	**14.8**

Now, Official Development Aid is only one element in the world "tax" which industrialized countries have been paying. Another element is the huge effect of inflation, which has turned loans to developing countries, often made on easy terms, into a net transfer of resources. The gap between the rate of inflation and the interest rates on the loans represents a subsidy, or net transfer, because it means that the borrowers pay back less than they borrowed in real terms. The size of the transfer can be estimated by calculating the difference between the world inflation rate and the average interest rate on the total debt of developing countries.

INFLATION AND THE DEBT OF LESS DEVELOPED COUNTRIES
(in billions of dollars)

TABLE 10

	1973	1974	1975	1976	1977
1. Total debt (annual average)	104.8	127.2	157.6	193.8	228.1
2. Debt service: interest payments	4.9	6.6	9.1	11.4	13.2
3. Average interest rate	4.7%	5.2%	5.8%	5.9%	5.8%
4. World inflation rate (Source: I.M.F.)	9.6%	15.3%	13.4%	11%	11.2%
5. Differential (4–3)	4.9%	10.1%	7.6%	5.1%	5.4%
6. Resource savings on credits (deriving from the inflation rate minus the interest rate applied to total debt)	5.1	12.8	12	9.9	12.3

Source: O.E.C.D.

Table 10 gives an idea of the size of the transfer of resources which has taken place. Through the effect of inflation on their debt, the developing countries saved $12.3 billion in resources in 1977. From 1974 onwards, the net transfer averaged about $12 billion each year. Of course, these are only rough estimates. The overall effects of inflation are complex and uncertain. Inflation benefits developed countries, for example, when they export manufactured goods mainly financed by these kinds of credits.[1] It also benefits them to the extent that they borrow on capital markets themselves. On the other hand, raw material-producing countries obviously gain from inflation when the prices of their exports increase.

Another major element in the "world tax" is the aid granted to LDC's by OPEC.

---

[1] It is possible that conventional calculations of the terms of trade of the Third World and of developed countries have been misleading us. The common wisdom is that the terms of trade of LDC's have been deteriorating. But if we took into consideration the "real" prices of our exports—i.e. including all the fringe benefits accruing to buyers such as subsidized credits with grace periods of 5 to 7 years—we would get a very different picture. We might find that the "real" prices of our exports—and our "real" terms of trade—have been declining for years.

This represents an indirect transfer of resources to the LDC's from the industrialized countries, which must pay OPEC for its oil. OPEC is a bit like Robin Hood, robbing the rich to give to the poor.

OPEC AID TO LESS DEVELOPED COUNTRIES
(in billions of dollars)

TABLE 11

	1973	1974	1975	1976	1977
1. Net aid contributions	1.3	3.4	5.5	5.6	5.7
Of which:					
2. Donations	0.8	2.2	2.6	3.5	3.5
3. Loans	0.5	1.2	2.9	2.1	2.2
4. Value of gift element of loans	0.2	0.5	1.3	0.9	1
5. Total donations (2 + 4)	*1*	*2.7*	*3.9*	*4.4*	*4.5*

Source: O.E.C.D./D.A.C.

Table 11 shows that OPEC gave an estimated $4.5 billion to the LDC's in 1977, comprised of $3.5 billion in donations and $1 billion in the form of the gift element of loans extended at below-market interest rates. The total transfer of resources to the LDC's from the industrialized nations, including these indirect transfers through OPEC, the resource savings for LDC's caused by inflation, and Official Development Aid came to $28.8 billion in 1977, as shown in Table 12. In 1978, the

THE TRANSFER OF RESOURCES TO LESS DEVELOPED COUNTRIES
(in billions of dollars)

TABLE 12

	1974	1975	1976	1977
Donations and the equivalent of donations from OPEC	2.7	3.9	4.4	4.5
(Gift element of loans)	(0.5)	(1.3)	(0.9)	(1)
Donations and the equivalent of donations from D.A.C. member countries . .	10.1	12.4	13.7	14.8
(Gift element of loans)	(1.8)	(2.2)	(1.9)	(1.8)
Sub-total: 1 + 2	12.8	16.3	18.1	19.2
Resource savings on credits	12.8	12	9.9	12.3
Gift element of OPEC loans .	−0.5	−3.1	−0.9	−1
Gift element of D.A.C. loans	−1.8	−2.2	−1.9	−1.8
Total	23.3	24.8	25.2	28.8

figure was probably around $35 billion taking into account the exceptionally high debt cancellation figure of $6.2 billion already mentioned.

To repeat, these are rough estimates, and must remain so, given the difficulty of assessing accurately the advantages and disadvantages of inflation for different groups of countries. However, what the estimates show is that the "world tax" payments by industrialized countries in favor of developing countries have been about double or more the ODA contributions with which the industrialized nations are usually credited.

In the absence of a classical tax administered by a world organization, of the kind proposed by theoreticians of the 1960's (the idea was an impractical one anyway), redistribution of resources was accomplished through market mechanisms, mainly soft loans.

In the final analysis, the motivation was not moral requirements, but the need to maintain world trade and support economic activity and employment levels in the industrialized world by preserving export outlets in Third World markets. What we have seen is a practical example of the classical theory according to which a seller of something varies his prices according to the ability of the market to pay—or in this case, the ability of the borrower to repay.

To a considerable extent, it was inflation which allowed the world to respond to the need to redistribute wealth from the richest countries to the less fortunate. It remains to be seen whether the inflation mechanism will function similarly in the 1980's or whether, on the contrary, it will have the effect of squeezing the resources being transferred to Third World countries.

PART THREE:
The Second Oil Crisis

Less than six years after the first oil crisis in late 1973, the second crisis began in early 1979 with the overthrow of the Shah of Iran and the rise of the Iranian Islamic Republic. Like the Yom Kippur war of 1973, events in Iran in 1979 acted as a catalyst for a leap in oil prices, accompanied by a new wave of inflation and soon followed by recession. History is trying to repeat itself. However, circumstances have changed. The first crisis broke at a time of detente, when the United States and the Soviet Union were moving away from confrontation towards an alliance of sorts. Today, we have returned to a tense international climate reminiscent of the Cold War.

This time around, side-by-side with the familiar economic dimension, the problem of higher oil prices has a strategic dimension which was lacking before. Furthermore, as we have seen, the positions of individual nations in the race for economic growth have changed dramatically since 1973.

The United States has left the Europeans behind, while Newly-Industrialized Nations have also spurted ahead. How will the race for growth be affected by the second oil crisis? Will international monetary disorder get worse? What role will be played by defense issues?

There are lots of agonizing questions, and no easy answers. What we can do is try to identify the problems. Already, it is clear that the cost of energy and the cost of defense represent two major obstacles to economic growth in the decade ahead.

CHAPTER 1
Unsolved Problems

The Shah of Iran departed from Teheran on January 16, 1979. Shortly afterwards, an Islamic Republic was proclaimed in Iran. Under the influence of these events, the price of oil, which had been subdued for some years, quickly began to rise. In 1978, the so-called reference price, the average posted price per barrel of Arabian light, stood at $12.70 compared to $9.30 in 1974, and only $1.20 in 1970. In 1979, it climbed to $18.65, and then to almost $32 in 1980.

On the unregulated spot market in Rotterdam, oil price movements were much sharper. In January 1980, the price per barrel hit $38 before falling gradually to around $32.

In 1979-1980, price increases boosted the oil import bill of the European Economic Community by almost $60 billion. For Japan, the increase was $35 billion, for the U.S. $36 billion, and for the non-oil developing countries $32 billion. As a percentage of GNP, payments for oil rose from 2.3 percent in 1978 to about four percent in 1980 for the E.E.C, from 2.6 percent to 5.8 percent for Japan, from 1.9 percent to 3.5 percent for the U.S., and from 3.2 percent to 5.3 percent for the Less Developed Countries.

The rise in the oil bill as a percentage of total imports was equally dramatic. In 1980, oil accounted for 28 percent of total imports in the E.E.C (up from 20 percent in 1978), 37 percent in Japan (up from 32 percent), and about one-third in both the U.S. and the LDC's.

Can the recycling process once again pull off the miracles it performed after the first oil crisis?

The Recycling Dilemma

The crisis created by the oil price increases of 1979-1980 is different in many respects from the first oil crisis. This time around, the producers have not only raised the oil price to a new all-time high, but have also demonstrated that their aim is to maintain or increase the price in real, inflation-adjusted terms.

Superficially, the context in which the crisis occurred was similar to the 1973 context, in that the world economic environment was characterized by rising U.S. inflation and strong dollar depreciation. Also, the world economy appeared about to gather steam again.

At the end of 1978, the U.S. economy remained strong and there were signs of a pick-up in economic activity in Europe and Japan.

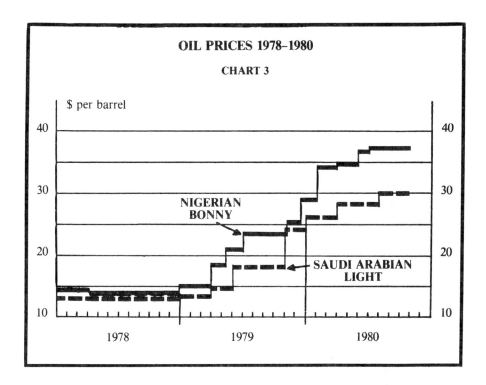

OIL PRICES 1978–1980

CHART 3

Consequently, the time seemed ripe for the oil producers to tighten the noose, i.e. to raise the oil tax which the world economy seemed able to pay without too much trouble. But the producers may have failed to take account of fundamental changes already caused by the first oil crisis.

A New Set of Circumstances

Since 1973, the whole climate has changed: the world has lost a number of shock absorbers which allowed it to cope with the first oil crisis without too much pain. The indebtedness of developing countries has more than doubled, from $157 billion in 1974 to $450 billion, and the Eurodollar market has also more than doubled in size, from $375 billion to over one trillion.

• Unemployment, generally speaking, is now about twice what it was.

• Economic growth rates are very low, on average about half of what they were.

• With the exception of the United States, productive investment is well below earlier levels.

• Major international banks, especially U.S. banks, are heavily burdened by the massive loans they have granted over the past several years to developing countries.

It seems doubtful that they will be able to take on the role of petrodollar redistribution on the same scale as before.

The Vicious Circle of the Oil Price Cycle

As we have seen, there were three main mechanisms by which the industrialized world was able to gradually lighten the burden of oil payments after the first oil crisis:

• An exchange rate mechanism, namely the depreciation of the dollar against other major currencies.

• A price mechanism, namely an improvement in the terms of trade of the industrialized nations to the detriment of OPEC.

• A volume mechanism: the volume of OPEC exports declined as a percentage of the GNP of industrialized countries.

However, this past experience teaches us hardly anything about how to cope this time around.

In the first place, the same mechanisms cannot work as before, with the oil producers determined to maintain or increase the real price of oil. Secondly, the OPEC cartel has a stranglehold on the quantities of oil produced and supplied.

The key difference between the first oil crisis and the second can be summed up as follows: in 1974-1975, the most important thing was the price of oil rather than the quantity of supplies; this time, it is the quantity which is important rather than the price. It must be realized that the producers have maneuvered themselves into the ideal position for sellers of something, which consists in increasing income even while reducing sales volume.

It must also be understood that there is a contradiction inherent in the producers' strategy: they call on the industrialized world to reduce oil consumption, but as soon as the industrialized world complies, they react by raising oil prices to maintain their surpluses. In other words, it is the very success of deflation policies followed by industrialized countries (except the United States) which seems to trigger oil price hikes.

The oil price cycle, as it has unfolded since the first oil crisis, gives rise to a sort of vicious circle, which must be broken if we are ever to find a way out of our crisis. The circle begins with an oil price rise, which causes increases in international liquidity and debt, and rising inflation accompanied by higher interest rates. Subsequently, there is a fall in economic growth rates, accompanied by a slowdown in inflation and falling interest rates, rising unemployment and declining oil consumption. Finally, the buying power of oil producing countries deteriorates: their surpluses decline, and some of them actually fall back into current account balance of payments deficit, as the real price of oil declines. This situation triggers another oil price rise, and the circle of hell is ready to start all over again.

Risk, Reward and Return on Capital: The Squaring of the Circle

Up to now the oil producers, in handling their petrodollar surpluses, have shown themselves to have three somewhat contradictory aims:

• To maintain the value of their capital, in a world subject to strong monetary erosion, where almost all investments fail to preserve buying power.

• To achieve high positive rates of return, in a world where interest rates are often negative and the profitability of capital investments is often low or zero, especially in Third World countries.

• To avoid risk, in a world where exchange rate fluctuations and political and economic uncertainties are liable to cause heavy capital losses.

It appears almost impossible at present to find investment outlets with the characteristics sought by the oil producers. Positive returns on capital imply risk-taking, while the absence of risk implies reductions in the value of capital through monetary erosion. These hard realities suggest that the oil producers will have to change their behavior from that of passive recipients of fixed incomes to that of active entrepreneurs.

The World Loses its Shock Absorbers

The search for a way out of our dilemmas is complicated by the fact that the industrialized world and the LDC's have lost much of their room for maneuvering during the past few years. Developing countries were able to absorb the shock of the first oil crisis through increasing external debt. But the dangerous rise in their external debt service ratios, which now average around 17 percent, means that further debt increases will not be possible without major risks.

Major international banks, which played a crucial shock-absorbing role last time around, have suffered a sharp deterioration in their balance sheets (falling capital-to-asset ratios, rising concentration of risk, and increases in the number of high-risk loans), which implies they will have to slow down in the international lending area, and become more selective in their choice of clients.

Industrialized countries have lost much of their ability to absorb higher oil prices through higher unemployment, slower rates of economic growth and rising prices. After the first oil crisis, there were cruel increases in unemployment in most industrialized countries, with the exception of the U.S. Today, with unemployment rates around five to six percent, any further increases would risk triggering serious political and social problems.

Similarly (again with the exception of the U.S.), economic growth rates were cut in half by the first oil crisis. In 1978-1979, because of a lightening of the oil payments burden, growth rates began to increase again. But another sharp fall would reduce resources available for investment, and would prove a severe blow to expectations of improved living standards, with severe repercussions both inside individual countries and internationally.

On the prices front, the first oil crisis was followed by a strong surge in world inflation. In many industrialized countries, inflation rates subsequently fell back gradually to threshold levels of between six and eight percent. But this still left "core" rates of underlying inflation way above those prevailing before 1973. Under the impact of the second oil crisis, world inflation risks getting out of control. This, then, is the world context in which the new effort to recycle petrodollars must be made.

The Obstacles

In 1979, oil prices rose by an average of 50 percent. In 1980, the new increase was greater than 50 percent, causing another dramatic surge in the quantities of petro-

TABLE 13: CURRENT ACCOUNT BALANCES OF OPEC, MAJOR DEVELOPED COUNTRIES AND LESS DEVELOPED COUNTRIES.

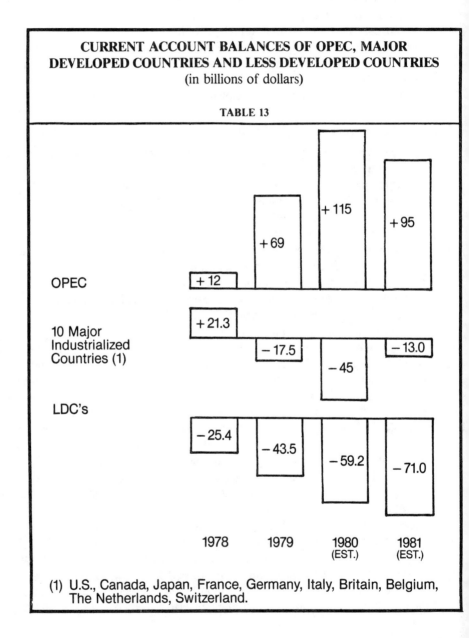

CURRENT ACCOUNT BALANCES OF OPEC, MAJOR DEVELOPED COUNTRIES AND LESS DEVELOPED COUNTRIES
(in billions of dollars)

TABLE 13

OPEC

| | +12 | +69 | +115 | +95 |

10 Major Industrialized Countries (1)

| | +21.3 | −17.5 | −45 | −13.0 |

LDC's

| | −25.4 | −43.5 | −59.2 | −71.0 |

1978   1979   1980 (EST.)   1981 (EST.)

(1) U.S., Canada, Japan, France, Germany, Italy, Britain, Belgium, The Netherlands, Switzerland.

CURRENT ACCOUNT BALANCES
OF MAJOR INDUSTRIALIZED COUNTRIES
(in billions of dollars)

TABLE 14

	1978	1979	1980 (EST.)	1981 (EST.)
10 Major Industrialized Countries	+ 21.3	− 17.5	− 45.0	− 13.0
Of which:				
U.S.	− 13.6	− 0.3	− 7.0	+ 2.0
Germany	+ 9.0	− 5.7	− 16.0	− 11.0
Japan	+ 17.6	− 8.8	− 12.0	− 5.0
France	+ 3.8	+ 1.2	− 6.5	− 3.6
Italy	+ 6.4	+ 5.2	− 4.0	+ 3.0
Britain	+ 2.0	− 4.9	− 1.5	+ 2.7

dollars to be recycled. The obvious question is whether recycling mechanisms can continue to function as satisfactorily as in the past. Remarkably, no one, either in government or in the private sector, seems to know the answer. What seems likely is that any new recycling mechanisms established in the 1980's will run into difficulties not yet encountered, primarily because of the unprecedented scale of the problem to be resolved. Specific obstacles include the difficulties which will be experienced by international banks, the deterioration in the financial health of developing countries and growing mistrust of the most important settlement currency, the dollar.

A Problem of Unprecedented Proportions

The quantities of money at stake are enough by themselves to create a problem of

119

unprecedented proportions. Total OPEC oil income rose from $130 billion in 1978 to $214 billion in 1979, and about $300 billion in 1980.

OPEC payments surpluses went from $12 billion in 1978 to $69 billion in 1979 and about $115 billion in 1980. Unless the real price of oil drops, this suggests that $100 to $120 billion will have to be recycled each year from now on. And this calculation is based on relatively optimistic assumptions concerning the capacity of OPEC countries to absorb imported goods and services.

The first issue to be faced is how the payments deficit corresponding to OPEC's surplus is going to be distributed among developed and developing countries. According to some preliminary estimates, the 1980 current account deficit of the major developed nations rose to $45 billion from $17.5 billion in 1979, while the deficit of developing countries increased to almost $60 billion from $43.5 billion. According to the same estimates, if the developed countries manage to cut their deficit to $13 billion in 1981, the deficit of developing countries will increase further to $71 billion.

Table 14 gives estimates of the varying performances of individual industrialized countries. Whatever happens, none of the industrialized countries will be able to escape in the near future from the balance of payments effects of the latest oil price increases. Escape would only be possible through drastic and ultimately unacceptable reductions of domestic demand.

The plight of the less developed countries is illustrated in Table 15.

FINANCING THE LDC DEFICIT
(in billions of dollars)
TABLE 15

	1978	1979	1980e	1981p
CURRENT ACCOUNT DEFICIT	25.4	43.5	59.2	71.0
EXTERNAL DEBT SERVICING	37.5	43.4	50.6	59.2
TOTAL FINANCING REQUIREMENT	**62.9**	**86.9**	**109.8**	**130.2**
NET FOREIGN INVESTMENT	4.8	5.5	7.0	8.5
CHANGES IN OFFICIAL RESERVES (A minus sign indicates a reserves increase)	− 14.2	− 5.0	5.0	10.0
EXTERNAL BORROWING (1): Estimate (2): Forecast	72.3	86.4	97.8	111.7

Apart from the increase in their overall current account balance of payments deficit, the LDC's will have to cope with a marked rise in the cost of servicing their outstanding debt. Overall, the financing requirements of the LDC's are seen more than doubling from $63 billion in 1978 to $130 billion in 1981. The LDC's are starting to pay bills by running down their foreign exchange reserves,[1] and they are con-

---

[1]This is a new development. In recent years, many LDC's (and Brazil in particular) have been taking advantage of relatively favorable international capital market conditions to borrow more than necessary and build up their reserves.

sidered likely to benefit from a slight increase in net investment inflows.

But the fact remains that only huge new foreign borrowing will allow them to balance their books. This borrowing is estimated at close to $100 billion in 1980, and over $110 billion in 1981. And that is on top of more than $400 billion of

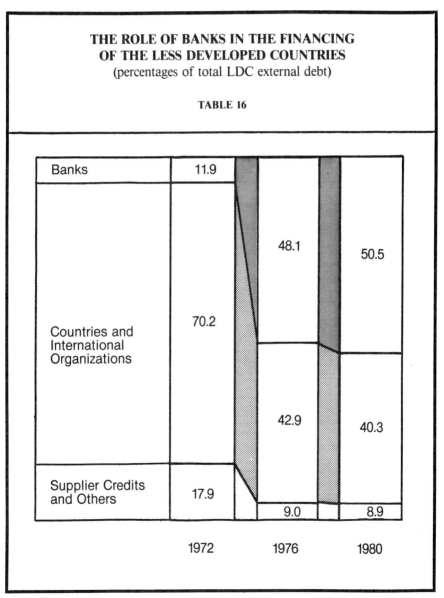

**THE ROLE OF BANKS IN THE FINANCING
OF THE LESS DEVELOPED COUNTRIES**
(percentages of total LDC external debt)

TABLE 16

government and government-guaranteed debt already outstanding at the end of 1979.

The Burden on the Banks

The capacity of major international banks to recycle petrodollars in the future will be limited by the recycling role they have already played in the past. International bank loans rose from about $170 billion at the end of 1973 to about $665 billion at the end of 1979. In 1980, international banks were financing more than 50 percent of LDC external debt, compared to 48 percent in 1976 and only 12 percent in 1972 (See Table 16).

This unprecedented lending splurge has had serious consequences for the banks, especially the major U.S. banks which have been most active in the international lending arena. The ratio of U.S. banks' foreign loans to total assets now stands at 33 percent, up from 11 percent at the beginning of the 1970's. Loans to LDC's, which represent especially vulnerable assets, account for around 10 percent of total assets, and in some cases more. U.S. banks account for around 45 percent of the total of bank loans outstanding to non-OPEC developing countries. For the 10 biggest U.S. banks, annual growth in profits from overseas operations was 23 percent from 1972 to 1977, compared to growth of only 5 percent in domestic profits. In some years, overseas operations yielded 70 to 80 percent of U.S. banks' total profits, with LDC loans playing a major role.

In the future, the U.S. banks will have to become more cautious in their overseas ventures. For one thing, their capital base has been eroded. The capital-to-asset ratio of U.S. banks has deteriorated to 3.5 percent from 4.5 percent. Another worry is their concentration of risk. Bank loans to Latin America represent two-thirds of

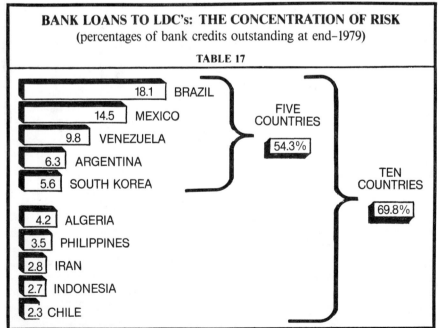

BANK LOANS TO LDC's: THE CONCENTRATION OF RISK
(percentages of bank credits outstanding at end–1979)

TABLE 17

18.1 BRAZIL	
14.5 MEXICO	FIVE COUNTRIES
9.8 VENEZUELA	54.3%
6.3 ARGENTINA	
5.6 SOUTH KOREA	TEN COUNTRIES
4.2 ALGERIA	69.8%
3.5 PHILIPPINES	
2.8 IRAN	
2.7 INDONESIA	
2.3 CHILE	

Source: BANK FOR INTERNATIONAL SETTLEMENTS

the loans granted to non-OPEC LDC's, and 10 countries share no less than 70 percent of LDC bank loans, with five countries (Mexico, Brazil, Argentina, South Korea and Venezuela) accounting for more than 50 percent.

Furthermore, the solvency of certain Third World countries has been deteriorating as the external debt burden has risen.

The following Table shows the surge in government and government-guaranteed debt of LDC's from 1972 to 1980. In 1981, as we have seen, total new financing requirements are likely to rise to $130 billion from $110 billion in 1980.

LDC DEBT
(government and government-guaranteed)

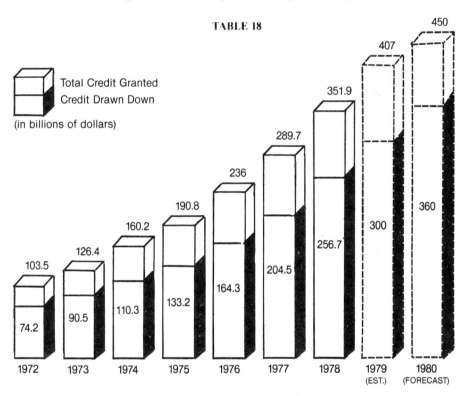

TABLE 18

The LDC's as a group are now using $60 out of every $100 borrowed simply to repay principal and interest on outstanding debt. Their average external debt service ratio (debt service payments as a percentage of exports), now around 17 percent, will continue to rise in the years ahead, reflecting the surge in debt outstanding and the fact that their export receipts will suffer from the slowdown of Western economies.

The Status of the Dollar.

Over the past decade, holders of dollars have developed grave reservations about the reliability of the U.S. currency. The dollar's share of the Eurocurrency markets has fallen significantly, as the following Table shows:

EUROCURRENCY DEPOSIT MARKET SHARES
(in billions of dollars)
TABLE 19

	Jan. 1, 1970	Jan. 1, 1974	March 31, 1980
Dollar	46.2 (81.5%)	131.4 (68.4%)	450.0 (66.6%)
German Mark	4.6	32.0	118.2
Swiss Franc	4.0	17.2	41.7
French Franc	0.2	2.1	11.6

Source: BANK FOR INTERNATIONAL SETTLEMENTS

The role of the dollar in official central bank reserves has not been reduced in a similar way, but only because of some special factors, notably the decline of the pound sterling as a reserve currency. This allowed the reserve roles of the German mark and Swiss franc to rise strongly without the position of the dollar being affected. But the dollar was more tolerated than wanted. As LDC's unloaded the U.S. currency to buy marks, Swiss francs and other strong currencies, Germany, Switzerland and other countries were obliged to buy dollars to prevent their own curriences from appreciating too strongly. Obviously, the petrodollar recycling process would be made more difficult if this mistrust of the dollar led the oil producers to go ahead with plans to create a new settlement currency as a substitute for the dollar.

In the short term, despite all the problems discussed, the recycling process could continue without major problems. There are a number of factors which could alleviate immediate difficulties. As far as diversification out of the dollar is concerned, OPEC's hands are tied by the sheer size of the dollar holdings it has already built up.

At the end of 1979, out of a total of $115 billion equivalent in OPEC bank deposits, $78 billion were in dollars, $6 billion in pounds sterling and $23 billion in currencies of other industrialized countries. Given the size of the dollar-denominated assets, and also the privileged relationship between the U.S. and Saudi Arabia—far and away the biggest investor—diversification out of the dollar can only take place at the margin, and then only gradually, otherwise the value of existing holdings would be at risk.

Secondly, the need for industrialized countries to finance balance of payments deficits will weigh more heavily than in the past on the strong-currency countries— Germany and Japan.

Thirdly, the demands of Soviet bloc countries on international capital markets should tend to stabilize. The Soviet Union itself hardly needed to tap international capital markets at all in 1980, thanks to gold sales. Furthermore, the high levels of external indebtedness already reached by some countries—Poland, for example— could cause a reduction in borrowing. The external indebtedness of the bloc as a whole stands at $74 billion.

Finally, non-oil developing countries will to some extent be able to draw on official reserves to cover financing requirements: from 1976 to 1979 their reserves increased by $42 billion. Nevertheless, serious risks of turbulence lie down the road. We could witness a new flight into gold. OPEC countries are now estimated to have 10 percent of their assets in gold, and further conversion of petrodollars into the yellow metal is always possible.

We could also experience new dollar crises. Since the beginning of the 1970's, the German mark has appreciated by 210 percent, the Swiss franc by 270 percent and the Japanese yen by 45 percent. And currency movements have been wildly irregular. In 1978 alone, the mark rose 15.6 percent, while the Swiss franc jumped 37.2 percent. The other way around, the yen plunged 20 percent against the dollar in 1979. Equally violent, if not more violent, exchange rate fluctuations cannot be ruled out in the future.

But the most serious prospect—and unfortunately the most likely one—is a resurgence of world inflation. High inflation rates recorded in 1980 in most industrialized countries do not augur well for the future.

The effect of the second oil crisis in boosting world inflation will make it difficult for industrialized countries to implement economic recovery policies in 1981, which clearly risks being a year of worldwide recession.

International Monetary Reform

As the 1970's drew to a close, the international monetary system was in a state of flux and dire uncertainty. The good news was that the major catastrophes so widely predicted had failed to occur. The capitalist system had not collapsed. On the contrary, it had been maintained and even strengthened somewhat in the United States. The international banking system, far from collapsing, had coped well with all the violent upheavals in international payments, as ingenious new payment mechanisms were rapidly set up. Floating exchange rates had proved to be neither our savior nor our downfall: they had not prevented monetary crises, but on the other hand they had allowed international trade to continue through thick and thin.

However, fundamental problems persisted. Through a fog of confusion, two facts clearly emerged. One was the return of gold to the monetary stage, and the other was the steady downtrend of the U.S. dollar.

Now, as we enter the 1980's, the situation of the dollar has been complicated by defense and security issues. In the wake of the Afghanistan affair and the war in the Near East, the dollar has risen, providing a spectacular illustration of the intimate links between external security and economic affairs. There are some fundamental economic factors in the dollar's favor, including a rise in U.S. exports, an improvement in the services component of the balance of payments, and the effect of recession in lowering U.S. imports. But a major role in the dollar's strength has been played by inflows of short-term and long-term capital fleeing parts of the world considered less safe than the U.S. The "errors and omissions" component of the U.S. balance of payments, a catch-all category which includes capital movements which cannot be readily identified, rose to $30 billion in the autumn of 1980, compared to $23 billion in 1970.

This is a sure sign of the times: when guns begin to fire, holders of capital, by nature circumspect, prefer to buy a ranch in Colorado or an apartment in New York rather than invest on the frontiers of the Elbe. Many Germans, Belgians and Swiss, for example, have contributed to the growth of capital inflows into the U.S.

The importance of defense and security issues will be discussed in detail later on. Leaving them aside for the moment, there are three basic international monetary policy issues to be considered—the role of the dollar, the maintenance of currency convertibility and the remonetization of gold.

The Risks of Collapse

A few years ago, there was a bestselling book called *The Crash of '79*. The author turned out to be wrong on two counts, but his intuitions remain valid. We know now that the Shah of Iran did not trigger a collapse of the international monetary system through a military invasion of Saudi Arabia—but Iran's war with Iraq does pose grave threats to the system. We also know that 1979 was not the year when the system fell apart—but 1981 could be.

In late 1980, there were two major causes for concern. In the first place, the international settlements system could be blocked by a drying-up of bank loans to Less Developed Countries and a consequent break in the petrodollar recycling chain. In the past, and especially during the last four years, the risk of world deflation has been averted mainly through a colossal increase in Third World debt, largely financed with Eurodollars.

But the system whereby banks transform short-term Eurodollar deposits into medium- and long-term loans on a massive scale is based on confidence. It's like riding a bicycle: you only keep your balance by moving ahead. A freeze on the movement of petrodollars would mean collapse of the system. In the wake of the Iranian crisis, payments difficulties caused by higher oil prices and higher interest rates could multiply. A world recession, which would cause a plunge in export receipts, would inevitably increase the threat of Third World insolvency. And we are faced with these possibilities at a time when the balance sheets of major international banks, especially those of U.S. banks, are obviously under severe strain. Their loans overseas, in particular their loans to risky country borrowers, which could go bad at the drop of a hat, are simply too big in relation to their other, safer loan assets.

Some U.S. banks, for example Citibank, decided several years ago to begin placing more emphasis once again on the domestic American market. And banks are already showing more caution in their choice of overseas clients. Under the pressure of events, this trend could strengthen, sharply squeezing the volume of foreign lending, and creating a full-scale payments crisis for certain LDC's. Quite simply, they would no longer be able to finance their external deficits by borrowing. This would cause a drop in their imports and a slowdown in their economic growth, which would have a deflationary effect on the world economy as a whole.

The second major threat to the international monetary system, equally serious, is the possibility of a loss of confidence in the dollar as a reserve and settlement currency. If, for example, certain oil producing countries effectively renounced the dollar, it would become necessary to increase supplies of other currencies—German marks and Japanese yen, for example—for settlement purposes. A part of dollar-denominated official reserve holdings could also be converted into Euromarks or Euroyen. Naturally, this would create strong downward pressure on the external exchange rate of the dollar. In effect, the value of the dollar would no longer be determined only by the usual demand and supply in the marketplace, but also by the size of outstanding dollar holdings accumulated during the long years of U.S. balance of payments deficits. This liquidity would swamp the foreign exchange markets, like water rushing through a broken dam. At that point, the U.S. would probably be forced to make a distinction between the external dollar, the one held by non-residents, and the domestic dollar, the one used by Americans.

For the external dollar, the U.S. could decree either total or partial non-convertibility. Total non-convertibility would mean a freeze, pure and simple, on U.S. external credits, and the value of the external dollar would decline sharply. The new value of the currency would depend on many things, especially the nature of guarantees which the U.S. could offer external dollar holders as security. But whatever happened, it seems obvious that the dollar would lose a very large proportion of its present value. The liquidation of external dollar holdings could be similar to the running down of Britain's external sterling balances after the war. The key question is whether the dollar liquidation would be carried out at one catastrophic blow, or whether it would be done gradually, through an acceleration of the dollar's depreciating trend against other currencies such as the German mark.

The end of dollar supremacy would probably cause a break-up of the international settlements system into four zones. One would be a German mark zone, grouping together the currencies of the European Monetary System. Another would be a dollar zone, which would include Canada, Mexico and Latin America. A third would be a Japanese yen zone, covering South East Asia. Finally, Middle Eastern countries, given their financial clout, would probably be able to set up a largely independent monetary zone of their own. It goes without saying that gold could serve as a common means of settlement among all these zones.

Fortunately, we have not reached this stage yet. For the time being, we should pay close attention to the role of gold, which could pave the way for a fundamental, long-term reorganization of the international payments system.

The Remonetization of Gold

In recent years, gold has received the explicit (though qualified) blessing of central banks, and the implicit blessing of the free market. The explicit approval came with the official role accorded to gold in the European Monetary System, set up in March 1979. The implicit approval was reflected in the leap in the free market gold price, which boosted international reserves and world liquidity.

The European Monetary System

In the EMS, deposits of gold give member countries the right to receive in return a new currency called the European Currency Unit (ECU). Before the EMS came into being, the central banks of Italy and Portugal had already received loans secured by portions of their gold holdings. But in those cases, gold was valued at around 20 percent below the prevailing free market price. The EMS took things a stage further by valuing gold at free market prices. Apart from giving EMS members the right to receive ECU's, gold can also function in the system as a means of settlement. It thus fulfills two of the functions of money—as a reserve instrument and as an instrument of payment. However, the EMS does not yet provide gold with the third function of money, as an instrument or standard of value. This means that the EMS does not contravene the IMF rules forbidding all reference to gold in the definition of currency values.[1] More fundamentally, it also means that gold's position in the EMS represents a reactivation of the metal's role, rather than full remonetization.

Even this limited reactivation has already caused some thorny problems. Originally, the EMS member countries had planned to complete the system by setting up a European Monetary Fund on March 31, 1981. The gold and dollar reserves which the members had already pooled together (representing 20 percent of their reserves), were to be placed in the new Fund, which was to have the authority to make loans to member countries in payments difficulties. However, when this plan was first drawn up, gold was worth no more than $180 an ounce, meaning that the resources at the Fund's disposal would have totaled no more than the equivalent of $13 billion (in the form of ECU's). Now, with gold at $600 an ounce, the Fund would control the equivalent of $50 billion, or $65 billion if reserve dollars are included—more than the combined GNP's of Peru, the Philippines and Portugal.

That would suit the Belgians and the Italians fine: they could draw on the Fund to support their currencies and delay the day of devaluation. But it would hardly serve the interests of West Germany, which is already worried by strains on the EMS created by the failure of countries to devalue their currencies promptly when required. Because of such conflicts of interest, the creation of the Fund has been put off. Even within the EMS, then, remonetization of gold raises political problems. Who decides whether to devalue or not? How long can the decision be delayed? Apparently harmless monetary policy techniques have been found to involve fundamental questions of national sovereignty. However, despite such setbacks, gold seems to be headed almost irreversibly towards remonetization in the long term—because of the hard realities of the marketplace.

The Gold Price Surge

These days, everyone hesitates to write about the price of gold, because it is likely to have changed before the ink is dry on the page.

At the end of 1979, the price began an unprecedented leap. One reason for this, generally recognized at the time, was international political tensions. A second reason, less clearly perceived, was major gold purchases by OPEC countries: today, about 10 percent of total OPEC assets are estimated to be held in the form of gold. Finally, there was a third reason, which went quite unnoticed. This was a change in the attitude towards gold of the United States.

The U.S., the world's biggest holder of gold, had promised demonetization of the yellow metal, which was henceforth to be considered a commodity like any

---

[1]The second amendment to the IMF statutes, formally approving demonetization of gold, took effect on April 1, 1978. It abolished the official gold price, and decreed that gold could no longer be used as a basis for currency values.

other. Accordingly, from May 1978 onwards, the U.S. Treasury sold about 500 tons of gold, and the IMF, at the instigation of the Americans, sold over 600 tons more. But these sales still left the U.S. and the IMF with gold holdings which today total 8,200 tons and 3,500 tons respectively. America's war chest of gold was hardly dented. But curiously, the U.S. Treasury suspended gold sales after November 1979 —just when sales were most needed to suppress the price. The fact is that having burnt their fingers, the Americans suddenly realized they were recklessly squandering priceless assets. So they withdrew from the market, and became implicitly committed to the gold remonetization process already begun with the setting up of the EMS.

Right now, it appears that several of the economic advisors to Ronald Reagan envisage the restoration of a gold standard in one form or another. The Republican party platform stated that "one of the most urgent tasks in the period ahead will be the restoration of a dependable monetary standard."

Already, whether it intended to or not, the U.S. has helped to restore the "refuge" value of gold in the minds of the public at large, by authorizing gold sales to individuals. There was a paradox inherent in that decision which deserved more attention than it got. Authorizing the purchase and circulation of gold is hardly the best way to destroy everyone's taste for it. Furthermore, the fact that central banks hold gold but refuse to sell it amounts to a recognition on their part that gold has a higher value than the other kinds of assets which they are prepared to liquidate.

Gold is not made to be exchanged or sold, but hoarded. It is the safe asset which holders only part with in emergencies—balance of payments crises, external threats, etc. Whatever the official U.S. policy may be, it is clear that the U.S. decision to end gold sales was a step in the direction of remonetization of gold.

Consider a few statistics. At $700 an ounce, gold represents close to 70 percent of total world reserves (not counting the IMF), and U.S. gold holdings are enough to cover half of the U.S. money supply, a quarter of U.S. Treasury public debt, and almost a third of all the Eurodollars in circulation. This is food for thought. Could high gold prices be the beginning of a miraculous solution to the problems plaguing the industrialized world?

The fact is that without the leap in the gold price, the long-term outlook was for bankruptcy, i.e. inconvertibility of dollar assets, and accelerated dollar depreciation. That would cause foreign exchange market chaos, and grief for everyone, in particular major dollar holders such as the oil producers. But the dizzying leap in the price of gold allowed the world to wipe the slate clean and start again from scratch. It was a bit like a conjuring trick, and all the world was pleased.

The United States was miraculously freed from the burden of dollar balances which could have caused its ruin, just as the sterling balances helped to ruin Great Britain. Holders of gold, including most industrialized countries, were obviously delighted, not to mention the Soviet Union, which produces around 400 tons of gold a year. Even dollar holders were pleased, because a way had been found to prevent depreciation of their assets, and to open up safe new investment outlets.

At any given moment, reform of the international monetary system could be begun simply by waving a magic wand and institutionalizing what has already occurred in the marketplace. Moreover, there is still considerable potential for further increases in the gold price, resulting for example from international crises. People have always run to the safety of gold in times of trouble, such as in 1940 and during the Korean War. Today, the ups and downs of the Middle East conflict undoubtedly have a major effect on gold's price.

Also, the recycling of petrodollars in 1981 and afterwards is going to present enormous problems, as we have seen. How will it be possible each year to find homes for about $110 billion surplus petrodollars, falling into the hands of a small number of oil producing countries, when major international banks, and especially U.S. banks, are already growing reluctant to act in the face of the strain on their balance sheets? If the OPEC countries decided to use half their expected surplus, say about $60 billion, to buy gold at $700 an ounce, their purchases would come to some 2,670 tons, equal to one and a half times total gold transactions in 1979, two and a half times world production (outside the Soviet Union), and one third of total U.S. gold stocks.

Gold provides a marvelous means of solving the energy supply problem, at least for a time, because income from gold, like income from oil, can be constantly increased even while sales volume remains the same. What is happening, willy nilly, is that a new relationship is being established, via the dollar, between the price of gold and prices of tangible goods, especially oil. In the process, world wealth is being redistributed. The Americans were wise to keep their hands on the biggest gold hoard in the world. Full remonetization of gold would mean dealing new hands to all the major players in the world economic game. Out of world gold reserves of 34,500 tons, close to 80 percent is held by the U.S., the IMF and a few European countries. French reserves of 3,200 tons, valued at $700 an ounce, would be enough for France to pay for two years of oil imports at current prices. Countries short of gold include Japan, Britain, Canada, the Scandinavian countries and, of course, the developing countries. The oil producing countries also belong in this list, although they are now busy making up for their past lack of the yellow metal.

The disturbing aspect of the sharp gold price rise, as interpreted by many commentators, is that it indicates widespread disaffection among the public with all paper currencies. However, this would only become really worrying if it led to galloping inflation on a worldwide scale. That could lead ultimately to an obliteration of currency values reminiscent of what happened to the mark in Germany in the 1920's. This is a real possibility, as we shall see later. But it is unlikely to happen in the immediate future.

The gold price is obviously not going to continue rising without interruption. Could it reach $1,000 or $2,000 an ounce? In the long run, nothing is impossible. But what appears likely is that the price will peak and then fall back significantly to a level which will be considered a reasonable point of equilibrium for several years. That, at least, is what past experience suggests. By itself, gold will not solve the basic problem of the international monetary system, which is how to limit or suppress the U.S. international currency printing privilege. But the rise in the gold price, paving the way for eventual remonetization of the metal, has brought closer the day when conditions will be ripe for meaningful reform of the system.

It should be made clear once and for all that remonetization of gold does *not* mean fixing the gold price as it was fixed under the old Gold Exchange Standard.

Under that system, the price remained unchanged at a theoretical $42 an ounce for half a century, which, after decades of inflation, obviously became absurd. The future world role of gold should be patterned on its role in the EMS, i.e. gold should be allowed to be re-integrated directly or indirectly into official reserves of countries. The second point is that the gold price should not be rigidly fixed, but merely stabilized.

For example, a range could be set within which the price would be allowed to fluctuate. This would mean applying to gold the principle of the European currency Snake—a *Golden Snake*. The permitted price range would itself fluctuate in line with world inflation.

To repeat, the aim would be only to stabilize the relationships between gold and currencies. This would be a more modest but also a safer objective than trying to fix those relationships permanently.

Another World Recession?

As we have seen, the first oil crisis triggered a severe worldwide recession, which began in the United States and spread around the globe. Only a few developing countries, like Brazil, managed to escape the general economic slowdown.

Will the second oil crisis produce the same effects? So far, it has not done so. The oil price increases at the beginning of 1979 caused no immediate economic downturn either in the U.S. or in European countries, where economic recoveries continued. Japan also took the oil price blows in its stride.

In 1980, however, the outlook started to cloud over, as oil price rises continued. The U.S. economy fell into recession in the second quarter of the year, with GNP plunging eight percent at an annual rate, and industrial production nosediving 19 percent. The depth of the U.S. recession came as a surprise, and a crisis mentality began to spread.

First West Germany, in the second quarter of the year, then France, around the middle of the year, began to feel the effects of the new oil shock. At the end of July, unemployment in the nine member countries of the E.E.C. totaled over 6.5 million, an all-time record. The unemployment total for all the industrialized countries of the OECD reached 24 million, and could rise to 25 to 27 million in 1981. OECD inflation reached 13.8 percent, up from 9.9 percent in 1979. As 1980 drew to a close, economic prospects for the industrialized countries were poor, and there was intense concern that certain Third World countries might not be able to jump the latest oil price hurdle.

The Mini-Recovery in the U.S.

In the U.S., the summer of 1980 proved to be a summer of false hopes. In June, there were signs that the recession was going to be one of the shortest—although also one of the deepest—of the postwar period, as unemployment stabilized, construction activity turned up again and auto sales increased. But by autumn, the outlook had changed. As it turned out, Detroit's launching of its new small cars was not the big success the manufacturers had been banking on. Inflation, predictably, took off again, causing the Federal Reserve to maintain tight monetary policies.

Rising interest rates proved a hard blow for the already suffering real-estate market. Last but not least, while consumer demand appeared to be growing stronger, widespread inventory liquidation took over as a major factor depressing economic activity.

Some hopes are now centered on the tax cuts promised by the White House. But given the slowness of budget deliberations, tax cuts will not be effective in stimulating the economy before the winter of 1982 at the very earliest. So for the U.S., there is the prospect of prolonged economic stagnation, or a return to recession.

The Synchronization Threat

Until recently, the justification for hoping that the world economic slowdown would remain limited was the belief that the U.S. and European economic cycles were out of step with each other. According to the optimistic scenarios, the U.S. was to emerge from a sharp but short recession by the autumn of 1980, just as Europe was beginning to run out of steam. This seesaw movement between the two economic zones would limit the scope of economic contraction.

However, the two cycles are now in the process of becoming synchronized, just as they were in 1974/1975—when synchronization made the worldwide economic crisis much more serious than it would otherwise have been. As we have seen, the best the U.S. can hope for in 1981 is a period of prolonged stagflation, with recovery likely to be weak or indecisive when it finally arrives. In the worst-case scenario, the U.S. could fall back into recession in the winter of 1982. Either way, the U.S. can hardly be counted on to lead economic recovery in the rest of the world.

In Europe, most economic forecasters are predicting a slight 1981 fall in West German GNP of about 0.5 percent, and a fall of about 1.2 percent in the GNP of Great Britain. They see economic growth in France of between zero and one percent, in Italy of about 1.5 percent, and in Japan of about three percent. These are only provisional forecasts, based on what is known so far, or what is hoped. The synchronization of the U.S. and European business cycles will reinforce deflationary tendencies, making the outlook more bleak than current forecasts indicate.

Another danger, even more serious, lies in the oil supply and price outlook. It is impossible at this stage to make meaningful predictions of the oil price a year or more from now. But what can be said with certainty is that beyond the current world recession the oil price will continue to rise. And there is not much the governments of industrialized countries can do about it.

The Limits to Growth

Major industrialized countries have very little scope for implementing economic recovery policies in 1981, for a number of reasons. Although some countries managed to slow inflation down through 1978, inflation rates generally have stayed very high: the average rate for the OECD industrialized nations is now close to the peak reached in 1974. Further, budget deficits in many countries have reached unacceptably high levels, and current account balance of payments deficits have risen to record levels in Japan, Germany and the Netherlands, severely limiting their room for economic policy maneuvering. It is clear that government efforts to stimulate economic activity will have to remain very limited.

Besides, governments appear to have become convinced that stimulation of demand is not the right way to solve their problems. Many industrialized countries are facing the need for a fundamental restructuring of their economies. Having failed to face that challenge quickly enough in the past, they must now learn to accept real reductions in living standards, not only because of the deterioriation in their terms of trade caused by higher oil prices, but also because of the need to free resources for productive investment and modernization of industry. Belatedly, Britain has decided to face the music; other countries—Belgium, Denmark, Sweden, the Netherlands and perhaps France—will have to do the same. So far, efforts to restructure economies have been based mainly on monetary policies, but these seem to have reached the limits of their usefulness. A return to fiscal policies and incomes policies now seems more appropriate, especially because the chances of winning a public consensus on the need for action are now better than they were.

In certain countries, the use of incomes policies could mean doing away with some forms of automatic indexation of minimum wages and social welfare benefits to inflation. The OECD has suggested that wage-earners not be compensated for price increases resulting from higher oil prices. Denmark has embraced this concept, while in Italy labor unions are fiercely opposing it.

Another approach is to force the consumer to shoulder the necessary burden of reducing energy consumption. Governments could raise the price of energy sharply through direct or indirect taxation. It may be a bitter pill to swallow. But it is the price to be paid by consumers in industrialized countries for having expected too much, and for not having reacted more quickly and more decisively after the first oil crisis.

The outcome of the current state of affairs, in all likelihood, will be a serious world economic crisis in 1981. It is not yet possible to predict how widespread the crisis may be, or how long it may last, although a world recovery in early or mid-1982 is likely.

What Future for the Third World?

Third World countries are obviously going to be severely hurt by the second oil crisis. According to the World Bank, their total oil import bill will rise from close to $30 billion in 1978 and $58 billion in 1980 to $200 billion in 1990. Their current account balance of payments deficit is seen rising from $27 billion in 1978 and $61 billion in 1980, to $104 billion in 1990.

Some Third World countries, including most of those in South America and certain countries in South East Asia, look sure to maintain positive growth rates, even if they are below recent levels. These are not the countries we have to worry about. The big problem lies with a small group of countries, about 10 at the most, including Turkey, Egypt and some Central African countries—Upper Volta, Zaire, Mali, Niger and Chad. These countries have extremely high external debt, and their solvency is in serious doubt. Furthermore, in most cases they have very low levels of income, in some instances below $150 per capita of population (in 1977); their industry accounts for 10 percent of GNP or less, they frequently suffer from serious food shortages and they are entirely dependent on imports to cover their energy requirements.

These countries, the so-called Least Developed Countries, face grave dangers to the extent that the petrodollar recycling process, as it has been carried out in the past, does not involve them. They are effectively dependent on international aid and will remain so. So far, the appropriate international aid mechanisms have still not been put in place, either by the IMF or by the World Bank, and time is running out. Basic problems of economic survival will soon begin to appear, and could lead to a fundamental breakdown in the system of international solidarity.

The oil price increases of 1979 did not provoke terribly pessimistic reactions from futurologists of the Third World. But the 1980 price rises were a different matter: they caused both the OECD and the World Bank to drastically revise their medium-term and long-term projections. In its third report on the developing world, the World Bank says developing countries generally will have to curtail economic growth sharply in order to improve their borrowing capacity. Competition on international capital markets is going to become very severe and, as a result, the report says, LDC's will see a sharp deterioration in the terms of their borrowings, with interest rates rising. The report projects an average three percent per year real increase in the price of oil, taking the cost of a barrel to $50 in 1985 and almost $80 in 1990. On that basis, the report expects the average annual economic growth rate of the Newly Industrialized Countries in South East Asia to slow to between 4 and 4.5 percent in the next five years, from between 5 and 5.5 percent from 1970 to 1980. As for the poorest developing countries, the report sees their growth rates falling to between 1.8 percent and 2.4 percent a year.

According to another report, prepared for President Carter by the Council on Environmental Quality, the population of the world will be well above 6 billion in the year 2000, with most of the increases coming in the poorest countries. The population of Mexico City is seen reaching 32 million. The gap between rich and poor countries is seen widening, with output per head in the U.S. exceeding $14,000, compared to $600 in the poorest countries. Still more serious, food prices are expected to double in real terms, mainly because of the effects of higher oil prices on agricultural production. The report also predicts regional shortages of water will be commonplace.

Other studies have reached similarly dark conclusions. The OECD's Interfutures report projects that income per head in black Africa in the year 2000 will be below $400 in terms of 1980 dollars, and according to the World Bank, 600 million people will be living in conditions of absolute poverty. The conclusions of the Brandt report point in the same direction.

Unless something is done to turn things around, almost one-third of humanity is going to be reduced to begging—and the oil crises will have played a predominant role in the process.

CHAPTER 2
The Burden of Defense

Economists often tend to ignore defense issues, on the grounds that defense does not really belong in the realm of economic analysis. I am convinced this is a major error. There are intimate links between defense policies and economic policies. Often, the two can be considered as opposite sides of the same coin.

Economic developments of the past 20 years cannot be properly understood without taking full account of defense problems and changes in the balance of power between East and West. Similarly, no analysis of the economic outlook for the 1980's is complete without taking into consideration the renewal of international tensions following the Afghanistan affair. These tensions are a direct result of the remarkable buildup of Soviet military power in the 1970's and the equally remarkable decline of the U.S. defense effort since the Vietnam war. They represent a crucial factor in world economic prospects, affecting the outlook for the dollar, inflation and world growth.

Economic Growth and Defense Spending

Classical economists, from Adam Smith to Jean Baptiste Say to Ricardo, all paid attention to the problem of financing national defense. It is highly curious that most economists today still choose to ignore its importance. The statistics speak for themselves. World defense spending totals about $500 billion a year. The U.S. and the Soviet Union alone spent over $2 trillion on defense between 1965 and 1975.

The first question to ask is whether there is a logical connection between the economic situation of a country and its defense effort. The few researchers who have studied this issue have tried to show that there is a direct relationship between the size of GNP and the size of the defense budget. One author, Fred Hoffman, has found it possible to assert that the percentage of GNP spent on defense rises together with increases in per capita income.

Some Marxists have gone further by setting forth a "law" according to which defense spending tends to increase in capitalist economies.

These theses, however, are simply not borne out by the facts. In the 1967-1971 period, for example, the countries which were spending close to 20 percent of GNP on defense, such as Egypt and Jordan, were far from being among the most prosperous countries. Of the 13 countries spending between 5 and 10 percent of GNP on defense, including Portugal, Iraq and the Sudan, 9 could be considered poor countries. On the other hand, of the countries whose defense outlays came to only two to five percent of GNP—countries such as France, Britain and Sweden—almost half were among the richest nations in the world.

Statistics seem to provide no support for the belief that increased defense spending is a function of rising national wealth, whether wealth is defined in terms of total GNP or in terms of income per head. On the contrary, it would even be possible to set forth a law stating that the more a country has the economic means to guarantee its security the less it is willing to make the effort, and the more it is subject to economic constraints the more it becomes willing to give security top priority.

National Income Up, Defense Spending Down?

The argument that defense spending should logically rise in line with economic growth as more resources become available crops up in all countries in discussions on budget allocations. But nowhere does it play a more prominent role than at the ministerial meetings of the North Atlantic Treaty Organization. The battle over who is in a position to contribute what to the common defense effort began with the birth of NATO after World War II, and is probably destined to continue as long as the alliance itself. The Europeans have argued that the United States, as the dominant power, must shoulder the main part of the burden. The U.S. has replied, with increasing bitterness over the years, that Europe's growing wealth justifies at least proportional growth in its defense contributions.

Whatever the merits of these arguments, the facts are that over the past 15 to 20 years, NATO countries have reduced their defense spending at times when they could have increased it without much trouble. Paradoxically, the Europeans have agreed to increase their defense contributions in times of economic difficulties, especially in the past few years. From 1956 to 1972, which was a period of exceptional prosperity for them, all the NATO member countries (with the exception of Portugal, because of its war in Africa) reduced their defense spending as a percentage of GNP. As a percentage of the national budget, defense outlays in the 1961-1971 period fell from 27 percent to 20 percent in France, from 33 percent to 29 percent in West Germany and from 28 percent to 19.5 percent in Britain.

From 1973 to 1975, on the other hand, when the first oil crisis had quadrupled oil prices and the industrialized world was suffering from recession, almost all NATO countries stopped reducing or actually increased defense spending as a percentage of GNP.

Then in May 1977, NATO ministers approved a plan calling for growth in defense spending by member countries of three percent a year in real, inflation-adjusted terms. That may seem a modest objective, but it is in striking contrast to the earlier decline in defense appropriations in real terms. France, which is not a member of the military wing of NATO, also plans to raise defense spending in 1977-1982 from 17 percent of the national budget to 20 percent, or 3.6 percent of GNP.

It seems that the worse their economies perform, the more countries spend on defense. A conclusion as surprising as that calls for some explanation.

Economic Logic and Defense Logic in the West

In advanced industrialized countries, defense spending seems to have become to a very large extent an autonomous economic variable. In the past 20 years or so, one factor responsible for declines in levels of defense spending in the West has been a growing feeling of security, resulting from a combination of factors, including membership in a long-standing military alliance and the gradual fading of memories of World War II.

But the most important factor, without any doubt, has been rising expectations, which have invaded Western social value systems. Everyone now expects his standard of living to go on getting better throughout his whole life. This is a completely new phenomenon. Previously, the idea of improvements in living standards, to the extent that it existed at all, was reserved for a small fraction of the population, which accepted that improvements could only come about gradually, over several generations. The result of the expectations phenomenon is that spending on defense is widely resented by the people. Rightly or wrongly, they see defense outlays as competing directly with their chances to improve their own lot, either through welfare handouts or simply through the benefits of economic growth. It is ironic that it was under President Nixon, generally considered a conservative if not a man of the Right, that this public resentment was at its strongest and most effective, causing the U.S. defense effort to stagnate and decline after the end of the Vietnam war.

Economic power is always the precondition for effective national defense. But it seems that once the economy has developed beyond a certain threshold point, the use of economic resources for defense purposes comes to depend on non-economic factors, which cannot be fully analyzed without delving into political complexities.

In the case of small high-income countries, reductions in defense spending can be explained by the fact that they are assured of a high degree of military security through their membership in a military alliance like NATO. For example, defense spending has fallen as low as 2.8 percent of GNP in Belgium, 2.1 percent in Denmark and 0.8 percent in Luxembourg. It is hardly surprising that it is the smallest NATO countries, with the lowest membership fees, which are the alliance's most ardent advocates.

But overall, the history of the past two decades or so shows that in the most advanced developed nations defense spending has been in conflict with the requirements of collective consumption and general prosperity.

For a long time now, defense budgets have been losing in this conflict, partly because of a widespread impression that threats to external security have lessened. Now, following a number of diplomatic and military shocks, it seems that we are witnessing the start of a spectacular turnabout in the trend—a swing back in favor of defense spending. The reasons for this turnaround lie in the dramatic reversal in the East-West power balance which took place in the 1970's in favor of the Soviet Union—where, as we shall see, defense spending conforms to a very different kind of logic than the West.

U.S./U.S.S.R.:
The Reversal of the Power Balance

In the early 1970's, having overtaken the U.S. in terms of military spending, the Soviet Union attained overall parity of military forces with the U.S., implying Soviet superiority in some areas. Outward signs of this new state of affairs included the Soviet role in the wars in Vietnam, Angola and Ethiopia, and in the Yom Kippur war. Later, of course, came the invasion of Afghanistan and the buildup of a powerful Soviet naval presence in all the waters of the world.

Soviet aggression finally caused the U.S. to make a thorough reevaluation of the Soviet arms buildup, which had been systematically ignored or underestimated during the period of Nixon and Kissinger. In their time, the watchword of U.S. policy was detente. It was important not to frighten American public opinion or America's allies with too realistic an assessment of the balance of power and of how it was likely to develop. Consequently, U.S. government officials deliberately ignored or distorted the evaluations made by their own experts. At the time when I was Chairman of the Economic Committee of NATO, U.S. delegates used to claim that Soviet military spending accounted for about six percent of GNP, about the same percentage as in the U.S. But calculations by the NATO secretariat, based mainly on data supplied by U.S. experts, showed the Soviet percentage to be 12 to 14 percent, at least double what the U.S. administration claimed. It was only several years later, after disillusionment with detente had set in, and after a change of presidents, that U.S. officials admitted the 12 to 14 percent estimate had been accurate.

This was not an isolated episode. In 1972/1973, U.S. experts already had information about Soviet experiments on the new generation of missiles which became known to us several years later as the SS 18 and SS 20. But the information was deliberately ignored by the administration in Washington.

Stripped of all equivocation, the key facts are as follows:

In constant 1976 dollars, Soviet military spending rose from $107 billion in 1965 to $144 billion in 1975. By comparison, the U.S. defense budget in 1975 was down more than one-third in real terms from the peak reached in 1968 during the Vietnam war, and down 15 percent from the level reached at the beginning of the 1960's.

Since 1975, the imbalance has shifted still further in favor of the Soviet Union. Right now, the Soviet defense budget is estimated to be at least 50 percent bigger than that of the U.S. A number of U.S. experts are speaking of a U.S. "vulnerability gap" lasting from now until 1985, during which time the Soviets will keep the upper hand no matter what the U.S. does to try to make up lost ground.

The Crushing Superiority of Soviet Military Spending

The Soviet Union has been steadfastly building up its military might, while the U.S. has been marking time. In some areas, the gap has been particularly striking. In 1975, for example, the Soviets were spending nine times as much as the U.S. on strategic defense systems (ABM systems, SAM rockets, interceptor planes), and twice as much on intercontinental missile systems.

From 1964 to 1976, the number of men under arms in the Soviet Union rose from 3.4 million to 4.4 million. In the U.S., the number has fallen from a peak of 3.4

million during the Vietnam war to 2.2 million today, the lowest level since the 1950's.

The number of Soviet intercontinental ballistic missiles (ICBM's) has risen from 225 in 1965 to 1,600 today, while the U.S. number has been steady at 1,200 for almost 10 years.

The number of Soviet submarine missiles has risen from 29 to more than 700, while the figure for the U.S. has held steady at 656 for several years.

In qualitative terms, the Soviets have also made huge strides.

Since 1965, the U.S. has developed only one new missile system, the Minuteman III. In the same period, the Soviet Union has developed seven new systems, the most recent being the medium-range SS 16 and the intercontinental SS 20. Three of the seven have multiple warheads. Furthermore, in coming years the Soviet Union is expected to test a further 10 to 15 new armed ballistic missile systems. Already, the improvement in the accuracy of Soviet missiles poses a serious threat to the security of the 1,053 ICBM's which constitute the spearhead of the West's strategic ground force. As for the U.S. strategic bomber force, it is still made up of aging B-52's, designed more than 20 years ago.

To complete the inventory, the Soviet arsenal of conventional weapons contains four times as many tanks as the U.S. has (40,000 against 10,000), two and a half times as much artillery, and 30 percent more combat planes.

Table 20, which takes into account the forces of allies on both sides, gives a pretty clear idea of the balance of power.

NATO vs THE WARSAW PACT

TABLE 20

The Balance of Power	U.S. and NATO*	U.S.S.R. and Warsaw Pact
Nuclear warheads	9,582	6,000
ICBM's	1,053	1,398
IRBM's and MRBM's..............	18	600
SLBM's (sub launched)	800	1,003
Manpower	6.7 million	7.1 million
Combat-ready divisions	95	159
Backup divisions	8	73
Tanks.........................	27,000	64,270
Strategic bombers	349	156
Combat aircraft.................	8,760	8,705
Aircraft carriers	30	4
Cruisers	30	37
Destroyers	164	76
Nuclear-missile subs	50	87
Artillery pieces.................	22,400	34,000

*Includes French forces
Source: INTERNATIONAL INSTITUTE FOR STRATEGIC STUDIES

The most significant phenomenon of the past five years has been the dramatic progress made by the Soviet navy, both in building new warships and in deploying them around the world.

The U.S. still leads in overall tonnage (4.8 billion tons against 2.8 billion), but the Soviet Union now has a much larger number of warships (almost 1,500 against 500 for the U.S.). The U.S. navy today has fewer nuclear submarines and submarine missiles than at any time since 1967. Because of the withdrawal from service of the Polaris submarine, the number of submarines in service has fallen below 41, and the first of the Tridents designed as replacements will not go into service until around mid-1981, more than two years behind schedule.

In addition, the Soviet Union now matches the U.S. in its ability to intervene from a great distance. The poker game played by John Kennedy over Cuba would no longer be possible today.

In the final analysis, the comparative statistics matter less than the state of preparedness of American troops, which was well illustrated by the failure of the hostage rescue mission in Iran.

The U.S. army is short 7,000 non-commissioned officers, and the navy is short 20,000 men. The qualifications of new recruits are dismally low, and many of them are incapable of using the sophisticated equipment at their disposal. The air force lacks the spare parts to stay in combat for more than a week. About half of the 13 U.S. aircraft carriers are not combat-ready, and the rest are considered "marginal." Only half of the air force is capable of carrying out its missions. As for the "Rapid Deployment Force," it would need three weeks to intervene in the Persian Gulf.

The How and the Why of the Soviet Arms Buildup

Calculated in constant roubles, the Soviet defense budget is believed to have grown from 40-45 billion in 1970, to 50-55 billion in 1975, and probably to 65-70 billion today. This means that between 1970 and 1980 the Soviets spent the equivalent of about $240 billion more on defense than the Americans. It also means that during the period of detente, marked by the SALT I agreement and crowned by the Helsinki Conference, the growth rate of Soviet military spending was about double the Soviet economy's overall growth rate of about two to three percent a year. Since 1970, the defense sector has accounted for between 12 and 14 percent of Soviet GNP, and has absorbed 20 percent of total industrial production.

These percentages are much higher than once thought in the West, indicating that the Soviet leaders have been much less willing to allocate resources to personal consumption than was once believed. The priority of priorities in the Soviet Union has remained national defense.

How should this be interpreted? Why did the Soviet Union continue its defense buildup despite its pronounced desire for detente with the U.S.? Why, after signing the SALT treaty in May 1972, did the Soviets maintain and even accelerate their development of strategic missiles? Were Soviet leaders guilty of duplicity? Did they deliberately set out to deceive world opinion in general, and the Americans in particular?

There are two possible explanations for Soviet actions. First of all, the Soviet

Union never really accepted the idea of Mutual Assured Destruction (M.A.D.), which holds cities on both sides hostage to nuclear devastation. For Americans, the annihilation of cities remains a theoretical concept, but it is very real for the Soviets, who saw their towns and villages razed to the ground during World War II.

Secondly, and this is fundamental, defense spending in the Soviet Union is built into the structure of the economy. The military and civilian sectors are closely linked. Contrary to what many Westerners still believe, Soviet defense spending is less the result of deliberate political or strategic decisions than it is a simple fact of economic life. This is the main reason the Soviet defense buildup continues regardless of shifts in Soviet diplomacy, and why the Soviets cheated the U.S. by failing to keep their side of the detente bargain. The defense buildup should not be interpreted as an indication of Soviet warmongering, but rather as a result of an ideological system, a historical tradition and an economic system which all converge and point in the same direction.

MILITARY SPENDING IN THE SOVIET UNION
AND THE UNITED STATES

TABLE 21

	Military spending in billions of dollars			Military spending per head of population in dollars			% of GNP		
	1973	1975	1979	1973	1975	1979	1973	1975	1979
Soviet Union	88-92	124	150	352-368	490	574	11	13	12 14
United States	74	84	108	372	417	520	5.6	5.5	4.6

Source: THE MILITARY BALANCE 1976-1977. INTERNATIONAL INSTITUTE FOR STRATEGIC STUDIES AND COUNCIL OF ECONOMIC ADVISORS.

The nature of the Soviet economic system is discussed in more detail in the next section. But let me say right here that in the years ahead, Soviet defense outlays will probably continue to grow at their past rate of about four percent a year, and faster at certain points in the production cycle of new weapons systems. This means that the Americans, after having tried to curb spending on defense in order to satisfy domestic economic and social requirements, will have to make a leap forward in the defense area just to maintain parity of forces.

It is a race between the Soviet tortoise, huge and slow but always in motion, and the American hare, which moves in leaps and bounds but stands still for prolonged periods.

The choices confronting the U.S. and its allies are not pleasant ones. If they keep playing the poker game with the Soviets, they risk sacrificing precious resources needed for economic growth and general prosperity; if they fold their cards, they risk finding themselves exposed a few years from now to all kinds of military and diplomatic blackmail.

Defense Logic in the Soviet Union

The Military-Economic Complex

In the Soviet Union, the military sector of the economy has absolute priority. The Soviet system has traditionally favored investment in defense and heavy industry to the detriment of consumption, which is seen as the residual element of final demand. This is the opposite, of course, of a free market economy, in which consumption often gets priority over other uses of resources.

All increases in available resources in the Soviet Union benefit the military sector first and foremost. Any benefits to the Soviet consumer are secondary—i.e. the increase in resources made available to the military sector relieves the pressures placed on consumption by military spending.

It is no exaggeration to say that the Soviet economy produces arms just as an apple tree produces apples. The military-industrial complex is not superimposed on the structure of the economy as it is in the United States: it is an integral part of the economic system, or, if you like, it *is* the system.

Paradoxically enough, the Soviet Union's behavior could be considered almost Ricardian, in the sense that the Soviets specialize in what they are most gifted at doing. The remarkable Soviet efficiency in producing arms contrasts sharply with the general inefficiency of Soviet industry and above all Soviet agriculture. It could be argued that the Soviets are simply exploiting a natural advantage which allows them to get the best possible returns on resources. Why try to sell cars of doubtful quality when there is such a good market for excellent T 72 tanks and efficient Kalashnikov rifles? Why struggle in the arena of international trade when the simple fact of owning the world's Number One war machine is enough to obtain the best of terms in trade inside Comecon, and even concessions from the West?

There is a certain economic rationality to Soviet behavior which cannot be ignored.

Soviet industry can be converted at extremely short notice from civilian production to military production, and the defense establishment is represented in all areas of economic life—in workshops, factories, research laboratories and universities—and almost automatically creams off the best brains, the best products, the best techniques. Hence the inexorable nature of the Soviet defense buildup. Throughout the period of detente which led to the Helsinki conference, while U.S. defense spending was declining in real terms, the annual growth of Soviet defense outlays never fell below four percent, and as we have seen, the percentage of GNP going to defense remained at 12 to 14 percent.

This was America's naive period. Nixon and Kissinger thought they could carry out detente and economize on resources which could then be allocated to other purposes—and they got cheated.

The Double Defense Budget of the West

There is a fundamental inconsistency in the idea of detente which supporters of East-West cooperation have never fully understood: in the Soviet Union, because of the very nature of the system, the military sector has always been one of the prime beneficiaries of cooperation and increased trade with the West. Consequently, the West, by promoting detente, may indirectly weaken its own external security. When a Western country helps a certain sector of the Soviet economy through exports or loans on easy terms, it is also aiding the Soviet defense sector.

The historian Alain Besancon described the Western countries as supporting a double defense budget, meaning that because of their cooperation with the Soviet Union they were paying for a part of the Soviet defense effort as well as for their own. Seen in this light, East-West economic cooperation is a bit like food which nourishes both the patient and the disease.

This line of reasoning should not be pushed to extremes. It must be borne in mind that the double budget mechanism generally functions only indirectly, via the pressures placed on consumption in the Soviet Union—in other words, the effect of East-West cooperation is to allow the Soviet Union to acquire the guns it would acquire in any case, but with the difference that there is some butter left over for the Soviet man-in-the-street.

But be that as it may, there are plenty of examples of Soviet utilization of Western technology for military purposes. U.S. companies sold more than $1.5 billion worth of equipment to the Soviet Union to build a truck factory on the Kama river. The trucks were supposed to be used for civilian purposes, but according to some sources of information they were used by the Soviet army during the invasion of Afghanistan. Another factory, also built with the help of U.S. equipment, is believed to be manufacturing not only trucks for military use, but also missile launching ramps.

A car factory in Gorky, which relies on U.S.- and Japanese-designed electronic equipment, is believed to be manufacturing amphibious assault vehicles and military-purpose trucks as well as civilian cars and trucks. More generally, it seems that the Soviets have made widespread use of U.S. electronic equipment, for example in the guidance system for the SS 18 missile, in the Backfire strategic bomber, in aerial defense networks, etc.

As for its own exports, the Soviet Union has halted export sales of titanium (it has a production capacity of 45,000 tons a year), which is used in the manufacture of submarines and missiles, in aeronautics and in the construction of nuclear power stations. Likewise, it exports none of its platinum or palladium, even though it controls one-third and two-thirds respectively of total world production of these metals.

The Soviets might argue, not without some justification, that sales of oil to the West end up fueling NATO planes. But the key point is the priorities observed in the allocation of resources. It is the priority systematically given by the Soviet Union to arms spending that marks the fundamental distinction between the Soviet system and the free market systems of Western countries, especially the United States.

Defense Logic in the United States

Traditionally, defense spending has played a considerable role in the U.S. economy. Defense outlays bolstered overall economic activity in the run-up to World War II. After the war came the birth of the military-industrial complex, a strong and profitable union of the industrial and military establishments. Furthermore, as we have seen, defense played a crucial role in postwar U.S. economic relations with its allies, as the U.S. traded military protection for Europe and Japan in return for the right to print virtually unlimited quantities of dollars.

In the Nixon-Kissinger period, however, a fundamental change took place in the U.S., even though it went largely unnoticed at the time.

What occurred was a major shift in emphasis away from defense towards social transfers. U.S. defense capabilities deteriorated, indirectly causing a major crisis within the NATO alliance and also between the U.S. and Japan, as the reduced value of U.S. military protection made the allies increasingly reluctant to finance the U.S. external deficit. This is part of the reason for the weakness of the dollar and the successive dollar crises of recent years.

The crises over Iran and Afghanistan finally provided dramatic illustrations of the weakening of U.S. military power. Public opinion in the U.S. woke up at last to the realities of the shift in the East-West power balance, and detente was decisively rejected.

If the present mood in the U.S. lasts, there is a strong chance that after declining in relative importance in the U.S. economy during the 1970's, defense spending in the 1980's will grow both as a percentage of the federal budget and as a percentage of the GNP. If that happens, it will have a major effect on inflation in the U.S. and throughout the world, and on the fate of the dollar.

The Decline of U.S. Defense Spending in the 1970's

U.S. DEFENSE SPENDING AND SOCIAL TRANSFERS
(as % of federal budget)

TABLE 22

Fiscal Year	Defense	Social transfers
1963	43.2	*18.2*
1965	38.8	19.2
1969	*42.2*	*26.5*
1970	39.2	28.5
1971	35.2	33.1
1972	32.4	35.1
1973	29.6	37.1
1974	*28.8*	*39.5*
1975	26.0	41.8
1976	24.0	43.9
1977	23.7	43.9
1978	22.8	42.1
1979	23.3	42.5
1980	22.9	43.3
1981	24.3	46.4

President Nixon, the bete noire of American liberals, has often been attacked as a warmonger, because of actions such as the invasion of Cambodia and the mining of Haiphong harbour. But the reality is quite different. In the Nixon-Kissinger years, for the first time since World War II, the U.S. undertook a deliberate and systematic effort to reduce military spending sharply—and the full consequences of their actions for U.S. and world security have still to be felt.

As Table 22 shows, the share of defense in the U.S. federal budget fell from 42.2 percent in 1969 to 28.8 percent in 1974. As a percentage of GNP, defense spending plunged in the same period from 8.1 percent to 5.4 percent (see Table 23). Later, the same trend was continued under President Carter, bringing defense spending in 1980 down to around 23 percent of the federal budget and 4.5 percent of GNP. But it was during the Nixon-Kissinger years that the decline began and that the rate of decline was the sharpest.

U.S. DEFENSE SPENDING AND SOCIAL TRANSFERS
(as % of GNP)

TABLE 23

Calendar Years	Defense		Social transfers	
	Billions of Dollars	%	Billions of Dollars	%
1963	50.3	8.5	29.2	4.9
1965	49.4	7.2	32.5	4.7
1969	76.3	*8.1*	52.6	5.6
1970	73.5	7.5	63.5	6.5
1971	70.2	6.6	75.2	7.1
1972	73.5	6.3	83.2	7.1
1973	73.5	5.6	95.8	7.3
1974	77.0	*5.4*	117.6	*8.3*
1975	83.7	5.5	149.1	9.7
1976	86.4	5.1	161.7	9.5
1977	93.7	4.9	172.7	9.1
1978	99.0	4.6	185.4	8.7
1979	108.3	4.6	209.9	8.8
1980*	121.6	4.8	233.4	9.2

*Second Quarter at an Annual Rate

Defense spending fell not only in terms of its share in the federal budget and GNP, but also in absolute terms.

Calculated in constant 1972 dollars, defense outlays fell from around $100 billion in 1968 to $63 billion in 1976, then recovered slightly to around $68 billion at the start of the 1980's. Again, President Carter simply continued a trend begun long before he came to power; in fact, it was Carter who began a slight reversal of the trend with a small increase in the military budget for 1980.

If the calculations are made in 1981 dollars, the picture looks the same, with the military budget falling from almost $200 billion in 1968 to $137 billion in 1975, then recovering to around $150 billion in 1980-1981.

U.S. DEFENSE SPENDING
(billions of 1972 dollars)

CHART 4

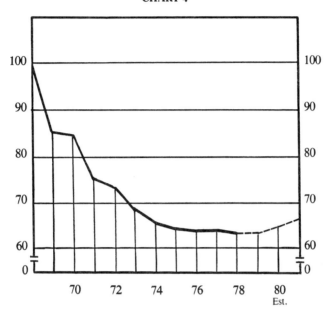

U.S. DEFENSE SPENDING

CHART 5

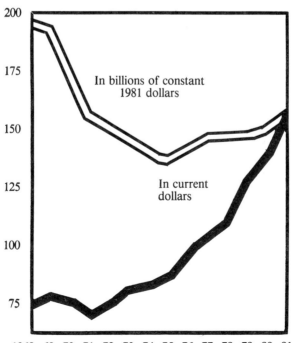

147

This unilateral act of relative disarmament was supported by the development of some very sophisticated theories, including the theory of Mutual Assured Destruction,[1] and theories on how to maximize the efficiency of budgetary expenditures.

The new ideas may have been very seductive, but their promoters were not without ulterior motives. The aim was essentially to convince American public opinion that it was quite possible, through rationalization, to reduce defense spending considerably and still preserve the same degree of national security.

With the advantage of hindsight, it seems that all the sophisticated ideas may have been used as pretexts to justify very deliberate policy choices. Perhaps because of a need to improve his personal image, Nixon may simply have decided to buy social peace at home through a massive increase in social transfers achieved at the expense of national defense capabilities.

What is certain is that the new policies were welcomed by the American public, which had been traumatized by the Vietnam war and was becoming intoxicated with the virtues of the ecology movement and preservation of the environment.[2]

As the preceding tables show, social transfers—spending on health, education and welfare—rose from 5.6 percent of GNP in 1969 to 8.3 percent in 1974. The jump to 9.7 percent in 1975 was partly the result of recession. But subsequently, social transfers continued to account for close to nine percent of GNP for the rest of the 1970's, despite one of the strongest and longest periods of economic expansion in postwar history. As a percentage of the federal budget, social transfers rose from 26.5 percent in 1969 to almost 40 percent in 1974 and over 43 percent in 1980.

The dramatic shift in U.S. priorities during the 1970's actually had its origins in the presidency of Lyndon Johnson. But it was implemented mainly by Nixon. Carter simply continued the trend.

It can be argued that this shift represented a deliberate decision to make massive reductions in defense spending in order to achieve domestic peace and harmony through huge federal assistance programs. In other words, in order to prevent racial riots and the burning of the ghettos, Nixon and his successors provided social aid to the fringe members of the U.S. population—blacks, hispanics and also some whites—making them a part of the consumer society (but *not* a part of the productive economy).

The consequent weakening of U.S. defense capabilities (which today is being publicly denounced by Kissinger, even though he was to a large extent to blame for it) can be held responsible for the Iran crisis, the Soviet invasion of Afghanistan and the increasing danger of a conflict over the Persian Gulf. History may judge harshly the men who upset the delicate East-West balance established by the Yalta agree-

---

[1] Roughly speaking, the M.A.D. theory states that it is unnecessary to pursue military efforts beyond the point at which both the U.S. and the Soviet Union have at their disposal enough nuclear arms to assure mutual destruction in the case of conflict.

[2] I have always interpreted the use of the ecological issue for political purposes in the U.S. as a sign of the weakening of the U.S. will to remain a world power. When you are "cultivating your own garden," as Voltaire expressed it in "Candide," you cease to worry about what your neighbor is up to. In April 1969, as I can personally attest, Nixon advocated the ecology movement to NATO, which resulted in the setting up of a special committee whose task was to decide how to respond to the challenges of modern society. The committee still exists. This comical episode helps to illustrate the psychological climate which prevailed at the start of the 1970's.

ment at the end of World War II. Because the breakdown of that balance is the origin of the threats to world peace which now loom in the 1980's.

Obstacles to U.S. Rearmament

The U.S. finally seems ready to make a sustained effort to strengthen its national security once again. The will to increase defense spending appears to be more than just an election-year flash in the pan. It is conceivable that by the mid-1980's the percentage of U.S. GNP going to defense will have returned to Vietnam war-era levels of around eight percent. The big question is this: Is U.S. industry up to the task of utilizing the funds made available?

In its issue of February 4, 1980, Business Week magazine published a detailed article on this subject which must have made very interesting reading for Soviet defense specialists. The article pointed to a number of bottlenecks in the U.S. defense industry, created in particular by shortages of qualified labor and skyrocketing labor costs, and by growing difficulties in securing supplies of key raw materials, including strategic metals. Delays in deliveries of titanium, for example, which is indispensable to the aeronautics industry, now exceed two years. Furthermore, while most major corporations are still able to respond to demand fairly rapidly, their sub-contractors are often not. For example, F-15 and F-16 aircraft have had to be built without engines, because of delivery delays. The same kind of problem afflicts the manufacture of integrated circuits.

The fact is that the government has been cold towards the defense industry for a long time, and the effects of this will now take a long time to wear off. Sensing the way the wind was blowing, many corporations, for example in the aeronautics industry, turned away from production for the military sector to concentrate on civilian markets which looked both safer and more profitable. Another obstacle to re-equipping U.S. armed forces is that a significant portion of U.S. arms production is earmarked for export rather than domestic use. U.S. arms exports during the past five years totaled around $50 billion.

It is clear that some hard choices will have to be made between production for the military sector and production for civilian areas of the economy. If need be, the government can always resort to a 1950 law giving priority to production for defense purposes in an emergency. But for the time being, the Pentagon is relying on makeshift solutions, such as installing new equipment in old planes for lack of new airframes. Whatever happens, no significant improvement in the situation is likely within two years, especially since a number of corporations are still waiting for confirmation of the administration's defense plans before they make fundamental changes in their production schedules.

One final point: at the end of 1979, the accumulation of funds authorized for military spending but still unspent totaled $82 billion (which, incidentally, is equal to four times the total military budget of France in 1980). This inability to spend available money is a good indication of the changes which have taken place in government attitudes towards defense, and in the defense industry, over the past several years. But on the other hand, $82 billion in spare cash is also a good indication of the substantial economic growth potential inherent in a U.S. rearmament program.

The Effect of Rearmament on the U.S. Economy

How will the U.S. economy react to increases in defense spending? Given lengthy and complex budget procedures, we cannot yet know for sure how big the increases in 1981 are going to be. But, for example, the defense spending increase originally foreseen by the Carter administration for 1981 of $5.4 billion would have the mechanical effect—given an estimated investment multiplier of 1.5 in the U.S.—of increasing GNP in one year by about $8 billion dollars, or 0.3 percent.

According to a study by Data Resources Inc., a $10 billion increase in defense outlays could have the following effects spread over three years:

TABLE 24

	1980	1981	1982
GNP	+0.4	+0.9	+0.8%
Unemployment rate	−0.1	−0.2	−0.3
Inflation rate	0	+0.2	+0.3
Interest rates	+0.1	+0.4	+0.7
Investment	+0.4	+1.3	+1.3

These are obviously very incomplete estimates, as are all calculations based on the purely mechanical findings of an econometric model. Taking into account changes in expectations and economic behavior, the effect throughout the economy would probably be bigger than the statistics in the Table indicate.

In the medium- to long-term, increased defense spending could play a role in U.S. economic recovery. It will also fuel inflation, raising prices of raw materials and the cost of skilled labor in defense-related sectors of industry. Externally, a major U.S. re-armament program would hurt the U.S. balance of payments performance, and the dollar could be hurt as well.

It is going to be difficult for the United States to strengthen its defense capability quickly. The situation of the U.S. has undergone fundamental changes since the days of the Korean war and even since the Vietnam war. The Americans have lost the illusion that they have the means to produce guns and butter at the same time. They no longer have the trade surpluses and the low inflation rate they once enjoyed. Above all, the dollar is no longer the unchallenged currency it once was.

The scope for undertaking a sustained rearmament effort appears to have been dramatically reduced after years of economic and social policies which have emphasized non-defense areas. If the U.S. government now promotes defense without slowing down activity in civilian areas of the economy, inflation will take off and could trigger a serious monetary crisis. On the other hand, if it tries to transform the economy into a war economy, the emphasis on defense spending will cause private sector demand to suffer. As always, the most likely outcome is a compromise between the two extremes—which may not prove to be particularly effective.

Whatever happens, defense and security issues appear likely to become once again a key factor in the U.S. and world economic arenas in the 1980's, after having taken a back seat during the past decade. Since it is politically very difficult to reduce social welfare spending significantly in the U.S., higher spending will probably mean higher inflation. U.S. inflation could rise to 15 to 20 percent in the 1980's. The other major industrialized nations could well follow the U.S. down the same inflationary path. If, on the other hand, they follow the monetary policy wisdom of West Germany and Japan and manage to keep their inflation rates below U.S. levels, the dollar will probably weaken and its position as a reserve and settlement currency will become more and more uncertain.

CHAPTER 3
Reflections on a Possible Future

After the first oil crisis, the industrialized world arrived at a crossroads—and it has been there ever since. Instead of making decisions on how to proceed, industrialized countries simply stopped in their tracks. That failure to act won us all a reprieve of a few years, as economic growth continued to be supported by cheap energy and cut-price national security. But those years represented the last rays of autumn sunshine. Now, winter is fast arriving. It is clear that those two essentials—energy and security—are again becoming rare and expensive commodities. The decisions that confront us cannot be deferred much longer.

What we need is not idealized notions of a new World Economic Order. Rather, we must learn to live in the Brave New World of an Oil Exchange Standard. We are going to need new and original contributions to solving the petrodollar recycling problem from commercial banks and from international institutions such as the International Monetary Fund and the World Bank. Longer term, if we are to keep body and soul together, it will be absolutely essential to develop new energy sources. To make the most of what we have already got, while laying the groundwork for a future equal to our past, we shall have to take a new approach to economic growth, moving closer to what I have termed a Stalinist model of consumption.

A New World Contract

Cooperation or Conflict

The first issue to be confronted is petrodollar recycling. For the second time in six years, investment outlets must be found for huge amounts of surplus petrodollars. In other words, ways must be found to re-inject into the world economy the buying power which the oil producers have taken out of it. Failure to find solutions would mean under-employment of resources and could turn the world economic clock back to the 1930's. However, recycling, as it has been carried out up to now, can itself be interpreted simply as a useful expedient, which has allowed the world to defer, but not to solve, the fundamental problem. In the long term, that fundamental problem is how to release the resources necessary to finance the development of alternative energy sources over the next 10 or 20 years. So far, no one has even tried to calculate the size of the financing effort required. No doubt it would be gigantic, perhaps on the order of $10 trillion. But it is the only way to prevent perpetually recurring and increasingly serious world crises.

What makes the energy problem so hard to deal with is the fact that production is concentrated on a small number of energy products—mainly oil, gas and to a lesser extent coal—and in a small number of countries, while consumption takes place throughout the world. To solve the problem within 10 or 20 years, it will be essential for all consuming countries to be able to develop their own energy production capacities, and move gradually towards self-sufficiency. This obviously requires setting up financing mechanisms capable of providing the necessary financial resources on the right terms.

Up to now, with rare exceptions (North Sea oil, the French nuclear program, coal in South Africa), developed countries have hardly begun the required planning and mobilization of financial resources. This harsh judgment applies perhaps particularly to the United States, but it also applies to all industrialized countries which have given priority to consuming energy rather than producing more of it. It is as if they decided to have one last holiday before coming home to face the hard realities of the 1980's.

The industrialized world is now running at least six years behind schedule in its development of new energy sources. The oil producers, for their part, have been no more courageous or clear-sighted than the industrialized nations, having invested less than five percent of their surpluses so far in the energy area.

Another imperative is to finance the development of agriculture, to prevent insurmountable problems from arising in developing countries by the end of the century.

It is obvious that solutions to the problems *will* be found. The only question is whether they are going to be found through international cooperation or through anarchy and conflict.

The Terms of a Reasonable Contract

The first task is to achieve once again a certain balance between the rights and the obligations of the various economic powers. The U.S., as we have seen, has long been paying for energy in terms of the face value of its currency only, thereby escaping from the constraints imposed on other countries. To face up to its obligations, the U.S. must start once again to play the game by the same rules as everyone else, which means paying its debts in real terms instead of simply by printing more money. That implies returning to balance of payments equilibrium, defending the dollar and controlling U.S. money supply. The gradual return to a gold standard should help the U.S. find its way back to the straight and narrow path.

As for the oil producers, they have been reaping the benefits of their position as oligopolistic sellers of energy to the rest of the world, without assuming the obligations and responsibilities which should go together with the greatest financial power in the world. These responsibilities require that the oil producers either hold the price of oil unchanged, or increase it only gradually, in such a way that the world economy is spared savage periodic blows. Commitments by the producers to stabilize the oil price in the long term are the only way to remove the uncertainties currently hanging over the future of the world economy.

The producers must also accept the risks which attach to great wealth. This means that in recycling their surpluses, they should shift from short-term to long-term investments, from bank deposits to direct investments, from speculative investments to productive ones, and from investments in developed countries to investements in developing countries. Only by giving up the cheating game and living up to their obligations can the OPEC countries make their financial power legitimate and lasting.

Towards an Oil Exchange Standard

Any monetary system functions only to the extent that it has a monetary unit capable of serving both as a standard of value and, directly or indirectly, as a medium of exchange. Gold fulfilled the role until the last world war. Subsequently the dollar took over, but then began to founder. Today, the predominant unit is the barrel of oil, whose value is supported by the strength of contractual agreements capable for the time being of exerting unrivaled economic and political power. Furthermore, oil is the origin of petrodollars, the monetary expression of which will soon be either the IMF's Special Drawing Rights (SDR's) or a new international monetary unit. We are thus going to be dealing with a medium of exchange based on an Oil Exchange Standard. How is this new international payments system going to function?

Recycling in the 1980's.

As we have already seen, petrodollar recycling in 1980/1981 presents new and very difficult problems. This time around, we cannot use the same recycling mechanisms as after the first oil crisis, at least not on the same scale. The facts show that in response to the changed circumstances, new recycling methods are already spontaneously emerging.

Contrary to what might have been expected, major international banks have not been submerged under waves of short-term petrodollar deposits, which they would not have known what to do with. In fact, in some cases and at certain times, the flow of petrodollars to banks actually appears to have come close to drying up.

OPEC Grows Bolder

In 1979, OPEC deposits in U.S. banks came to $16 billion, more than a quarter of the total OPEC surplus of $60 billion. In the first part of 1980, the deposit total was only $3.7 billion. In the Eurodollar market in London, OPEC deposits in mid-1980 rose only very moderately, despite a sharp rise in the OPEC surplus. A similar trend is revealed by statistics from the Bank for International Settlements, which keeps track of deposits throughout the international banking system. So where are the newly-generated petrodollars going?

The answer is that while still increasing their bank deposits, the oil producers have begun to diversify their investments, both geographically and by category of investment. Major new beneficiaries of petrodollar inflows have been West Germany and Japan. OPEC investors, and especially the Arabs, have become more bold and self-confident. They are no longer content to invest their money timidly in short-term deposits in major international banks. Instead they have decided to start running some financial and industrial risks. For example, they have become heavy buyers of stocks and bonds in Tokyo. OPEC investments in Japan at end-1979 already totaled $10 billion, and have leaped since then. OPEC buying of securities in Germany, France and the U.S. is also likely to increase.

Furthermore, Arabs are laundering money and channeling it into unidentified investments in the U.S., including real estate, shareholdings in companies, etc. These capital movements help to account for the increase in the errors and omissions component of the U.S. balance of payments, which incorporates all capital inflows whose origin cannot be identified with precision. What all this means is that OPEC investments are becoming more diversified and are reaching all sectors of the economy. So far, the diversification process has not caused problems, and it has helped to ease the petrodollar burden on the banks.

The oil producers are also broadening the scope of their Third World-related activities. Over the past six years, OPEC's international aid totaled about $33 billion, mostly benefiting a small group of countries, either Moslem countries or extremely poor ones. Now, the oil producers are participating more and more in Eurodollar lending activity. Some of them are also venturing into direct loans on easy terms to countries such as Mexico and Venezuela. The OPEC aid fund has been increased to $4 billion, and a proposal has been made to raise the total sharply to $20 billion. The producers still need to do much more in the Third World area. But their actions so far provide at least an encouraging sign.

The Role of the Banks

For some years now, major U.S. banks have been adopting a more and more cautious approach towards overseas lending. With huge amounts of loans already on their books, they have increased their lending to foreign borrowers by only 13 to 14 percent a year since 1976 (although their loans to a dozen particularly shaky non-oil developing countries, including Argentina, Chile, South Korea, Thailand and Brazil, have continued to rise at an annual rate of about 17 percent).

Meanwhile, commercial banks in Europe, Canada and Japan, which came to recycling later than the U.S. banks, have continued to increase their lending overseas very rapidly, at a rate of 33 percent a year (40 percent in the case of the dozen countries referred to above). The outlook now, however, is for a slowdown in the overall growth of commercial bank lending to foreign borrowers, perhaps to around 15 percent a year. The non-U.S. banks will be able to maintain higher rates of expansion than that, while the U.S. banks will be more or less forced to stay below the 15 percent mark because of the size of the loans already on their books. This overall slowdown means, without any doubt, that a gap will emerge between the financing requirements of the non-oil developing countries and what the banks are able to provide. No one knows how big this money shortage is going to be. Between now and 1985, it could total anywhere between $10 and $50 billion. Thus, the developing countries are going to be faced with a choice between reducing imports, which could trigger worldwide recession, and seeking financing elsewhere. In the circumstances, "elsewhere" means international organizations, and in particular the IMF and the World Bank.

The Grand Ambitions of the IMF and the World Bank

The annual meeting of the IMF and the World Bank in the autumn of 1980 took place at a critical moment in recent world economic history; and the decisions outlined at that meeting will play a major role in our economic future.

The first lesson to be drawn from the discussions was that given the choice between economic growth and control of inflation, both industrialized and non-industrialized countries seem to be inclined towards the first option, namely growth, even if the price to be paid is more inflation. This is of fundamental importance. It indicates that the majority of countries might be ready to create huge amounts of new international liquidity to satisfy everyone's needs.

A second point of major importance concerns the fate of the IMF itself. Since its creation in 1947, the IMF has acted as the guardian of international monetary orthodoxy. Now there is the possibility that it will be turned into a bank like any other bank, operating on a world scale and borrowing and lending almost without conditions and restrictions.

The advantages of such a change are obvious. Above all, the Third World would no longer risk suffocating for lack of funds. But we have to know what we are getting into. The remedy could turn out to be worse than the illness. The transformation of the IMF could remove the last barrier standing in the way of the rising tides of international liquidity and inflation. The stakes are extremely high. So far, no decision has been reached. But the possibility has been raised, and it goes to the very nerve center of the international monetary system.

IMF Resources

From 1974 to 1979, the IMF played only a modest recycling role. Its loans, to a dozen non-oil developing countries and to a few small industrialized countries, hardly exceeded $500 million a year. Right now, the Fund controls perhaps $30 to $40 billion, counting lending facilities created in recent years plus previously available funds. Another 20 billion SDR's or so are expected to be provided by the seventh increase in member countries' quotas currently underway. This may sound like a lot of money. But the modus operandi of the IMF means that the money it is actually able to lend is much less than the figures indicate. That is why the Fund wants to increase its resources. It tried for example to borrow $8 to $10 billion a year from OPEC, but the idea had to be shelved because of political problems, specifically the issue of recognition for the Palestine Liberation Organization (PLO).

Another idea was a Substitution Account at the IMF, which would receive deposits of dollars from central banks and issue in return assets denominated in SDR's, the IMF's currency. That idea has also been put aside for the time being, after running into various technical difficulties. One problem is that to make the Account attractive enough to central banks, the return on the newly-issued SDR's would have to be higher than the return on SDR's currently in existence. (In passing, it might be noted that the IMF decided in September 1980 to reduce from 16 to 5 the number of currencies used as the basis for calculating the SDR's value. This was not a fundamental change, but it did simplify matters, and could facilitate the use of SDR's by banks, and perhaps one day allow SDR's to enter into regular international use).

What remains is the possibility of the IMF borrowing on the open market, like any other bank. However, unlike any other bank, the IMF does not have the capital to guarantee its borrowings. It has its gold, but it cannot use that without the approval of 85 percent of its members.

In the final analysis, the Fund's assets are its good reputation and its prestige as the guardian of international monetary orthodoxy. As we have said, no decision has yet been made on whether the Fund should be transformed in this way. At this stage, it remains an idea—and one which is vigorously opposed by some IMF member countries, in particular West Germany and France.

IMF Lending

At least as important as the question of how the Fund is going to secure new resources is the question of how those resources will be used. When I was a young economist at the IMF about 20 years ago, the rule was: "No money without a rigorous economic stabilization program." Today, however, the "conditionality" rules attached to IMF loans have been relaxed considerably. Countries can now borrow more than before (200 percent of their quota instead of 125 percent), and for longer periods (three years instead of one year). Also, interest payments by the poorest borrowing countries are going to be subsidized, and there are plans for new mechanisms designed to provide special loans to poor countries to cover payments for imports of oil and foodstuffs.

The changes taking place represent a fairly radical shift in IMF policies. In the past, the IMF only intervened on the demand side. In other words, loans were designed solely to provide a country with additional overall resources to give it the time needed to put its house in order through changes in fiscal and monetary policies. Now, the IMF is going to be intervening on the supply side, for example by encouraging energy savings or domestic energy production. This means that the Fund's activities will tend to become more and more similar to those of the World Bank. This is good to the extent that the two institutions, by operating more in concert with each other, should become more responsive to the needs of their member countries. But there is also a danger in the IMF's new approach. Through a preoccupation with medium-term and long-term financing of energy projects, the IMF risks losing its role as the protector of monetary orthodoxy. It is not possible to be judge and defendant at one and the same time.

An Enlarged Role for the World Bank

For the World Bank, there are no problems of role changes. Increasing its resources and the scope of its activities is fully consistent with its permanent vocation, which is to act as the Good Samaritan helping the world's poor. As things stand, the Bank's authorized capital (of which less than 10 percent is paid in) is going to be raised from $45 billion to $85 billion, and the resources of its soft loan affiliate, the International Development Agency, are to be raised to $12 billion.

Other ideas include raising the maximum permitted ratio of loans to authorized capital above the current ceiling of 1, and increasing authorized capital without increasing the amount of capital paid in.

In addition, there is a proposal for creation of a World Bank subsidiary which would have the specific task of financing energy development projects.

Cooperation between the IMF, the World Bank and Commercial Banks

Right now, international monetary experts are bubbling over with proposals on how to solve the recycling problem—which is a welcome change after the dearth of new ideas in recent years.

Among the suggestions is the idea of constructing some kind of bridge between the commercial banks, which have borne the brunt of recycling up to now, and the IMF and the World Bank, which are going to assume major recycling roles in the future. It must be said that up to now examples of cooperation between private sector banks and the two international organizations have been rare and exchanges of information between them have been very limited. There are various ways in which bridges could be built. One proposal is simply for the IMF, the World Bank and commercial banks to get together and make joint loans, in the same way that banks currently form lending consortia among themselves. Another approach would be for the IMF and the World Bank to provide guarantees for commercial bank loans, to encourage the banks to make or renew loans in particularly risky cases.

Yet another idea is for the World Bank to pass on part of its loan portfolio to commercial banks. This would allow the World Bank to build up needed liquidity, while allowing the commercial banks buying the loan assets to benefit from the technical studies which the World Bank conducts when it makes loans.

As for cooperation among commercial banks themselves, Chase Manhattan Bank Chairman David Rockefeller proposed in the spring of 1980 that the banks set up a common "safety net," allowing banks to bail each other out in cases of difficulties in their Eurodollar market operations.

All of the proposals are interesting, and they all point in the same direction, that of increasing the overall amount of resources available, and strengthening cooperation among private and public sector institutions.

Cooperation Among Central Banks

The search for new procedures in international monetary affairs could lead to bilateral agreements between central banks providing for the substitution of other currencies for the dollar. For example, surplus countries could exchange some of their dollar holdings for German mark-denominated assets from the Bundesbank, the German central bank. The Bundesbank would then invest the dollars with the U.S. Treasury. Such transactions affect only the accounts of central banks; they have no impact on foreign exchange markets or money creation.

For surplus countries, one of the principal attractions of this approach is that it would give them a means of holding a bigger portion of their assets in strong non-dollar currencies, whose value they could monitor fairly easily.

Switzerland is known to be studying the possibility of offering special investment instruments to oil producing countries which want to diversify their reserve assets.

The Governor of the Swiss central bank has mentioned opening up interest-bearing Swiss franc deposit accounts at the central bank, as well as issuing special Swiss franc securities. It is thus clear that the Swiss banking authorities are taking into account the possibility that the Swiss franc will be in growing demand as a reserve currency, and the Germans seem to be moving in the same direction.

The problem with all the measures discussed above is knowing how far to go and when to call a halt. The possibility of transforming the IMF, for example, and thereby creating new liquidity without limit, represents both a strong temptation and a grave threat to world monetary stability. All the measures, if and when they are implemented, will tend to have the effect of extending to all countries, both rich and poor, the privilege of running "deficits without tears," a privilege previously reserved for the United States. The U.S. will not lose its right to print international currency or its freedom to finance domestic deficits with an external deficit. But that right will cease to constitute a privilege because everyone else will be enjoying similar freedom. This will serve the cause of fairness, but it is a safe bet that it will also fuel inflation.

The proposals and trends which I have described all point towards the birth of an Oil Exchange Standard. The world monetary system is already becoming more and more centered on the price of a barrel of oil, which serves as a standard of value through the establishment of the informal gold/oil exchange rate. The emerging Oil Exchange Standard would be strengthened by indexing of the price of oil, which would further enhance oil's role as a world standard of value.

The crucial point to be borne in mind is that the creation of huge amounts of new liquidity is only a beginning. All it does is prevent an immediate collapse of the system and the demise of the poorest countries. The most fundamental requirements are to stabilize the price of oil, and to solve the world's energy problem by developing new energy sources both in the industrialized countries and in the poorest countries on earth. The difference between success and failure in meeting those requirements could be the difference between world peace and world war in the years ahead.

Indexing the Oil Price

Stabilization of the price of oil is absolutely essential. Nothing is more harmful to world stability than the staggering blows inflicted by periodic energy crises. Price stabilization proposals have already been drawn up by OPEC experts. But beware. What they are seeking is not a stable price but *a stable rate of price increase.* The "noose effect" described earlier would become institutionalized. The skimming off of resources from oil-importing countries would persist. We would continue to be strangled by an invisible hand, only the pressure would be applied more evenly and the process would be somewhat less painful than before.

The OPEC proposals call for the oil price to be indexed to three variables (regardless of conditions on world oil markets):

• *Prices of industrial goods imported by OPEC countries.* The choice of this inflation criterion rather than price levels in industrialized countries represented a concession to hawks within OPEC. OPEC imports are mainly comprised of capital goods with high skilled-labor content, which are more inflation-prone than other products.

• *Movements in a basket of 12 currencies, including the U.S. dollar.* This index-ing link is designed to protect the oil producers from fluctuations in the dollar's value.

• *Economic growth in industrialized countries.*

Indexing of this kind would almost certainly increase the oil payment burden of industrialized nations. The real price of oil would probably rise by close to five per-cent a year, with three percent accounted for by economic growth and one to two percent by the difference between OPEC import price inflation and inflation in the industrialized world.

For oil import payments to remain unchanged as a percentage of the GNP of in-dustrialized countries, they would have to reduce oil consumption per unit of GNP by close to five percent a year, which looks like a difficult objective to achieve in the short term. However, without indexing, the oil payment burden looks certain to grow heavier anyway. The estimate of a five percent a year rise in the real oil price is about in line with current forecasts which do not take indexing into account.

Chart 6 illustrates the actual rise in the real oil price since 1974, and how it would have risen with the kind of indexing now being proposed:

OIL PRICES, 1974–1980

CHART 6

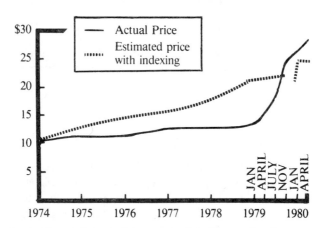

The chart clearly shows that total payments for oil over the six year period would have been greater with indexing than they actually were. On the other hand, the sec-ond oil crisis would have been largely avoided with indexing, and the oil price would be little different today from what it actually is.

In effect, indexing would mean that the more industrialized countries increased economic growth, the more they would have to pay in OPEC "taxes"— regardless of their success in conserving energy.

But it would also have one huge advantage: it would reduce uncertainty, which is the natural enemy of economists, industrialists and financiers. The damage done to the world economy by oil price hikes so far, especially the harmful effects on investment and savings, has been caused to a large extent by the growing element of uncertainty in all economic planning. With indexing, plausible forecasts could once again become a part of economic calculations. Whatever happens, however, payments for imported oil are going to continue inexorably taking a heavy toll. That is why it is essential that oil be replaced as the world's basic source of energy.

Development of New Energy Sources: A Categorical Imperative

The oil price cycle, as it has developed over the past seven years, is slowly but surely robbing industrialized countries of control over their economic destiny. One day it could rob them of their political sovereignty. It is bad enough for independent sovereign nations to have to stand by and watch their economies thrown into confusion every five or six years by massive and totally unpredictable increases in the price of the energy on which they depend for economic growth and, ultimately, for their very survival.

But there is a potentially even more serious consequence of oil price increases, and it is one which oil price indexing will do nothing to prevent. This is the takeover by outside interests of some of the levers of financial and industrial power inside the industrialized countries. The oil producers' constant accumulation of wealth gives them increasingly ample room for maneuver to carry out the most extensive usurpation of economic power ever accomplished by peaceful means. There is only one way to prevent this: the industrialized world must succeed in developing new energy sources to replace oil.

After the first warning of 1973, the West was guilty of failing to take the alternative energy objective seriously, even though it was already clear how the oil price cycle was going to develop. In the United States, the public preferred to daydream and to indulge in the illusion that a plot had been hatched by major oil companies, rather than tackle the real problem at its roots.

In Europe, countries sought relief in supposedly privileged bilateral oil supply deals, which did nothing to solve the fundamental problem. Only France, to some extent, can be considered an exception to the general rule, because of its nuclear program and its final acceptance of the need to reduce oil consumption and increase investment in energy projects. History will no doubt condemn the politicians who allowed a state of affairs so prejudicial to the sovereignty of their countries to continue.

The Birth of OPEC Financial Power.

Five years ago, an extrapolation by the World Bank indicated that OPEC, and in particular surplus countries such as Saudi Arabia and Kuwait, would build up immense financial power. After gaining widespread attention for a while, this forecast was soon consigned to oblivion, and oil consuming countries went back to consuming without restraint. Today, we find out that the Middle East members of OPEC are setting up a new international banking system to allow them to take control during the coming decade of a substantial part of the world's financial resources.[1] After wielding the oil weapon successfully in the 1970's, they plan to add to it a money weapon in the 1980's.

At the end of 1980, the assets of the Persian Gulf members of OPEC amounted to $350 billion, three times what they totaled five years earlier, and more than the combined assets of the five leading U.S. banks—Bank of America, Citicorp, Chase Manhattan, Morgan Guaranty and Manufacturers Hanover.

In five years from now, if the oil price remains stable in real terms, the resources of these OPEC members in the Gulf—just five countries, with a combined population of less than 12 million—could reach one trillion dollars, or one-third of the GNP of the U.S.; if the oil price rises, even at a slower pace than in the past, the figure could double or even treble—in which case these countries would have enough money to buy the United States. There is much more. For one thing, the lines between banking power and political power are blurred in the Gulf countries. In Kuwait, the Kuwait Investment Office acts on behalf of the Treasury. The Saudi Arabian Monetary Agency acts both as a merchant bank and as an agent of the Saudi Treasury. What this means is that the entry in force of Gulf banking institutions into world financial markets would cause a marked politicization of the international financial system.

Furthermore, Gulf investors are stepping up their purchases of shareholdings in businesses in the West and in Japan. Kuwaiti interests already hold about 25 percent of the capital of 20 leading American banks, as well as chunks of Eastern Airlines, Texaco, Getty Oil, Mobil and Exxon. Altogether, Kuwaiti and other Gulf investors have shareholdings in several hundred top U.S. corporations. Gulf interests are also participating in a major way in Japanese banking activities. The financial power of the Gulf countries is beginning to make itself felt. For years, Gulf financiers left the management of their assets to American or European advisors. Now, however, Gulf banks have taken over from Western institutions in the Middle East. Kuwait was one of the first oil producing countries to set up its own institutions to manage directly its petrodollars. A new generation of financiers is emerging in the Gulf, "Westernized" and perfectly capable of doing without the help of outside advisors.

So it seems that the days of passive OPEC investments in Treasury bills are over. As we saw earlier, Gulf financiers are now turning to long-term investments in stocks and bonds. They are diversifying currency risk. And they are investing in advanced technology industries, notably in Japan. For the time being, their behavior as shareholders is discreet. But it goes without saying that sooner or later they will want to have a say in the management of the companies in which they have invested, just as they already claim a say in the functioning of the world economic system.

However threatening this may be for the economic sovereignty of industrialized countries, it must be said that it is a perfectly natural development. The industrialized countries allowed OPEC to build up its immense wealth, and encouraged OPEC investors to buy shareholdings and take risks. They are now living with the inevitable consequences of their own actions.

---

[1]Business Week, October 6, 1980.

Cutting OPEC down to Size

The only way for industrialized and non-industrialized countries to head off the economic and political threats inherent in growing OPEC power is for them to retake control of world energy sources. The task is a gigantic one. After all the illusions about various substitutes for consumption of oil, we must recognize that there are really only three: coal, nuclear energy, and energy conservation.

Potential world reserves of coal total 11 trillion tons, and production, which amounted to 2.7 billion tons in 1978, could be dramatically increased in the decades ahead. Installed nuclear energy production capacity should triple by 1990. As for energy conservation, the elasticity ratio between energy consumption and economic growth could be cut to below 0.6—meaning that a one percent increase in economic growth could be achieved with a rise of less than 0.6 percent in energy consumption. The huge problems to be solved include how to cope with damage to the environment and where to find the enormous amounts of financing required.

The Obstacles

Abandoning use of oil will cause massive environmental problems. Coal, for example, gives off large quantities of carbonic gas which is harmful to the climate. Extraction of oil from shale in the U.S. will involve massive consumption of water and considerable atmospheric pollution, not to mention the problem of waste disposal. As for nuclear energy production, we are all familiar with the kind of pollution problems that can create. But as I have said, we hardly have any choice but to press ahead. Time is running out.

Energy development projects have certain key characteristics. In the first place, lead times are very long. The delay between the start of investment to prove a deposit and the moment when production begins averages five to eight years in the case of hydrocarbons, and eight to 10 years in the case of coal.

Secondly, energy investments are extremely capital-intensive. The ratio between investment costs per unit of annual production capacity and the price of that unit of production is close to three in the case of coal, compared to only one in manufacturing industry. And it can go much higher—to seven, for example, in the case of North Sea oil. For some years now, this ratio has been rising at an ever-quickening pace, which means that unit investment costs have been increasing faster than the nominal selling prices of energy products and faster than world inflation.

There are several reasons for this, including increased difficulty of access to deposits (such as offshore oil and gas deposits), sharp increases in wage and equipment costs, and extra investment outlays needed to protect the environment. The result is that the already-huge sums required for energy projects are growing rapidly. It has been estimated that from now to 1990 France will have to spend between $2.5 and $5 billion on overseas energy development projects. For European countries taken together, the figure rises to between $25 and $30 billion. According to some experts, the required total of energy investments worldwide in the decade will be between $1.5 and $2 trillion, more than half the GNP of the United States. Just recently, a West German organization forecast that between now and the year 2000, the world will have to spend $10 trillion on energy development projects, including $4.7 trillion on nuclear energy and $3.2 trillion on hydrocarbons.

No one can know for sure how accurate such forecasts will prove. All we know with certainty is that the amounts involved will be gigantic, and that they will require the countries concerned to mount an effort such as they have not undertaken since the last world war.

Some Possible Solutions

The continuing crisis in the Middle East means that Europe must diversify its oil supply sources away from that area. Currently, more than two-thirds of Europe's oil comes from the Middle East. This is an untenable situation in the long term, because Europe cannot go on living with the daily threat of a government being overthrown in one Middle Eastern country or another. All estimates show that whatever happens, Europe will have to remain heavily dependent on imports in the coming decade to satisfy its energy requirements. Consequently, it must seek new overseas supplies.

It so happens that hardly any of the continents in the world contain greater energy treasures than North and South America. Tarsands in Canada and Venezuela and oil shale in the U.S. and Brazil represent reserves equal to 10 trillion barrels of oil. Recovering just 10 percent of that would be enough to satisfy the energy requirements of the the American continents for 100 years. Add in exploitation of American coal and gas reserves and the figure could rise to 300 years.

The main obstacle is the huge cost of solving environmental problems, arranging transportation and developing technology up to the task. Europe has advanced technology and considerable financial means. The possibility of joint European-American exploitation of American energy resources deserves close examination. As for the problems facing the Third World, the World Bank has estimated that the oil import bill of developing countries in constant dollar terms will double from between $50 and $60 billion in 1980 to $110 billion in 1990. After the most recent oil price increases, that estimate now looks to be on the low side.

World Bank president McNamara proposed a $25 billion dollar aid program spread over the next five years to develop new energy sources in Third World countries. The program would be carried out by a new World Bank agency set up specially for the task, and would supplement the Third World activities of major oil companies, which often balk at the political risks involved in exploiting energy resources in developing countries.

The global scale of the energy problem, and the enormous investments required to develop new energy sources, could make it necessary to formulate some kind of World Energy Plan. A special new international financial organization, such as a World Bank for Energy, could be established to mobilize resources and coordinate plans. The essential requirement for both industrialized and non-industrialized countries is to release the financial resources necessary for developing new energy sources, be they new sources of oil to replace OPEC oil, or substitute energy sources. To do this, it will be necessary to increase savings rates significantly, which means that the kind of relationships among savings, consumption and investment which have prevailed for the past 30 years will have to be fundamentally altered. The massive financing required for energy investments cannot be mobilized without a major impact on domestic savings, aid to the Third World, interest rates and international credit market conditions. In the circumstances, the dire possibility of a world capital shortage, which has long haunted the imagination of economists and financiers, could become a reality.

A New Kind of Economic Growth

What is going to happen in the years ahead?

Will there be a leap in inflation in industrialized countries to offset the effects of higher oil prices? Even if there is, the oil producers will almost certainly react to cancel out inflation's effect. Paying higher prices for their imports comes to the same thing as accepting payment for their oil in depreciating currency, and they will no longer do it. Increases in the price of industrialized countries' manufactured goods exports will be quickly matched by increases in the price of oil.

Will there be armed conflict? Will the industrialized countries attempt to take over the sources of their oil supplies by force? Even if they succeeded in doing so, they would only be delaying the inevitable, to the extent that the real power of the OPEC cartel lies in the last analysis in the fact that oil is a rare and non-renewable commodity.

The final possibility, and the most likely outcome, is that the industrialized world will acquiesce in paying its oil taxes in real terms. That means real incomes will have to decline. The oil importing countries will have to return to balance of payments surplus. They will have to cut economic growth still further in order to reduce oil imports. And they will have to increase domestic savings in order to release the resources necessary to finance enormous investments in energy savings and development of alternative energy sources. Levels of real income will have to decline, or at best stagnate, to allow for higher levels of production.

These simple imperatives are still not understood by the public at large, which remains attached to anachronistic notions, such as the need to make life more comfortable, which belong to an era which is now over, the era of falling energy costs. *It is obvious that the imperative now is not to work less and live better, but to work harder for less reward.* Politicians have the difficult task of bringing home this harsh, simple truth to voters who have been softened by years of easy living and expectations of still better conditions to come.

The industrialized countries are likely to become victims of slower economic growth, rising inflation caused by higher energy costs, and rising unemployment. In the immediate future, the odds heavily favor a major world recession, as the economies of the U.S., Europe and Japan all decline. This time around, the U.S. is likely to be slow to recover, as Europe and Japan were after the first oil crisis. For a period of several years, the industrialized world must expect a dull and uncertain economic performance, of the kind Europe experienced after the first oil crisis and up to 1977-1978. When that period is over, certain structural changes in industrialized economies will become evident.

In the first place, growth in energy consumption will be slower than overall economic growth. This means that industrialized economies will become more and more oriented towards services. Already, the industrial base of developed countries has contracted sharply. West Germany has lost a million industrial workers in four years, and Japan just as many. This trend is destined to continue.

Secondly, the interruption in the historical process of substituting machines for men will continue, at least temporarily. Increases in the price of capital, caused mainly by rising energy prices, will encourage replacement of capital by labor.

Thirdly, economic growth will be sustained more and more by investment, rather than by consumption as in the past. The restructuring of industry, the search for new energy sources and the development of energy-saving methods will demand an enormous financing effort. Industrial equipment will have to be adapted to the task. Research and development expenditure will eat up a growing proportion of available resources.

Credit will become more expensive and more difficult to get. The balance between consumption and savings will tip in favor of savings, which implies a major change in economic behavior, since savings rates have been declining everywhere— even in Japan—in recent years. Consumption will come to be considered more and more as a residual element of final demand, rather than as an engine of growth. This does not mean a sudden revolution in consumption habits, but rather a reduction or withering away of certain kinds of consumption.

Everything implying physical movement and heavy energy consumption will be penalized: vacation trips, the skiing industry, hotels, restaurants, road construction and non-essential public works.

Everything implying sedentary, stay-at-home activities will be promoted: television, telecommunications, telephones, video-cassettes, etc.

Obviously, the automobile industry will be affected. But the development of engines consuming less gasoline, or even alternative fuels, should lead to a new kind of vehicle industry. Suburban home-building will suffer as urban centers are renovated. Public transport systems will be developed more than private means of transport.

It is unlikely that a change in patterns of consumption on the scale described will occur spontaneously as a result of market forces alone. So governments will have to make it occur. The current efforts of governments to disengage themselves from economic life may prove to be obsolete before they really get underway.

The ecology movement, efforts to improve the quality of life and the environment, efforts to improve working conditions and shorten working hours—all of these will prove to be victims of history, anachronistic relics from an earlier and easier period. Such hopes and aspirations, however legitimate they may be, will be in conflict with the overriding need to develop new sources of energy. Born and nourished in a context of wealth and abundance, they risk dying in a severer, more restrictive economic environment.

All of this was actually foreseeable years ago, in the wake of the first oil crisis. But from 1974 through 1978, the industrialized world retreated, in the hope of being in a better position to attack later on. Now it seems that our fate has been decided. We are in for a long desert crossing, which will require us to suffer much hardship, and to demonstrate all the resourcefulness at our command.

CONCLUSION
What Can We Expect?

The key to world economic prospects in the coming decade can be found in a simple equation, written as follows:

$$Oil + Defense + Social\ Welfare = Inflation$$

Massive investments will be necessary to exploit new oilfields and develop alternative energy sources. Defense spending will rise as a result of international tensions. Social transfer payments inherited from the past period of prosperity will be increased by an inevitable rise in unemployment. This combination of expenditures will strain resources to the limit.

The huge demands on available revenues will become manageable only through a dramatic strengthening of state control, and with the help of new mechanisms designed to stem the inflationary tide. But however effective such mechanisms may prove to be, inflation is still likely to be the means employed for resolving social conflicts.

It is obvious that the general trend is towards accelerating inflation. The trend is visible even—and especially—in the United States, where the principle of indexing is spreading to all sectors of the economy. Indexing applies not only to wages, but also to financial markets and social welfare payments. Everyone is more or less protected against the effects of inflation—except the world's poorest.

Inflation rates in the industrialized world of 15 to 20 percent are a near-certainty in the 1980's. But the outlook is not for an inflationary surge of the Brazilian or Argentinian kind. Rather, we can expect inflation Italian-style, with its highs and lows.

In the area of national security, the 1980's will be a decade of destabilization and unprecedented tension. The threat of the use of force to solve otherwise insoluble economic problems will linger in the background of international diplomatic relations, as we enter the period of the "vulnerability gap" which will last until 1985 at least.

Will Reagan be the John Foster Dulles of the 1980's, calmly walking the edge of the precipice with nuclear thunderbolts in one hand and an olive branch in the other?

Two things are virtually certain. The first is that defense spending will rise as a

170

proportion of national budgets and Gross National Products, not only in the U.S., where the trend has now been guaranteed by Reagan's victory, but also in Japan and throughout Europe. West Germany and Britain may balk at the prospect, but the general trend is clear: defense spending is going to have to play a bigger role in the economies of the industrialized world. Protestors will object that defense build-ups are unnecessary because the Soviet empire is going to break apart. It may—but only in 20 or 30 years. A lot can happen in the meantime.

Secondly, Reagan can be expected to demand from America's allies that they assume a bigger share of the common NATO defense burden. As a Reagan advisor put it recently, the allies can ask the U.S. to shoulder the burden of defending the free world and abandon its other world financing responsibilities, or they can ask the U.S. to shoulder the burden of world financing and abandon its defense responsibilities. But they cannot ask the U.S. to do both things at the same time.

For this reason, the 1980's could open up a new era in the long-standing rivalry between Europe and the U.S. As we have seen, the first round of the struggle went to Europe, while the second round was won by the U.S. Who will win in the play-offs?

The U.S. looks to be in a good position. An America back on the road of savings would once again become a formidable economic adversary. We have already seen a remarkable recovery in U.S. investment in advanced technology industries. The fact that one part of the U.S. economy is *developing towards under-development* must not make us forget that the other part is very advanced and continuing to progress at a rapid pace.

What will become of the dollar? Will it yield to its new rivals, the Euromark and the Euroyen? Is the gold/oil exchange rate going to be stabilized? Are we heading towards remonetization of gold? All of these are plausible working hypotheses. But remember one thing: currencies are the clothes of power. If the U.S. regains its position of world dominance, it will have no trouble winning respect for the dollar. A stronger dollar would in no way be incompatible with remonetization of gold. With Europe and Japan assuming a fairer share of the common defense burden, U.S. resistance to rehabilitation of gold could fade and even turn into support for the idea, insofar as it could once again serve U.S. power.

And the Third World? The Least Developed Countries, those excluded from the process of economic growth, seem destined to become world beggars. On the other hand, the heavyweight developing countries, such as Brazil, India and China, seem perfectly capable of continuing to grow at their own speed and in their own way inside zones of interdependence.

The One World concept may have gone the way of a quickly-faded rose. We must start to think in terms of regionalization—of trade, international payments and economic development. Because from now on, it is probably inside interdependent development zones that world growth is going to take place.

Is this world growth really going to slow towards zero, as some pundits predict? It would be suicidal to resign ourselves to that prospect. Growth can and must continue. But it will have to be a new kind of growth. We shall have to accept less consumption and more savings. If the change is not accomplished by voluntary means, it will have to be forced upon us, and the most likely means of coercion is inflation without indexing.

As regards oil, the big challenge is to loosen the noose which OPEC has placed around our necks. The way to do this is obvious. To borrow a phrase from the Venezuelans—who have hardly practiced what they preach in this respect—we must *sembrar el petrolio,* or *sow* the proceeds from oil. Not in Monte Carlo or in real estate investments, but in oil itself. We must plow proceeds from oil back into investments in oil. We must seize some of the oil revenues and mobilize them to explore and exploit new energy sources. Can we do all this without a World Energy Plan? Can we do it without stronger government intervention? Neo-liberalism and its substitutes—monetarism and gradualism, are unlikely to survive the second oil crisis for long. Even fashions must yield to facts, especially when the facts are obstinate ones, like the facts of oil.

Are we going to witness a new, Yalta-style partition of the Middle East? Will the Soviet Union, after grabbing Afghanistan and its enormous natural gas resources, take control of Iran? This has been a distinct possibility ever since the start of the Iran-Iraq war. As we saw in the Ethiopia/Somalia conflict, the Russian bear always chooses the fattest prey. If it captured Iran, Iraq would slip into the American fold. That would undoubtedly stabilize oil supplies. Middle Eastern oil at fixed prices would be swapped for military protection, which would be a new variation on the 30-year old NATO theme of swapping U.S. military protection for piles of depreciating dollars.

Such are the twisting paths disappearing into the fog of the future. The period ahead will not be kind to the weak. The laws of the economic jungle will prevail. It will be neither a golden age of computerization, nor the age of grisly nuclear holocaust. It is a future which will remain dominated by the same fundamental imperative as the past—the need to share use of time and space among a constantly growing number of human beings. At some point, no doubt, the process of substituting machines for manual labor will start again, and we shall be free, as always, to make the best or the worst of what we have.

Walking alongside the river one day, Confucius came across a child holding a bird. When he asked the child what was in its hands, the child replied that it was a bird, and asked what he should do with it, hold on to it or allow it to fly from his grasp. Confucius replied simply: "Look at it. It is in your hands, in your hands and no one else's."

Just as our future is in our own hands, in our hands and no one else's.

POSTCRIPT I
Austerity and
Economic Growth

In very simplified terms, the growth in savings and the reduction in consumption necessary in industrialized countries in coming years can be estimated as follows:

Right now, generally speaking, consumption accounts for around 60 percent of the GNP of these countries, while investment and defense expenditures account for about 20 percent. Over the next 20 years or so, the portion of GNP spent on defense will have to be increased by at least 2.5 percentage points to bring it up to the five to six percent level, and a minimum of five percent of GNP will have to be set aside for investments in energy. This extra 7.5 percent of GNP which will have to be saved or spent on national security will have to come out of consumption, which should thus fall as a percentage of GNP from 60 percent to 52.5 percent.

It goes without saying that a change of this magnitude will be easier to accomplish in an expanding economy than in a stagnant one. For example, if GNP growth were zero for the next 20 years, the value of consumption would have to decline by around one percent a year. But if GNP were to expand by two percent a year, consumption would rise by around 1.3 percent a year.

In an optimistic scenario, with the multiplier effect of rising investment functioning to the fullest extent, GNP could grow by five percent annually, and consumption by 4.3 percent.

Consumption *can* continue to expand in the difficult years of adjustment ahead, but only if overall economic growth rates can be increased.

POSTCRIPT II
Lafferism, Reaganomics and the No Work Society

Lafferism aims to increase productivity by encouraging savings and investment through progressive reduction of taxes, in particular taxes on high incomes. Lafferites believe tax cuts would lead to increases both in production capacity and in rates of productivity; the emphasis on leisure at the expense of work would be reversed, and the underground economy would be discouraged. Lafferites also hope that increased investment demand created by tax cuts would take over from consumption as the main engine of economic growth.

What are we to make of Professor Laffer's theories? A few observations:

In the first place, there are few precedents in economic history for massive tax cuts, and the ones there are are open to a number of interpretations. Take the Kennedy tax cut of February 1964—which of course was implemented by neo-Keynesians like Walter Heller, while today's tax-cut advocates are supply-side economists. Neo-Keynesian analysts have pointed out that the non-inflationary economic boom which followed the Kennedy tax cut (economic growth reached five percent a year for two years, while wholesale prices rose only 0.2 percent) was not the result of a clearly defined economic mechanism. In other words, no economic model or econometric analysis reveals an automatic link between tax cuts and increased production (the kind of link which is inherent in the investment multiplier effect or the demand accelerator effect). The most serious studies seem to indicate that the link, insofar as it exists at all, is an indirect one, resulting from changes in psychology— i.e., tax cuts trigger a surge of confidence, which leads to increases in savings, investment and production.

Secondly, a word about the famous Laffer Curve, which tracks the fiscal income received at different rates of taxation. At its extremes, the Curve simply reveals a self-evident truth, that tax income is zero both when tax rates are zero and when they are 100 percent. What matters is the idea of an optimum fiscal point, below which increases in the tax burden raise fiscal income, but above which increases in the burden actually reduce fiscal income. Laffer believes that any reduction in the tax burden would increase fiscal income.

Another Laffer hypothesis is that the optimum point for fiscal income corresponds to the optimum point for the economy as a whole. Above that point, he believes, everyone comes to consider public spending as inefficient, and works less in order to escape from a tax burden considered too heavy. In reality, however, it is doubtful that everyone has as precise an idea of the usefulness or otherwise of public spending as Laffer supposes. There is no obvious reason why the optimum point for fiscal returns coincides with the optimum point for the economy. There is thus an element of arbitrariness, i.e. a doctrinaire, a priori element hidden in the apparent scientific rigorousness of the Laffer Curve concept.

Thirdly, it should be noted that Lafferites believe tax cuts must benefit the rich, who are considered to have the highest propensity to save and the highest efficiency in overall economic terms. Lafferism thus represents a radical rejection of the trend towards greater equality of income, which began after the Second World War in most industrialized countries (the most striking examples being Britain, Sweden and the Netherlands), and which has been pursued through systems of progressive taxation, through social transfer payments and through direct action to narrow the gap between the top and the bottom of the income scale.

Finally, it should be borne in mind that for Laffer it is increased production which holds the key to stimulation of the economy. This represents in effect a return to the classical law of Jean Baptiste Say, which is explicitly quoted by supply-siders in support of their theories: *Supply creates its own demand.*

The belief is that tax cuts encourage investment, while increases in the working hours of skilled employees free production bottlenecks and open up the whole economy. While the short-term aim may be to trigger a burst in economic activity, the fundamental purpose is a structural reform of the economy, designed to guarantee permanently rapid growth in production capacity. Believing that the effect of tax cuts will be automatically compensated for by strong economic growth, the most extreme of the supply-siders consider budget cutbacks to be pointless. Reagan however has adopted the empirically wise approach of trying to link cuts in public spending to the tax cuts.

This, in fact, is the true revolutionary element of Reaganomics—the will to cut public spending, which means reducing the role of the federal budget in GNP, and reducing the role of government in the economy. The tax cut proposals are merely an alibi, or a pretext.

At first sight, Lafferism and Keynesianism look more complementary than contradictory. However, close analysis reveals the existence of irreconcilable differences between the two doctrines. Keynesianism was assimilated into the theories of the Welfare State, and is distinguished by elements of state planning and a belief in social equality. The supply-siders, on the other hand, want to return to the sources of economic liberalism, which means encouraging work and the entrepreneurial spirit. The emergence of their theories, together with a renewed interest in monetarism, represents a reaction against the economic evolution of advanced industrialized countries since 1945. The supply-siders consider that this evolution, tending towards a reduction of economic inequalities, has demobilized the forces of dynamism within economies, and has thus proved a failure.

The debate on supply-side theories is now in full swing, and it could continue for a long time, since it is critical in its political and social implications not only for the U.S. but also for Europe and for the whole of the industrialized world.

* * *

The process of increasing state control over the economy has been underway for a long time in industrialized countries around the world. The United States, the undisputed champion of economic freedom, was the first country to raise the standard in the anti-tax crusade; two presidential candidates in succession have now won office in the name of the struggle against big government. Nonetheless, one American in four or five still depends on government handouts, and social transfer payments —for health, education and welfare—account for close to 10 percent of GNP and 50 percent of the federal budget.

In France today, taxes and social security contributions together account for 41.5 percent of GNP. In West Germany the figure is 39 percent, in Britain 37 percent, and in the U.S. 35 percent. (At the top of the list are Norway, Sweden and the Netherlands, where the figure is over 50 percent of GNP; these are also countries which are experiencing insidious socio-economic crises, and now appear destined to succumb to socialization without putting up a fight).

In France, in the recent Presidential elections, the programs of the three or four main candidates appeared different, but were in fact identical in one fundamental respect: despite ideological differences, they were all proposing increases in public spending, social transfers, and taxes and social security contributions—in short, they all planned to strengthen the role of the public sector in the French economy. During the past seven years, France has been led by a liberal President, Valery Giscard d'Estaing, and for the last five of those seven years the President's Prime Minister, Raymond Barre, has tirelessly proclaimed the virtues of free market economics. And yet what has happened? The process of establishing state control over the economy has actually been accelerated.

In Britain, Mrs. Thatcher has done the exact opposite of what she promised. Her whole election campaign two years ago was based on the need to cut government spending. But the last budget approved by the House of Commons provides for a sharp increase in government spending, increased social transfers and higher taxes.

In Germany, Chancellor Schmidt—even though he is a Social Democrat—came to power with the aim of presiding over an economy based on free market principles. And yet during his time in office, state control of the economy has increased sharply, and the budget deficit is hovering around five percent of GNP. Obviously, the forces pushing in the direction of increased state control are extremely powerful. What are the consequences?

It is first necessary to go back to the great Cambridge master, Lord Keynes— whose teachings have been so misunderstood and so badly applied. The fact is that while it was legitimate and even indispensable when Keynes wrote 50 years ago to stimulate the economy through increased public spending, it is absurd to try to do the same thing today when average income levels have tripled. State planning, justifiable at low income levels, becomes perverse at levels of income three or four times as high. The reasons for this have to do with the nature of productive effort—without which our industrialized nations cannot survive. The distinction that should be made when discussing productive effort is not between manual labor and intellectual labor. Both the garbage collector and the research worker are indispensable for different reasons; the development of computer technology does not mean that we have any less need for a plumber than we had 100 years ago. Rather, the key distinction is between what encourages productive effort of all kinds, and what discourages it.

At low levels of income, close to subsistence levels, a rise in government spending in accordance with Keynesian principles increases productive effort because job seekers wish to enter the labor market. At income levels three times higher, increased government outlays and higher taxes and social security contributions actually reduce productive effort: available jobs remain unfilled.

This situation has been lazily tolerated in industrialized nations for a long time. Governments have chosen to subsidize unemployment, and bring in immigrant workers—in Britain and France, for example—to do menial, poorly-paid work. This is an utterly perverse situation, and one which is full of risks—as London's recent Brixton riots showed.

It is also an utterly immoral situation, with three different kinds of victims: the employed, who are overtaxed; the subsidized unemployed, who are stripped of their dignity as men; and the first-generation immigrants, who are being unduly exploited (the second generation rebels).

It takes political courage to stop this scandal. Governments must cease applying the old Keynesian remedies in a socio-economic context radically different from that for which the remedies were devised. This implies recognizing that after the oil crisis it is no longer possible to pay for work at the old price. And it implies a halt to automatic subsidization of unemployment.

State control of the economy discourages productive effort both at the top and at the bottom of the income scale. At the top, an excessive tax burden encourages leisure—year-round holidays, golf or possibly work in the underground economy. At the bottom, the result is similar, because of transfer payments. A potential job-seeker will quite rationally opt for government handouts and freedom from work if the only alternative is a job which promises him only slightly more net income while taking away most of his leisure time.

A society which rejects productive effort becomes a society addicted to leisure, games and distractions generally. It is a society which loses interest in research and which enters, inevitably, a process of stagnation and decay. This is where economic issues join with cultural and moral ones. It is not a matter of capitalism or socialism. We are talking about a law which has no exceptions, one which operates in industrial terms rather than political or ideological terms.

The Soviet Union serves as a laboratory experiment in this respect. For the past 15 years, the economic growth rate in the Soviet Union has been falling by around 0.5 percent every five years. Twenty years ago, the annual growth rate was five percent. Today, it is down to 3.5 percent, and is expected to drop to hardly more than two percent within two years. This is essentially the result of stagnation of worker productivity. The Soviet worker has absolutely no incentive to increase his productive effort, since increased effort will not raise his income and his buying power, while reduced effort will not be punished by an insupportable loss of income. Thus he avoids work, and takes refuge in other pursuits—as the high alcoholism and absenteeism figures in the Soviet Union show.

But the really striking thing is that a similar process is now underway in the

United States, where worker productivity has not stopped deteriorating for 20 years. In Europe, the best example of the same trend is provided by Britain, with its combination of generalized welfare and tax rates which limit workers to very modest living standards. This combination has steadily destroyed incentives to work and Britain has fallen into chronic economic regression.

All of this would not be so bad if we lived in isolation from each other. But we do not. In the next 20 years, we must face two enormous economic challenges. The first is the technological challenge, without precedent in world history, represented by the arrival at adulthood of 3.5 billion human beings—who will have to be first fed and then provided with productive employment if humanity is not to be transformed into a vast sanctuary of beggars.

These challenges demand that industrialized nations increase their productive efforts and build up savings, rather than reduce those efforts. Current talk about reducing working hours is positively archaic. What we need to do is just the opposite of what is now being discussed: we need to work more for less reward. In France, a recent report on poverty talked about providing a kind of minimum income for everyone. This is exactly the opposite of what must be done, unless the productive effort of France is to be held in check indefinitely.

Ten years ago, it was fashionable to condemn the consumer society and its misdeeds. This was manifestly absurd. Consumption is not only legitimate, it is indispensable insofar as it causes increased productive effort. The mortal danger facing developed nations is not consumption, but the *No Work society,* which leads inevitably to a process of social decay.

In this context, the coming to power of a Socialist party in France, with firm ideas on expanding the public sector and increasing social transfers, cannot be viewed without some alarm.

Following the virtual failure of the Thatcher experiment in Britain, the Reagan program represents the only attempt by a major industrialized nation to stem the tide of state control over economies, which has been rising almost irreversibly for 50 years. This fact alone indicates how closely we must watch the development of Reaganomics. Remember, what is important is not the tax cuts, but what hides behind them. Tax cuts have little virtue if they are not accompanied by cuts in government spending, which are the essential requirement. If the Reagan experiment is a success, there is no doubt it will serve as an example for the rest of the industrialized world. A new chapter is now being written in our economic history.

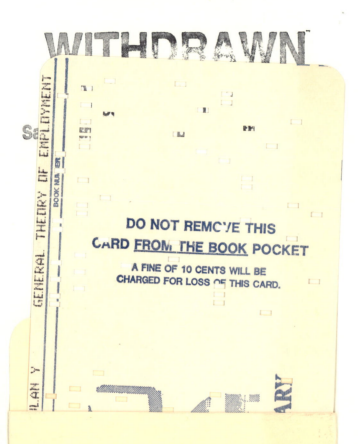